THE CENTURY OF TASTE

THE CENTURY OF TASTE

The Philosophical Odyssey
of Taste in
the Eighteenth Century

George Dickie

New York   Oxford
OXFORD UNIVERSITY PRESS
1996

Oxford University Press

Oxford   New York
Athens   Auckland   Bangkok   Bombay
Calcutta   Cape Town   Dar es Salaam   Delhi
Florence   Hong Kong   Istanbul   Karachi
Kuala Lumpur   Madras   Madrid   Melbourne
Mexico City   Nairobi   Paris   Singapore
Taipei   Tokyo   Toronto

and associated companies in
Berlin   Ibadan

Copyright © 1996 by Oxford University Press, Inc.

Published by Oxford University Press, Inc.
198 Madison Avenue, New York, New York 10016

Oxford is a registered trademark of Oxford University Press.

Library of Congress Cataloging-in-Publication Data
Dickie, George, 1926–
The century of taste : the philosophical odyssey of taste in the
eighteenth century / George Dickie.
p.   cm.
Includes bibliographical references and index.
ISBN 0-19-509680-0
1. Aesthetics, Modern—18th century.   I. Title.
BH181.D53   1996
111'.85'09033—dc20   94-49131

MUST
IAHK2725

1 3 5 7 9 8 6 4 2
Printed in the United States of America
on acid-free paper

For Ruth Marcus

Foreword

This is an original and refreshing assessment of the development of a philosophical interest in the idea of taste. It is characteristic of George Dickie's philosophical sensibility: it insists on direct, simple expositions of arguments, and it refuses to accept or even to tolerate obscure theses. In the end, it is a celebration of Hume. It takes Hume to be more sophisticated than Hutcheson, Gerard, and Alison, and it presents him as both more accurate and infinitely clearer than Kant. Thus Hume's theory is the high point in this philosophical narrative, and Kant is the beginning of a disastrous decline.

Everyone will profit from this study. Some will be offended by it. Those will be the students of Kant and his successors, who will find Dickie intolerably impatient with their hero. Dickie not only confesses an inability to find sense and coherence in Kant's doctrines, but he has the temerity to assert that there is not much useful sense to be found. I do myself find this dismissal hasty, but I think Dickie is right—and characteristically right—to dare to suggest that Kant begins a descent into self-deluded pomposity. It remains for his defenders to defend him: Dickie has pointed to just what needs defending.

During the last twenty-five years, as the history of philosophy has again become interesting to analytically inclined philosophers, Kant's texts in moral philosophy and aesthetics have been recovered. That is a real achievement. But it is time to ask whether, if those texts are not the dictatorial, jargon-ridden morass they had earlier been thought to be, they are really as profound throughout as their current expositors take them to be. Do we have to take either all of Kant or none of him? I hope not. Dickie is one of the first among contemporary philosophers to suppose that the eighteenth century offers us important, defensible philosophy in aesthetics, while continuing to insist that Kant is not so good.

Dickie's background and energy suit him perfectly to place Hume's remarks on taste in their context, for he has worked long and well on the texts of Hutcheson and Hume's other near-contemporaries. Dickie's temperament makes him impatient with Kant, and even angry at Kant for dissipating Hume's achievement. His background, energy, and instincts give Dickie a philosophical voice worth listening to. It should not be ignored, and especially not by those who love Kant. Dickie is giving them a chance—slim as Dickie thinks it is—to show they have not been taken in. Good luck to them. And thanks to George Dickie.

Ted Cohen
University of Chicago

Acknowledgments

This book is the culmination of a career-long interest in eighteenth-century theories of taste.

My greatest debt is to Ted Cohen, who read the whole manuscript. His comments—especially those on Hume and Kant—were of enormous help. Ralf Meerbote read early versions of the Hutcheson and Kant chapters, and his comments—especially on the Kant chapter—were exceedingly valuable. Robert Yanal and Joyce Carpenter read an early version of the Kant chapter and gave me much useful advice.

I also wish to thank Susan Carbone, Todd Hochenedel, Heidi Nelson, Timothy O'Connor, Robert Richardson, Robert Rupert, and Doran Smolkin, who were members of my 1989 graduate seminar and who studied with me the writings of Hutcheson, Gerard, Alison, Kant, and Hume.

I want to thank the following for leave time during which this book was written: the National Endowment for the Humanities for a Fellowship for University Teachers for the 1989–90 academic year, the Research Board of the University of Illinois at Chicago for leave for the fall semester of the 1991–92 academic year, and the University of Illinois at Chicago for a sabbatical leave for the fall term of the 1992–93 academic year.

Contents

THE CENTURY OF TASTE

Introduction

It is an undoubted fact that we take pleasure in mountain vistas, the sight of a rose, the viewing or hearing of works of art, and the experience of many other things. We also make distinctions among the objects of such experiences, saying of the experienced objects (or their properties) that they are beautiful, sublime, delicate, and so on. Certain sights and sounds displease us, and these also involve various distinctions. Almost from the beginning, philosophers have been concerned to have a theoretical understanding of these experiences and their objects. And we continue to the present to try to give an account of these experiences and their objects. The notion of the aesthetic attitude, the idea of aesthetic experience, and Frank Sibley's conception of aesthetic qualities are recent examples of attempts to theorize about these matters. The theory of taste was eighteenth-century philosophy's attempt to give an account of such objects and of the pleasure and displeasure taken in them, and it is with this particular philosophical theorizing that this book is concerned.

The eighteenth century *was* the century of taste, that is, of the theory of taste. At the beginning of the century, the focus of theorizing about experiences of the kind under discussion shifted from objective notions of beauty to the subjective notion of taste. A little later in 1725, Francis Hutcheson gave the English-speaking world its first relatively sophisticated theory of taste. Hutcheson was, of course, not the first English-speaking thinker to talk about taste, but he was the first to give a systematic, philosophical account of it. Shortly after the middle of the century, David Hume's brief essay "Of the Standard of Taste" provided the best expression that the theory of taste was ever to achieve. As the eighteenth century drew to a close, the extravagant, unrestrained theorizing of the associationist Archibald Alison and the obscure, misguided speculations of Immanuel Kant were burdening and bringing thinking in the taste mode also to a close. A few representatives of the theory of taste lingered on into the early nineteenth century, but theorizing

3

in the taste mode was, alas, dying and being replaced with a very different kind of thinking.

This book is concerned with five theorists of taste, four of whom were mentioned just above. The views of these five can be seen as the beginning, the high point, and the fading away of the theory of taste as a way of philosophizing. I have two main theses. The first thesis is that after Hutcheson laid down the basic—limited but promising—theory of taste, Hume, following Hutcheson in his own way, all but perfected the theory of taste. The second thesis is that the associationists—Alexander Gerard and Alison—led the theory of taste into one kind of blind alley and that Kant led it into another kind. The sad fact is that the eighteenth-century philosophers who came after Hume did not heed his promising leads; as a result, at least in part, theorizing in the taste mode died out. In drawing the conclusions about Hume and Kant that I do, I am not suggesting that Hume did and Kant did not influence the development of what is now called "aesthetics." Hume has had little influence because the theory of taste died out. Kant has had great influence because, although the theory of taste died out, elements of his theory were transformed into the theory of the aesthetic attitude.

Dozens of theories of taste were worked out during the eighteenth century. I have focused on the theories of only five philosophers. Hutcheson's theory is an obvious choice, as it is the philosophical beginning of the theory of taste in the English-speaking world. I have chosen to discuss Gerard and Alison's associationism because it was such a popular view in its day and because its blurring of taste notions led, I believe, to a loss of confidence in theorizing in the taste mode. I have chosen to discuss Kant's theory because it is so widely revered and so often regarded—mistakenly, I believe—as the high point of philosophizing in the taste mode. Kant's theory is usually addressed only by Kant scholars, who have little interest in the theory of taste as such. I think it is important for Kant's theory to be addressed within the context of an examination of other theories of taste and by someone whose primary interest is the theory of taste. I have chosen to discuss Hume's theory because I believe it is the most successful of the theories of taste. Hume's theory, while it is, of course, stated in the language of the eighteenth century, is in many ways like a twentieth-century theory. For example, he makes no attempt to draw conclusions about the nature of or even about the existence of a *faculty* of taste, which was a set piece for eighteenth-century theorizing. Moreover, he does not try to limit his discussion to a few categories such as the beautiful and the sublime. He speaks casually of many "beauties" and "blemishes"; in this regard, his theory in important ways resembles Frank Sibley's notion of aesthetic qualities.

Despite my remarks about the baneful results of associationism and Kant's theory, I shall not be concerned with the historical influences of any of the five theories of taste I discuss. My primary interest is to give expositions and evaluations of these theories.

There are, I think, in these expositions and evaluations a number of new ideas or approaches. The following are among the more important. I give a detailed account of the argument that underlies Hutcheson's conclusion that there is an internal sense of beauty. I have noticed, I think for the first time, that the associationists rely not only on the well-known notion of the association of ideas to produce the central and distinctive feature of their theory but also on a dubious notion that I call "the coalescence of ideas." I show how, in order to understand Kant's theory of taste fully, it must be seen as nested within his teleology. The teleology of the second half of the third *Critique* is typically ignored as uninteresting or irrelevant by persons interested in the theory of taste, and this is, I believe, a mistake. I have, by the way, not attempted to respond to or otherwise use the enormous second-ary literature that exists on the third *Critique*. I have tried, by focusing on Kant's teleology, to make sense of the third *Critique* as a whole. I have also tried to present a kind of middle-sized account of Kant's theory—one that is not so long that keeping all the parts in mind is difficult and one that is not so short that it cannot do justice to all the many parts of the theory. I show that Hume more than just mentions rules or principles of taste and that his theory contains a successful account of the nature of such principles and of how they are to be discovered.

I shall not discuss these five theories in strict chronological order. I discuss Hutcheson's theory (1725) first because in one way or another it is the source of the other four theories. I then discuss the associationists—first Gerard's theory (1759) and then Alison's (1790) in chronological order. I discuss Kant's theory next—the third *Critique* and Alison's *Essays* were pub-lished in the same year. I discuss Hume (1757) at the end of the book, very much out of chronological order, because I wanted to save the best for last.

1

The Basic Theory of Taste:
Francis Hutcheson

Francis Hutcheson's argument for his theory of taste in his *An Inquiry into the Original of Our Ideas of Beauty and Virtue* (1725) occurs in the first of the two essays that comprise the book. The argument of this first essay, entitled "An Inquiry Concerning Beauty, Order, Harmony, Design," proceeds in four steps, with each of the last three steps presupposing and building on an earlier step or on several earlier steps. Step 1, which occupies the Preface and Section 1, attempts to prove that there is an *internal sense of beauty* that produces *pleasure* when triggered by a characteristic or characteristics of perceived objects. Step 2, which takes up Sections 2–4, is concerned to show that the sense of beauty is triggered by and only by the characteristic *uniformity amidst variety* in nature, nonrepresentational aspects of art, theorems, and representational art. Step 3, which is confined to Section 6, attempts to prove that the sense of beauty is *universal* in human beings. Step 4 is a twofold thesis concerning *displeasure* and *pleasure* in the experience of beauty. The first claim argued for in Section 6, along with the universality thesis, is that any *displeasure* in the experience of beauty must have a source other than the sense of beauty. The second claim that takes up Section 7 is that the *pleasure* taken in beautiful objects derives not from custom, education, and/or example but from the sense of beauty.

These four steps are discussed in the next four sections of this chapter. Notice that in the preceding outline of the four steps Section 5 is not mentioned. Section 5, which is the longest single section in Hutcheson's book, is devoted solely to the design argument for the existence of God. This excursion into theology is not essential to the understanding of his theory of taste. At the end of his account of his theory of taste, Hutcheson brings up the theological topic of final causes as it related to his theory; I shall discuss the topic briefly. In developing my account of Hutcheson's theory, I shall follow the same order of topics that he does in his book. I shall be concerned with

Hutcheson's theory of taste as it is presented in the "Inquiry Concerning Beauty"; he made some alterations in his theory in his later work, but it is the "Inquiry Concerning Beauty" that was influential on later thinkers.

External Sense and Internal Sense

John Locke in discussing ideas, which he takes to be the raw materials of knowledge, says that the source of all ideas is experience. There are, he says, two sources of ideas in experience. One source involves objects external to our minds—tables, chairs, and the like. Locke calls this source *sensation* and says that ideas from this source depend on the senses, by which he means vision, hearing, touch, and the like. This source of ideas is what Hutcheson has in mind when he speaks of "external sense." The other Lockean source of ideas involves objects internal to the mind, namely, the operations of the mind itself. Locke calls this source *reflection* and says that ideas from this source come from the perception of the operation of our own minds. By the operations or acts of the mind, Locke means perception, thinking, doubting, believing, and the like. In reflection, the mind turns in on itself. Of reflection, Locke says that it is enough like sensation that it "might properly enough be called internal sense."[1] For Locke, external sense and internal sense (reflection) are both cognitive; that is, both are sources of ideas that are involved in bringing information to the mind.

Hutcheson, who was a follower of Locke, accepts his notions of sensation and reflection, as well as the rest of Locke's epistemological framework. Hutcheson, however, uses the expression "internal sense," not as a synonym for the cognitive notion of "reflection," but in an entirely different way. In his "Inquiry Concerning Beauty," Hutcheson uses "internal sense" to refer to an innate power to respond with pleasure when external senses perceive certain properties. So for Hutcheson, an internal sense is not a cognitive but a responsive or reactive mental faculty, the function of which is to produce pleasure. On his view, internal sense and external sense are connected; external sense is required to bring an object into the mind for internal sense to react to and produce pleasure. Alexander Gerard notes at the beginning of his *Essay on Taste* that Hutcheson in the "Inquiry Concerning Beauty" spoke of internal senses but that in his later works Hutcheson spoke of such senses as "subsequent and reflex senses; subsequent, because they always suppose some previous perception of the objects about which they are employed [to produce pleasure] . . . reflex, because, in order to their exertion [to produce pleasure], the mind reflects upon, and takes notice of [an] . . . object . . . perceived."[2]

Thus, Hutcheson and Locke both use the expression "internal sense,"

---

1. John Locke, *An Essay Concerning Human Understanding* (New York: Dover Publications, 1959), vol. 1, p. 123.

2. Alexander Gerard, *An Essay on Taste*. 3d ed. of 1780, Walter J. Hipple, Jr., ed. (Delmar, N.Y.: Scholars' Facsimiles & Reprints, 1978), pp. 1–2.

but they mean entirely different things. Shaftesbury and even earlier thinkers are sources for Hutcheson's notion of internal sense.[3]

The Internal Sense of Beauty

In the Preface to his "Inquiry Concerning Beauty," Hutcheson states and gives a bit of argument for the basic conclusions of both his theory of taste and his moral theory. His arguments in the Preface take the form of reporting the results of reflection or introspection. The arguments here relate directly only to his theory of taste, although he states that his "principal design is to show that human nature was not left quite indifferent to the affair of virtue. . . ."[4] Hutcheson apparently thinks that it is easier to make a case for the theory of taste and that doing so first will make it easier to persuade his readers of the correctness of his moral theory. So, in the Preface, his arguments are directed solely to the theory of taste, and the first half of his book is devoted exclusively to the theory of taste, with moral theory discussed in the second part of the book.

The three basic conclusions of the Preface concern the senses.

1. There is mental machinery similar to the external senses (seeing, hearing, etc.) but sufficiently different so as to deserve the name "internal sense."
2. Both the external and internal senses are natural and function independently of the will (*necessarily*).
3. Both the external and the internal senses have their *separate pleasures*.

Hutcheson continues his statement of and arguments for his basic conclusions in Section 1 of the "Inquiry Concerning Beauty." He begins this argument in the Preface by first stating some things about the pleasures of the external senses that he thinks everyone will agree to. On this basis, he then generalizes his conclusion to all pleasures, focusing on the pleasures derived from the arts and related areas. He begins by saying,

> In reflecting upon our external senses, we plainly see that our perceptions of pleasure or pain do not depend directly upon our will. Objects do not please us according as we incline they should. The presence of some objects necessarily pleases us, and the presence of others as necessarily displeases us. . . . By the very frame of our nature the one is made the occasion of delight and the other dissatisfaction. (p. 24)

(Note that in this passage Hutcheson speaks of "our perceptions of pleasure and pain." This shows that he is using the notion of perception in a broader way than it might ordinarily be understood today; he uses the notion to cover both feelings of pleasure and pain as well as cognitive awarenesses.)

3. Peter Kivy, *The Seventh Sense* (New York: Burt Franklin & Co., 1976), pp. 1–21.

4. Francis Hutcheson, *An Inquiry Concerning Beauty, Order, Harmony, Design.* Peter Kivy, ed. (The Hague: Martinus Nijhoff, 1973), p. 25. All subsequent internal page cites in this chapter to Hutcheson are to this edition.

What Hutcheson is saying in this passage is that the external senses (seeing, hearing, etc.) furnish us with perceptual objects (colors, sounds, etc.), which in turn cause pleasure or pain (or, I suppose, leave us indifferent) quite independently of our deciding or willing. The fact that we are pleased independent of the will—that is, necessarily—Hutcheson takes to prove that these pleasings are innate, that is, occur "by the very frame of our nature." He then generalizes that all our pleasures and pains are independent of the will and gives the following example. "Thus we find ourselves pleased with a regular form, a piece of architecture or painting, a composition of notes, a theorem. . ." (p. 24). These pleasures are also taken to be necessary and innate. He then claims that the pleasure of such taste experiences "arises from some uniformity, order, arrangement, imitation, and not from the simple ideas of colour or sound or mode of extension separately considered" (p. 24). Perhaps when we are pleased with a *regular form* the pleasure derives from uniformity, order, and the like and not color or sound separately considered, but, contrary to Hutcheson, when we are pleased with a piece of architecture, a painting, or a composition of notes, the pleasure may arise both from uniformity, order, and the like *and* from color or sound separately considered. What accounts for Hutcheson's odd conclusion about color and sound?

In Section 1, Hutcheson seems to contradict his earlier statement. There he writes,

> Thus every one acknowledges he is more delighted with a fine face, a just picture, than with the view of any one colour, were it as strong and lively as possible. . . . So in music, the pleasure of fine composition is incomparably greater than any one note, how sweet, full, or swelling soever. (pp. 33–34)

Here, Hutcheson, while suggesting the superior importance of uniformity, order, and the like, implies that color and tone separately considered give pleasure also. Hutcheson's odd earlier conclusion seems to have been contradicted, and he now seems to hold that color and sound separately considered both do and do not produce pleasure.

The apparent contradiction is easily resolved. The paragraph in which Hutcheson allows that color and sound separately considered give pleasure begins with his noting, "The only pleasure of sense which many philosophers seem to consider is that which accompanies the simple ideas of sensation" (p. 33). And he goes on to say, "But there are far greater pleasures in those complex ideas of objects, which obtain the names of beautiful, regular, harmonious" (p. 33). Here Hutcheson is just assuming without argument that the beauty of objects and its connected pleasure derives from complex ideas of sensation and that simple ideas of sensation such as color and sound make no contribution to the beauty of objects and the pleasure connected to it. But this is just sheer prejudice.

Hutcheson builds this prejudice into his theory by means of his distinction between external and internal senses. He remarks casually in Section 1, "It is of no consequence whether we call these ideas of beauty and harmony perceptions of the external senses of seeing and hearing, or not. I should rather choose to call our power of perceiving these ideas our *internal sense* . . ." (p. 34). But it is crucial to Hutcheson's theory that he distinguishes between external and internal senses and connects beauty to an internal sense. And, it is by means of this distinction that he builds the formalism of complex ideas as the cause of beauty into his theory. What he does is to associate the pleasures that accompany the simple ideas of sensation with the external senses; these pleasures thus become the pleasures of the external senses. But the pleasures that accompany some complex ideas of sensation have a different source; they derive from the internal sense of beauty or harmony. (Later, when Hutcheson raises the question of what kind of experience produces the beauty pleasure, the answer will have to be some kind of complex idea.) Thus in Hutcheson's view there is a division of function between the external and internal senses such that they sort out pleasures into different bins.

Hutcheson goes on in Section 1 to justify his use of the notion of internal sense by the following three arguments: First, many persons can see and hear simple ideas in a completely accurate way (discern color, shapes, sounds, etc.) and take pleasure in them but "find no pleasure in musical compositions, in painting" (p. 34), and the like or have but a weak pleasure as compared to what others enjoy. What Hutcheson's argument shows, if it is successful, is that some persons receive pleasure from both simple and complex ideas and that some receive pleasure from only simple ideas. He takes this alleged fact to show that there is an internal sense that some persons have and that is weak in others. His argument works only if the pleasure in music, painting, and the like, which some persons have and some persons lack, cannot be tied to the external senses or some other source and must therefore be attributed to an internal sense.

A few lines later, in a passage introduced in the fourth edition, Hutcheson repeats this same argument but introduces a new consideration.

> Let us consider, first, that 'tis probable a being may have the full power of external sensation, which we enjoy, so as to perceive colour, line, surface, as we do; yet, without the power of comparing, or of discerning the similitudes of proportions. Again, it might discern these also, and yet have no pleasure or delight accompanying these perceptions. (p. 35)

The new consideration is Hutcheson's introduction of the notion of "the power of comparing, or of discerning the similitudes of proportion." Here, three things are mentioned: (1) the powers of external perception, (2) the powers of comparing and discerning similarity, and (3) the power of taking pleasure in what one is aware of. The discerning of colors and sounds (simple ideas) clearly belong, for Hutcheson, to the external senses, as does taking pleasure in these simple ideas. Presumably, the discerning of similarity, for Hutcheson, belongs to the internal sense, although Hutcheson does not actually say this. Usually when Hutcheson speaks of an internal sense, he is concerned only with an affective function—the power of feeling pleasure from the awareness of complex ideas.

There is an important kind of asymmetry between the external senses and the internal sense as Hutcheson usually treats them. The external senses are cognitive senses that connect the mind to the external world. But the sense of beauty, which is the internal sense I am concerned with, as Hutcheson defines it in all four editions of *An Inquiry into the Original of Our Ideas of Beauty and Virtue,* is not cognitive at all. He writes, "These determinations to be pleased with certain complex forms the author chooses to call senses, distinguishing them from the powers which commonly go by that name by calling our power of perceiving the beauty of regularity, order, harmony, an *internal sense*" (p. 24). Here the internal sense of beauty is defined as a "determination to be pleased." As thus defined, the sense of beauty does not bring any cognitive thing into the mind; it reacts to the presence of something already in the mind. But in the passage cited just before this last quotation, Hutcheson strongly suggests that the sense of beauty has a cognitive dimension parallel to that of the external senses. He clearly thinks that the external senses have cognitive and affective aspects, and the earlier of the previous two passages suggests that the sense of beauty also has a cognitive as well as an affective aspect. The passage that speaks of discerning similarity was introduced into the fourth and final edition of the *An Inquiry into the Original of Our Ideas of Beauty and Virtue.* Perhaps Hutcheson was beginning to see that he had to locate the power of discerning similarity somewhere and that it did not fit comfortably into the machinery of the external senses.

This is a good place to make the following point. Some persons take Hutcheson to be trying to argue that, to use the parlance of a later day, "x is beautiful" is analogous to "x is red." They thus think Hutcheson owes us an account of the standard conditions for perceiving the beautiful that is analogous to the standard conditions for perceiving red. But Hutcheson is not trying to do this sort of thing at all. He conceives of the sense of beauty as an affective faculty, not a faculty by means of which we perceive beauty as we perceive red by means of vision. The external senses, for Hutcheson, are both cognitive and affective, but the internal sense of beauty is similar to the external senses only in the respect that it is affective—a power for feeling pleasure.

A second argument for an internal sense of beauty, which Hutcheson places between the two versions of the argument that has just been discussed, runs as follows: "we discern a sort of beauty" and derive pleasure from it in such things as theorems and universal truths in which experiences of the external senses do not play a significant role (p. 35). Hutcheson's argument is that here is a case of beauty in which the external senses do not play a central role; therefore, an internal sense must be responsible for the pleasure. This argument works only if the pleasures in question cannot be tied to the external senses or given some other source and if a sense of some kind is necessary to have the pleasure.

These two arguments of Hutcheson are aimed at establishing that there is a sense that is *internal,* that is, a sense different from the external senses that has different objects that cause pleasure. *Both of his arguments require that pleasure be derived from a sense.* In the second argument, which concerns theorems and the like and the pleasures they cause, since the external senses are not involved and thus cannot be the source of pleasure, he thinks he can conclude that there must be an *internal* sense that is the source of pleasure. In the first argument, after noting that a person with good external senses who takes pleasure in simple ideas may be unable to take pleasure in complex ideas (music, etc.), he concludes that such a person lacks an ability to have pleasure. Because Hutcheson assumes pleasure is tied to some sense or other and the person in question has perfectly good external senses, he concludes that the person lacks a sense—an internal one.

A third argument for an internal sense of beauty, which Hutcheson commingles with his first argument, involves the relation of knowledge to experience. Earlier in Section 1, in a passage in which I take him to be talking about only simple ideas, Hutcheson asserts, "Many of our sensitive perceptions are pleasant, and many painful, immediately, and that without any knowledge of the cause of this pleasure or pain, or how the objects excite it. . . ." (pp. 31–32). He later notes that a person of good taste may enjoy the pleasure of beauty "at once without much knowledge" of similarity of proportion (p. 36). Here he is claiming that the pleasure of beauty can be had "without much knowledge." He goes on, however, to make the stronger claim: "This superior power of perception is justly called a *sense* because of its affinity to the other senses in this, that the pleasure does not arise from any *knowledge* of principles, proportion, causes, or of the usefulness of the object, but strikes us first with the idea of beauty" (p. 36). This parallel between the immediacy of the relation between simple-idea pleasures and knowledge, on the one hand, and the immediacy of the relation between complex-idea pleasures and knowledge, on the other hand, is taken as a justification for using the notion of internal sense, although in this third argument, Hutcheson is focused on justifying the *sense* aspect of the notion of internal sense.

Early in Section 1, Hutcheson plants a clue as to how he plans to deal with disagreements over taste. He affirms the belief that human minds are pretty much the same and suggests that disagreements over pleasures of both simple and complex ideas are to be accounted for by the association of ideas. He is suggesting that experiences of certain sorts can undermine the pleasures of the innate sense of beauty and of the innate external senses. This theme is developed at length later in his book.

I now turn to Hutcheson's view of the referent of "beauty." He announces his view in Section 1 in an often quoted passage.

> Let it be observed that in the following papers the word *beauty* is taken for the idea raised in us, and a sense of beauty for our power of receiving this idea. Harmony also denotes our pleasant ideas arising from composition of sounds,

and a good ear (as it is generally taken) a power of perceiving this pleasure. In the following sections, an attempt is made to discover what is the immediate occasion of these pleasant ideas, or what real quality in objects ordinarily excites them. (p. 34)

The first two sentences of this quotation do not really make it clear whether "beauty" and "harmony" refer to feelings of pleasure or to the characteristics of objects of experience which cause feelings of pleasure. "The idea raised in us" and "pleasant ideas" might refer to either. In a parallel way, "our power of receiving this idea [beauty]," and, as Hutcheson conceives of "a good ear," leaves open the possibility that these powers produce feelings of pleasure or discern the characteristics of objects of experience that cause feelings of plea- sure. The final sentence in the quotation, however, makes it clear that "beauty" and "harmony" refer to feelings of pleasure, for it states that later in his essay he will try to discover the characteristics of objects of experience that cause the pleasant ideas. One curious result of this understanding of this passage is the meaning it gives to the expression "a good ear." Hutcheson writes that "a good ear (as it is generally taken) [is] a power of receiving this pleasure." This means that a person with a good ear is one who receives pleasure from music. The expression "good ear" is ordinarily understood to mean that a person with a good ear is one who can discern fine musical distinctions. Whether a person with a good ear receives pleasure from the distinctions made is ordinarily understood to be an additional and different question. This passage dates from the first edition, and it appears, as noted earlier, that it had only started to dawn on Hutcheson with the fourth edition that there was a question of how complex ideas are discerned. He does not introduce the cognitive notion of discerning similarity into this passage even in the fourth edition. Thus, he leaves in place his view that "beauty" refers to pleasure and his misinterpretation of the notion of "good ear."

Hutcheson's official view, as given in his definitional passage, is that "beauty" refers to a certain pleasure. But he uses "beauty" sometimes to refer to pleasure and sometimes to refer to the characteristics of an object of expe- rience that cause pleasure, seemingly without noticing that there is a prob- lem. For example, he writes, "And farther, the ideas of beauty and harmony, like other sensible ideas, are necessarily pleasant to us . . ." (p. 36). Here he has to be saying that certain characteristics of objects of experience are innately pleasant; otherwise, he would merely be asserting the triviality that pleasure is pleasant. In other places he is quite explicit in using "beauty" to refer to characteristics of objects of experience, as when he writes, "Beauty in corporeal forms is either original or comparative" (p. 38). When Hutche- son uses "beauty" and "beautiful" to refer to characteristics of objects, he does so in what might be called a derivitive way; that is, beautiful objects are beautiful because they are objects that trigger the sense of beauty, which in turn produces pleasure (beauty in his basic or definitional sense).

Early in the Preface, Hutcheson stresses the *necessity* with which some perceptual objects please and displease us, by which he means that these dispositions to be pleased and displeased are built into "the very frame of our nature"; that is, they are innate. At the end of Section 1, he again notes this necessity and adds that these pleasures and displeasures are also *immediate*. Hutcheson takes the immediacy of the pleasures and displeasures to show that they cannot be the products of self-interest, presumably because self-interest involves calculation, and calculation takes time. Furthermore, he adds, we often pursue beauty in ways contrary to our own self-interest: "Now this shows us that however we may pursue beautiful objects from self-love, with a view to obtain the pleasures of beauty . . . yet there must be a sense of beauty, antecedent to prospects even of this advantage, without which sense these objects would not be thus advantageous" (p. 37). Hutcheson moves from the immediacy of the pleasure of beauty to the conclusion that this pleasure cannot be a self-interested one. He then uses this conclusion as more evidence that there is a sense of beauty that underlies the pleasure of beauty and that is therefore antecedent to any self-interested pleasure.

At the end of Section 1, Hutcheson raises the question of the last element of his theory—the nature of the characteristic or characteristics of objects of experience that trigger the sense of beauty. He begins this passage, "Beauty in corporeal forms is either *original* or *comparative;* or, if any like the terms better, *absolute* or *relative*" (p. 38). Here he is clearly using "beauty" to refer to objects of experience. The basis for Hutcheson's distinction between absolute and relative beauty is the notion of representation; some beautiful objects are representations, and some are not. Comparative or relative beauty is representational beauty. Original or absolute beauty is nonrepresentational beauty. When the details of this last element of his theory have been worked out in the next three sections, representational beauty will have been reduced to being a special case of nonrepresentational beauty.

In the last paragraph of Section 1, Hutcheson makes clear that in speaking of absolute beauty he is not making any claim about beauty as a property of objects independent of minds. According to his view, beautiful objects are beautiful only in relation to human minds. In stating this point, he makes some confusing remarks about primary and secondary qualities, which I do not believe have any particular implications for his theory and which I shall ignore.

Before proceeding to Hutcheson's discussion of absolute and relative beauty, I want to note that in the Preface and Section 1 Hutcheson has not just been giving an outline of his theory. He has already begun to argue for his theory and thereby to eliminate certain choices. His tying of simple ideas and their pleasures to external sense and complex ideas and their pleasures (beauty) to internal sense has ruled out the possibility that simple ideas separately considered can contribute to beauty and has dictated that what triggers the sense of beauty must be some complex idea or ideas.

Uniformity amidst Variety

In Section 2, Hutcheson discusses absolute beauty. In Section 3, he treats the beauty of theorems, which is clearly just a special case of absolute beauty. Beauty of theorems is given its own section presumably because, unlike the cases discussed in the earlier section, the external senses do not play any direct role here. In Section 4, he discusses representational beauty, which not so obviously also turns out to be a special case of absolute beauty.

Hutcheson opens Section 2 with this remark: "Since it is certain that we have ideas of beauty and harmony, let us examine what quality in objects excites these ideas, or is the occasion of them" (p. 39). Here "beauty" and "harmony" clearly refer to pleasure, since it is the characteristic of objects that is the cause of the idea of beauty that he seeks to discover. In the very next sentence he uses "beautiful" to refer to a characteristic of objects. "And let it be here observed that our inquiry is only about the qualities which are beautiful to men. . . ." (p. 39). What he is doing in this last quoted sentence is to qualify his earlier claim that beauty is relative to minds by observing that he is talking only about human minds. Animals appear to have different preferences.

Hutcheson proposes to begin his inquiry into what triggers the sense of beauty with a consideration of the "simpler kinds, such as occurs to us in regular figures" (p. 40). He then suggests that what triggers the sense of beauty in the simpler cases may also trigger it in more complicated cases. His way of proceeding suggests the possibility that in simple cases one characteristic of objects may trigger the sense of beauty and that another characteristic may trigger it in complicated cases, but I do not think he seriously considers the possibility of multiple causality here. He proceeds to the simpler cases of regular figures:

> The figures which excite in us the ideas of beauty *seem* to be those in which there is uniformity amidst variety. There are many conceptions of objects which are agreeable upon other accounts, such as grandeur, novelty, sanctity. . . . But what we call beautiful in objects, to speak in the mathematical style, *seems* to be in compound ratio of uniformity and variety: so that where the uniformity of bodies is equal, the beauty is as the variety; and where the variety is equal, the beauty is as the uniformity. This may *seem* probable, and hold pretty generally. (p. 40; italics mine)

In this passage Hutcheson uses "seem" or "seems" three times, presumably to indicate that he is just stating his conclusion in a tentative way. Having stated his conclusion, he will subsequently give it support. The way he is proceeding (stating his conclusion first and then giving the support for it) is obscured by the last sentence of the passage just quoted, "This may seem probable, and hold pretty generally," which is just a concluding remark to what he has been saying. In the three earlier editions of *An Inquiry into the Original of Our Ideas of Beauty and Virtue*, this last line reads, "This will be plain from examples," which indicates that the examples that follow are supposed to be the support for his conclusion. He then proceeds to give a long list of examples that he apparently thinks are obvious and sufficiently support his conclusion about uniformity amidst variety. He begins with a discussion of regular figures.

Although Hutcheson does not put it in quite so explicit a way, I take the structure of his argument to be: (1) Here are some examples of pairs of objects (regular figures), which everyone will agree trigger the sense of beauty differentially; (2) an examination of these pairs of objects will reveal the property or properties of the objects that trigger the sense of beauty. An example of the first kind of pair is Hutcheson's claim that a square is more beautiful that an equilateral triangle. These two figures are equally uniform, so uniformity cannot be the characteristic that is responsible for the difference in beauty. The square has more variety (more sides); therefore, it must be the greater variety that is responsible for the greater beauty. An example of the second kind of pair is Hutcheson's claim that an equilateral triangle is more beautiful that a scalene triangle. These two figures are equally varied (have three sides), so variety cannot be the characteristic that is responsible for the difference in beauty. The equilateral triangle is more uniform than the scalene triangle; therefore, it must be the greater uniformity that is responsible for the greater beauty. This is Hutcheson's argument for his conclusion that the compound ratio of uniformity and variety triggers the sense of beauty. (Notice that he does not say of a pair of objects that one is beautiful and one is not. He speaks of "more beautiful than"; that is, he speaks of pairs of objects having more or less of the beauty-making characteristic.)

There are a number of difficulties with Hutcheson's arguments involving regular figures. First, his claim that a square is more beautiful than an equilateral triangle is counterintuitive. I think that an overwhelming majority of people would disagree with his claim. The lack of the universal agreement he is assuming here means that his argument for variety as a beauty characteristic is undermined. I am not, however, suggesting that variety cannot contribute to beauty.

Second, his claim that an equilateral triangle and a scalene triangle are equally varied seems false. The two triangles have the same number of sides and angles, but the scalene triangle's unequal sides make it more varied. Hutcheson's conclusion that an equilateral triangle is more beautiful than a scalene triangle is plausible, but his reasoning is faulty.

The greatest difficulty with Hutcheson's argument, however, is not the small-scale kind just discussed but the fact that he starts with regular figures *and* proceeds as if he can find *all* the characteristics that trigger the sense of beauty among the properties of regular figures. Geometric figures, for example, lack color, which is of the greatest importance in matters of beauty. (Hutcheson can, of course, account for color *harmony* on his theory as a kind of uniformity, but I am thinking of the sheer beauty of color, which is quite different.) Of course, Hutcheson thinks he has ruled out color "separately considered" as contributing to beauty because it is tied to the external senses. If Hutcheson had begun with more complicated objects than geometric figures, perhaps he would have drawn different conclusions. I do not wish to suggest that Hutcheson is wrong in concluding that uniformity and variety are beauty-making characteristics; I do wish to suggest that his method of argument severely and adversely limits the conclusions he can draw.

Having drawn his basic conclusions from geometric figures, Hutcheson turns to beauty in nature. He asserts without argument, "The same foundation [as with geometric figures] we have for our sense of beauty in the works of nature" (p. 41). He then proceeds to illustrate at very great length that uniformity and variety abound in every part of nature that we call beautiful. He first notes the large-scale aspects of the universe: the spherical forms of the heavenly bodies, their periodic motion, and so on. He then describes the earth's surface as mostly covered by "a very pleasant inoffensive colour" greatly diversified by light, shade, and various surface features. (Notice that it is the uniformity of color that he thinks important for beauty, not the color "separately considered.") He goes on at length to cite the uniformity and variety in plants, animals, fluids, and sounds. His examples tend to be quite abstract: the uniformity that results from all the members of a species resembling one another and the variety that results from there being many individual members of the species; the variety of means of movement (walking, crawling, flying, etc.) and the uniformity of its accomplishment (muscle contraction).

He concludes Section 2 with this remark:

> . . . in all these instances of beauty let it be observed that the pleasure is communicated to those who never reflected on this general foundation, and that all here alleged is this, that the pleasant sensation arises only from objects in which there is uniformity amidst variety. We may have the sensation without knowing what is the occasion of it, as a man's taste may suggest ideas of sweets, acids, bitters, though he is ignorant of the forms of the small bodies, or their motions, which excite these perceptions in him. (p. 47)

Except for a slip when he writes in his discussion of birds about "the beauty of lively colours," Hutcheson never considers whether any characteristic other than uniformity and variety contribute to beauty. This may be due to his having started with geometric figures and having been fixated on the kind of properties that they have, or he may have become fascinated with uniformity and variety at an even earlier stage. Whatever the explanation, Hutcheson just goes on and on, illustrating the great number of beautiful things that have uniformity and variety.

In Section 3, which is entitled "Of the Beauty of Theorems," Hutcheson continues his illustration of uniformity and variety in beautiful objects by giving a large number of instances, in these cases intellectual rather than sensory objects. He gives as examples such things as Euclidean propositions and the theory of gravitation. In such cases the proposition or theory unifies a great variety of truths or phenomena.

Hutcheson remarks that difficult theorems give us more pleasure than easy ones because difficult solutions have some element of surprise, which is pleasant. It is hard to see the point of his remark, assuming he is right, because he clearly does not and cannot regard surprise as contributing to beauty. Perhaps he is just cataloging the various pleasures that derive for intellectual exercises.

More to the point, he notes that our desire for uniformity is so powerful that it has misled a number of philosphers. He mentions Descartes's desire of deducing all knowledge from one proposition and Leibniz's use of the principle of sufficient reason as well as several other cases.

At the end of Section 3 in a subsection devoted to works of art, Hutcheson illustrates the occurrence of uniformity and variety in various kinds of architecture. Why a discussion of works of art, especially architecture, is included in a section on the beauty of theorems is a mystery. In any event, he concludes this subsection on what is really his view on the nonrepresentational beauty-making characteristic of architecture with the following, not so surprising claim: "The same might be observed through all other works of art, even to the meanest utensil, the beauty of every one of which we shall always find to have the same foundation of uniformity amidst variety, without which they appear mean, irregular, and deformed" (p. 54).

In Section 4, the final of the three sections on the characteristic of objects that trigger the sense of beauty, Hutcheson discusses what he calls relative or comparative beauty. Relative beauty "is that which is apprehended in any object commonly considered as an imitation of some original" (p. 54). Having characterized relative beauty, Hutcheson, without any justifying argument, offers an explanation of how it comes about: "this beauty is founded on a conformity, or a kind of unity between the original and the copy" (p. 54). The original of an imitation may be either an actual thing or a fictional object, which Hutcheson characterizes as "an established idea." Relative beauty in no way depends on any beauty in what it represents, although a likeness of an object with absolute beauty will have two sources of beauty.

There is a kind of paradox about Hutcheson's notion of relative beauty. He speaks of relative beauty as being apprehended *in an object,* which sounds analogous to the way absolute beauty (uniformity and variety) is apprehended in an object such as a natural object or a piece of architecture. But relative beauty cannot be *in an object* that is a representation in the way that absolute beauty is *in an object.* On Hutcheson's account, relative beauty is based upon the resemblance between a representation and its subject matter, which means that the beautiful object is the complex object, *the representation plus its subject matter* with a resemblance relation between them. Relative beauty is just a special case of absolute beauty in which one element of a complex object of absolute beauty is a representation and the other element is the represented thing. The paradox is that as Hutcheson explains relative beauty it is just another instance of absolute beauty and not another kind of beauty.

The fact that Hutcheson's account of relative beauty makes it a complicated kind of absolute beauty means that his theory is more highly unified than it would be if there were two different kinds of beauty with two different bases. What Hutcheson has done is this. He sees that representation is a valuable thing, and he incorporates this value into his theory by presenting it as a kind of uniformity, a notion that already stands at the center of his theory. His procedure, however, misrepresents the way in which we value representation. First, it is the representation itself that we value, not a complex of which a representation is an element, although, of course, the valuing involves the representation standing in relation to subject matter. Second, we do not value the representation as a case of beauty; we might say of a representation, "That's a beautiful likeness," but what we mean is that there is a high degree of resemblance, not that the representation as such is beautiful.

Universality of the Sense of Beauty

Section 6 is entitled "Of the Universality of the Sense of Beauty among Men." At the beginning of his "Inquiry Concerning Beauty," Hutcheson tries to prove that there is an internal sense of beauty. Next, he tries to prove that uniformity in variety triggers the sense of beauty. Now he is going to try to prove that the sense of beauty is universal in humans.

The test of the universality of the sense of beauty that Hutcheson proposes is one that parallels the test of rationality. He writes,

> And as we allow all men reason, since all men are capable of understanding simple arguments, though few are capable of complex demonstrations, so in this case it must be sufficient to prove this sense of beauty universal if all men are better pleased with uniformity in the simpler instances than the contrary. . . . (p. 76)

When Hutcheson says that "all men are better pleased with uniformity in the simpler instances than the contrary," I take him to mean that all men are better pleased by greater uniformity than by lesser uniformity. I give this interpretation because every object will have some degree of uniformity, which means that uniformity in one object cannot be contrasted with non-uniformity in another object. (Note that Hutcheson focuses entirely on uniformity with no mention of variety; this happens with some frequency in the "Inquiry Concerning Beauty." Note also that he assumes that being pleased by uniformity is conclusive evidence for the existence of the sense of beauty.) Hutcheson makes his argument manageable, he thinks, by focusing on simpler rather than complex cases because complexities introduce difficulties. For example, a complicated object with a high degree of uniformity might not please someone because its very complexity prevents that person from perceiving its uniformity. If, however, simpler cases are considered, everyone will be able to comprehend the degree of uniformity of the simpler cases, and they will function as an accurate test of people's true preferences.

Hutcheson asks a series of questions about pairs of objects of greater and lesser uniformity. Although he does not remark on it, the pairs of objects differ widely in their degree of uniformity. In each case he thinks—and, I think, correctly—that it is obvious that everyone will prefer the more uniform object. The universal preference for uniformity (greater uniformity) proves, he thinks, the universality of the sense of beauty. The first of Hutcheson's questions is ". . . did ever any man make choice of a trapezium, or any irregular curve, for the ichnography or plan of his house, without necessity, or some great motive of convenience?" (p. 76). He thinks everyone will answer in the negative. He ends his series of similar questions with this passage.

> Who was ever pleased with an inequality of heights in windows of the same range, or dissimilar shapes of them? With unequal legs or arms, eyes or cheeks in a mistress? It must however be acknowledged that interest may often counterbalance our sense of beauty in this affair as well as in others, and superior good qualities may make us overlook such imperfections. (p. 77)

The answer to these two questions is also obviously in the negative. Hutcheson thus proves the universality of the preference for greater uniformity and believes himself to have proven the universality of the sense of beauty. His method of argument is to choose pairs of objects of such simplicity that any normal person will be able to perceive the degree of uniformity in them. Once the choices are clear, Hutcheson thinks it is obvious that, everything else being equal, everyone will choose the greater uniformity.

The Origins of Displeasure and Pleasure

Having shown the universality of the preference for uniformity and, to his own satisfaction, the universality of the sense of beauty, Hutcheson turns to questions concerning the origins of displeasure and pleasure.

If uniformity universally pleases the sense of beauty, is there any form— that is, complex idea—that displeases it? His answer is ". . . there is no form which seems necessarily disagreeable of itself" (p. 74). He might have argued, but does not, that every individuated object will have *some* degree of uniformity and, hence, affect the sense of beauty positively in support of his claim that the sense of beauty gives only positive pleasure. Of course, this argument would not show that there are no complex ideas that displease the sense of beauty. If, however, the sense of beauty is not a source of displeasure, what is the origin of the displeasure that often occurs in our experiences of art and nature?

Hutcheson finds a number of different origins. Many simple ideas (smells, tastes, etc.) positively displease the *external* senses, and, if these ideas are present in a uniform object, they can give rise to positive displeasure. Such experiences would have positive displeasure from, say, a smell and positive pleasure for the uniformity. Also, we are sometimes displeased because an object has less uniformity than we expected it to have or than we think it should have had. This displeasure, however, is disappointment at not having received more pleasure than we expected or think we should have received, not displeasure from the sense of beauty. Such experiences would also be compounds of pleasure and displeasure (disappointment).

The association of ideas is a further source of displeasure (and pleasure) that can complicate an experience in which pleasure is had from the sense of beauty. Hutcheson discusses the association of ideas as something that can have an impact on our experience of art and nature in at least four different places in Section 6. He thus devotes a great deal of space to the topic, but the following passage gives the gist of what he has in mind.

> We know how agreeable a very wild country may be to any person who has spent the cheerful days of his youth in it, and how disagreeable very beautiful places may be if they were the scenes of his misery. And this may help us in many cases to account for the diversities of fancy, without denying the uniformity of our internal sense of beauty. (p. 81)

There is, Hutcheson maintains, a kind of mistake that is sometimes made in judgments of beauty in which a lesser beauty is mistakenly taken to be the greatest possible beauty. This error in large part is possible because uniformity is so widely diffused through the universe. Hutcheson gives the following quaint example of this kind of mistake: "A Goth, for instance, is mistaken when from education he imagines the [Gothic] architecture of his country to be the most perfect" (p. 77) and, hence, more beautiful than Roman architecture. The Goth is right, says Hutcheson, in thinking Gothic architecture beautiful because it has uniformity in variety but wrong in thinking it more beautiful than Roman architecture because the curve of the Roman arch is continuous and, hence, more uniform. (One might turn the argument against Hutcheson here, arguing that Gothic architecture is more varied than Roman.) The Goth's supposed mistake may derive from either or both of two sources: (1) his parochial education or (2) his association of hostile ideas with Roman buildings.

Hutcheson concludes the section on the universality of the sense of beauty with the following remark: "Grandeur and Novelty are two ideas different from Beauty, which often recommend objects to us. The reason of this is foreign to the present subject. See *Spectator* No. 412" (p. 82). Presumably the intent of his remark, in addition to referring the reader to Addison, is to note that there are some still further things that can have an effect on our experiences of beauty. We might be more pleased with a less beautiful object than with a more beautiful one because the former is grand or novel.

In Section 7, which is entitled "Of the Power of Custom, Education, and Example, as to Our Internal Senses," Hutcheson tries to counter rival theories and thereby reinforce his own view. Unspecified opponents have alleged that custom, education, and/or example are responsible for "our relish for beautiful objects," and he denies this (p. 82). Custom, he points out, is simply the result of frequent repetition. And while such repetition can increase our ability to perceive or understand something, mere repetition cannot cause us to be pleased by something if we were not originally disposed to be pleased by it. He concludes that "had we no natural sense of beauty from uniformity, custom could never have made us imagine any beauty in objects" (p. 83).

By education, Hutcheson seems to understand essentially the association of ideas. His argument appears to be that the association of ideas can never cause us to take pleasure in any characteristics of objects if we do not have natural *senses* capable of producing pleasures. He mentions here again his example of the Goth who mistakenly thinks Gothic architecture more beautiful than Romanesque architecture. The Goth, he claims, could never have formed this mistaken belief if he had not had an antecedently existing sense of beauty.

Example is dealt with in a manner similar to that used on custom and education. The example of others can guide and direct us to experience, say, certain works of art, but example cannot cause us to take pleasure in those works. Of course, example may lead someone to pretend to be pleased by some work, but actually receiving pleasure from a work of art presupposes a "natural sense of beauty" (p. 86).

Because the notion of the association of ideas plays a small, important role in Hutcheson's theory and a very prominent role in the theories of Gerard and Alison, a general account of the notion is useful at this point.

First, these eighteenth-century philosophers, following Locke, conceive of perceptions of the world, memories, thoughts of things, and pleasures and pains as *ideas*. "Idea" for these philosophers means "object of awareness." Such things as feelings of pleasure and pain are ideas because they are objects of awareness. For example, these philosophers conceive of the seeing of an apple as a situation in which a person is aware of a complex idea (the perceived apple), which is made up of simple ideas such as perceived redness, perceived roundishness, and so on; in turn, at least some of these philosophers conceive of the complex idea (the perceived apple) as the causal effect of a physical object that lies outside the person's experience.

The general schema of the association of ideas is that the occurrence of an idea *A* in some person's mind will cause an idea *B* to occur in that person's mind because idea *B* is associated in some way with idea *A* in the past experience of that person or because idea *B* and idea *A* have some relation, say, resemblance. The assocation may be, on the one hand, of a *natural* kind, as when *A* and *B* are causally connected, or resemble one another, or are markedly dissimilar. The perception of smoke calls to mind the causally associated idea of fire. The perception of John may call to mind the idea of his identical twin brother, James, who exactly resembles him. On the other hand, the association may be of an *accidental* kind. Hutcheson's example of a present perception of a beautiful place being found disagreeable because it was in the past the scene of a person's misery is an example of an accidental association of ideas at work. An accidental association of ideas may be a very powerful connection of ideas, as in Hutcheson's example.

Hutcheson uses accidental association to try to explain why persons can have different experiences of the same object at the same time. When a person experiences idea B, the association of ideas may import into that person's experience at a particular moment an idea A that that person accidently associates with idea B. Another person who lacks this accidental association of the ideas A and B may not have idea A in his experience at the same particular moment when he experiences idea B. Gerard and Alison use both natural and accidental association of ideas in developing their theories.

Final Causes

In the final section of his essay, Hutcheson rounds off his theory with a discussion of final causes. Why did God create us with a sense of beauty at all and why with uniformity as its object? We could have been created without a sense of beauty or with one that is pleased by irregularity, that is, by objects with low degrees of uniformity.

Because we are beings of limited understanding, our knowledge of the world must be a knowledge of general causes and theorems; we are too intellectually limited to have knowledge of large numbers of particular truths. Thus, our cognitive powers are oriented toward uniformity. If our sense of beauty were pleased by irregularity, our cognitive powers would drive us one way and our affective nature would drive us in the opposite direction. Our knowledge of general causes is necessary for our welfare and survival, but we would take no pleasure in this knowledge. If we lacked a sense of beauty altogether, a somewhat similar result would ensue. As it is, our cognitive powers and our affective natures are oriented in the same direction.

Finally, God's giving us senses of beauty and a world replete with uniformity ensures us of great happiness. God is a utilitarian.

It is worth noting that Hutcheson's theological conclusions do not function to support his theory of taste; they just round off the theory of taste. His arguments for his theory of taste are independent of his theology.

Critical Evaluation of Hutcheson's Theory

In preparation for a critical examination of Hutcheson's theory of taste, let me summarize the arguments he uses to support his theory. First, his argument for his conclusion that there is an internal sense of beauty (step 1) seems to go like this:

1. There are external senses. Common agreement

2. The objects of the external senses are simple ideas, never complex ideas. Hutcheson's assumption

3. Some objects of the external senses produce pleasure, and the pleasure derives from the external senses. Hutcheson's assumption

4. Every pleasure derives from a sense.	Hutcheson's assumption
5. There are only external senses and internal senses.	Hutcheson's assumption
6. There are complex ideas of beauty (musical compositions, paintings) that produce pleasure.	Common agreement
7. The pleasure produced by complex ideas of beauty cannot derive from the external senses.	From 2, 3, and 6
8. The pleasure produced by complex ideas of beauty must derive from some sense other than an external one.	From 4 and 7
9. This nonexternal sense must be an internal sense; that is, there is an internal sense of beauty.	From 4, 5, and 8
10. This internal sense is the source of the pleasure from complex ideas of beauty.	From 4, 7, and 9

There are no doubt a number of ways in which to attack Hutcheson's argument. I wish to focus attention on premise number 4, "Every pleasure derives from a sense." This premise is necessary for Hutcheson's argument because without it the pleasure produced by complex ideas (musical compositions, etc.) does not require some sense or other to be responsible for the pleasure. And without the requirement of some sense or other for producing pleasure, it cannot be inferred that an internal sense (of beauty) is responsible for the pleasure. But it is unclear to me why pleasure would have to be derived from a sense. Consider the external senses, say, vision. It is true that in order to take pleasure in a perception of a color (a simple idea), it is necessary to have the external sense of vision operate first; that is, one must first see the color in order to receive pleasure from it. But it does not follow from this that the pleasure received derives from the external sense of vision. Vision is a cognitive function, and taking pleasure in a visual object is an affective function. But I see no reason to conclude that vision as such has cognitve *and* affective aspects. Consequently, it seems to me that there is no good reason to assume with Hutcheson that every pleasure derives from a sense. But if Hutcheson does not have the premise that every pleasure derives from a sense, he cannot conclude that there is an internal sense of beauty. This means that he has no reason to attribute some pleasures to the external senses and some to internal senses, and this in turn means that there is no good reason to exclude simple ideas from the domain of the beautiful.

Peter Kivy, in his book *The Seventh Sense,* argues very persuasively that Hutcheson's criteria for being a sense—independence of the will, innateness, independence of knowledge, and immediacy—do not do the job that Hutcheson thinks they do.[5] Hutcheson thinks the fact that the phenomena he focuses on exhibit these four characteristics means that the phenomena must be attributed to a sense. Kivy argues that these four characteristics are also characteristics of the workings of reason as Hutcheson and his contemporaries understood reason. The implication of Kivy's view is that Hutcheson had just as much justification to attribute the phenomena he was concerned with to reason as to sense. Kivy's argument, if successful, is also sufficient to derail Hutcheson's conclusion that there is a *sense* of beauty. Kivy's argument can be shown to yield the same result as my argument: Hutcheson does not show there is a *sense* of beauty; hence, he does not show there is an internal sense of beauty, so he has no way to exclude simple ideas from the domain of beauty.

Hutcheson's argument for his conclusion that it is uniformity amidst variety that triggers the sense of beauty (step two) seems to go like this: First, he examines pairs of relatively simple objects that trigger the sense of beauty differentially. He thinks that if the two objects in a pair are different in only one characteristic, then it must be the differing characteristic that is responsible for the greater beauty of the more beautiful object. That characteristic is thus a beauty-making characteristic. For example, he claims that a square is more beautiful that an equilateral triangle and that the two figures are equally uniform and differ only in variety—the square has more angles and sides. He concludes that variety is responsible for the square's greater beauty and is thus a beauty-making characteristic. Using a similar argument, he concludes that uniformity is a beauty-making characteristic. The two premises (1) uniformity is a beauty-making characteristic and (2) variety is a beauty-making characteristic are Hutcheson's support for his conclusion that the compound ratio of uniformity and variety is what tiggers the sense of beauty. He then goes on to give additional support for his conclusion by giving example after example of more complicated beautiful objects that exhibit the compound ratio of uniformity and variety. The large inductive sample presumably shows that all beautiful objects possess the compound ratio.

Despite the difficulties in his argument, I believe Hutcheson is right that uniformity amidst variety is a beauty-making characteristic. He clearly also concludes, however, that it is the *only* beauty-making characteristic, but his argument just as clearly has nothing relevant to say about his exclusivity claim. He, of course, thinks (mistakenly) that in step 1 he has ruled out any simple ideas as beauty-making. But even if he had ruled out all simple ideas,

5. Kivy, *The Seventh Sense,* pp. 37ff.

there are numerous complex ideas other that uniformity amidst variety that he has not ruled out—elegant shapes, gracefully curving lines, and the like.

There is another problem—a problem of omission in Hutcheson's theory and in the theories of many of the taste theorists. He and a number of others do not distinguish between an object's having a beauty-making characteristic or characteristics and an object's being beautiful. Hutcheson speaks of objects with uniformity amidst variety as beautiful objects, but this cannot be right because virtually every object has uniformity amidst variety and not all of these objects are beautiful. What he really means is that objects with uniformity amidst variety are objects with a beauty-making characteristic. Thus, Hutcheson (and many other taste theorists) never raises the question of how much of or what degree of the beauty-making characteristic is required to make something beautiful. "Beautiful," "aesthetically good," and other specific evaluational notions are *threshold* concepts. For example, on a theory such as Hutcheson's, the term "beautiful" would become applicable only when there is an object with a relatively high degree of uniformity amidst variety.

When Hutcheson comes to the third step in his argument—proving the universality of the sense of beauty—he thinks he has already shown that there is a sense of beauty with uniformity amidst variety as its *only* object. He thus believes that he knows the *nature* of both the sense of beauty and its object. He presumably thinks, however, that it is possible that only he or perhaps a few persons possess this faculty. Thus, he undertakes to show that it is universal in all humans. His method is to use a test to which *all* humans are sensitive—the method of comparisons of very simple pairs of objects of greater or lesser uniformity. There is perhaps a problem about variety here, because Hutcheson does not say anything about it in his universality argument. Perhaps he thinks that because he already knows that uniformity amidst variety is the only object of the sense of beauty, he need only concern himself with one aspect of uniformity amidst variety, namely, uniformity. In any event, when his test successfully shows that all humans prefer greater uniformity to lesser uniformity, he thinks he has shown that the sense of beauty with uniformity amidst variety as its only object is universal in humans.

However, since he fails to show in step 1 that there is a sense of beauty and in step 2 that uniformity amidst variety is its only object, all that the third step shows is that all humans prefer greater uniformity.

Since Hutcheson has not proven that there is a sense of beauty, the two questions addressed in step 4—whether the sense of beauty is ever a source of displeasure in experiences of beauty and whether the sense of beauty is the only source of pleasure in experiences of beauty—cannot be answered. Hutcheson, in trying to answer these questions, nevertheless, does draw some conclusions that are defensible, although these conclusions themselves raise additional problems for his theory.

Having asserted somewhat dogmatically that no complex idea "seems necessarily disagreeable of itself" (p. 74), Hutcheson needs to explain the source or sources of the displeasure that sometimes occurs in experiences of beauty. The first source of displeasure he mentions comes from the domain of simple ideas. Smells and the like (simple ideas of the external senses, as he calls them) can be responsible for displeasure in experiences of beauty. Hutcheson is certainly right that simple ideas can be a source of displeasure in experiences of beauty. The topic of simple ideas, however, raises a difficulty for Hutcheson's theory. Simple ideas are pleasant as well as unpleasant. Since he has not shown that there is a sense of beauty that reacts only to complex ideas and is the *sole* source of pleasure in beauty, he has no way to show that the pleasure produced by simple ideas is not part of the beauty pleasure.

The second source of displeasure in experiences of beauty that Hutcheson identifies is the association of ideas. He is certainly right also that the association of ideas can be responsible for displeasure in experiences of beauty. But here again his argument raises a difficulty for his theory. The association of ideas can produce pleasure as well as displeasure, and since he has not proven the existence of the sense of beauty that is the *sole* source of the pleasure in beauty, his theory does not show that pleasures derived from associations are not part of the beauty pleasure. This chink in Hutcheson's theory leaves an opening for the later associationist theories of taste.

Hutcheson is also certainly right about disappointment—his third candidate for producer of displeasure. Disappointment when we expect better can be a displeasure in the experience of beauty. But again there is a difficulty. In the absence of a proof for the existence of the sense of beauty that is the *sole* source of pleasure in beauty, his theory does not show that the pleasure of satisfaction in getting as good as we expected is not a part of the beauty pleasure.

Hutcheson's remarks about sources of displeasure in our experiences of beauty are clearly an attempt to combat the problem of relativism—"to account for the diversities of fancy." Disagreeable simple ideas, disappointment when we expected better, and associations of ideas can import displeasure into the experiences of beauty and cause disagreement among persons about those experiences. Hutcheson, of course, thinks that it is clear that these three are irrelevant distractions that have no bearing on beauty and, hence, give no support to relativism. At the end of his discussion of the universality of the sense of beauty, his remarks about grandeur and novelty no doubt serve a similar purpose. Grandeur and novelty are sources of *pleasure* but are different from beauty, and if disagreements involved in experiences of beauty are caused by pleasure imported by concurrent experiences of grandeur or novelty, this does not give support to beauty-relativism.

Of course, for Hutcheson, the "relativism" being avoided here is not really relativism; he is trying to account for diversities of fancy that arise not from disagreement over the beauty of objects but from pleasure and displeasure imported into experiences of beautiful objects by other things—associations of ideas, grandeur, and the like. Real relativism for Hutcheson could occur only if people disagree over whether uniformity amidst variety gives pleasure, and he has shown that there is a universal preference for this characteristic. Of course, he does not show that uniformity amidst variety is the only source of beauty pleasure, and if people disagree over other characteristics, then relativism still looms as a problem.

The second question of step 4 is whether custom, education, and/or example can be sources of the beauty pleasure. Hutcheson wants to show that, contrary to what some have alleged, custom, education, and/or example cannot be sources of the beauty pleasure and that the sense of beauty is.

Consider custom first. Suppose we listen repeatedly to a piece of music and become accustomed to it. Suppose, as a result, we come to perceive the various sound qualities of the music and find them beautiful (that is, receive pleasure from them). Custom (becoming accustomed) thus plays a role in our coming to find beauty in the music. It is not custom, however, Hutcheson argues, that causes the pleasure; custom is merely the mechanism that enables us to come to notice the musical qualities. Once the qualities are noticed, we are then pleased by them. He writes that

> had we no natural sense of beauty from uniformity, custom could never have made us imagine any beauty in objects. . . . When we have these natural senses antecedently, custom may make us capable of extending our views farther and of receiving more complex ideas of beauty in bodies, or harmony in sounds, by increasing our attention and quickness of perception. (p. 83)

Hutcheson is right about custom, but he is not justified in claiming that there is a "natural sense of beauty" that is antecedent to custom. He would be justified in claiming that a disposition to be pleased by uniformity (or perhaps other characteristics) is antecedent to custom. Remember that the sense of beauty is a disposition to be pleased by a particular complex idea and *no other* complex or simple idea and that Hutcheson has not shown that such a *specific* disposition exists.

Hutcheson's argument against education as a source of the beauty pleasure is not very clearly stated, but I take it to be along the same lines as his argument against custom. We can be instructed about paintings, music, and the like, and such instruction can enlarge our knowledge of such arts and their qualities and thus increase the number and range of things we can take pleasure in. But education, like custom, is simply a mechanism for increasing our knowledge. Such increased knowledge of and attunement to the qualities of things will not by themselves cause us to take pleasure in these qualities or things; a disposition to receive pleasure from such qualities is also required. Hutcheson assumes that this disposition is the sense of beauty. The criticism leveled against Hutcheson's analogous conclusion in connection with custom applies here also.

The argument against example is the same as that against education. The example of others can call beautiful things to our attention, but we could not take pleasure in them without an antecedent disposition to take pleasure in them, that is, without a sense of beauty. The criticism against custom applies here also.

2

The Association and Coalescence of Ideas: Alexander Gerard

In Hutcheson's theory of taste, the association of ideas plays a wholly negative role: It is used to explain why there are deviant preferences. For example, the association of ideas is used to explain why someone prefers an object of lesser uniformity (lesser beauty) to one of greater uniformity (greater beauty), and a typical explanation would be that such a person associates a certain pleasant thing or event with the object of lesser uniformity such that the pleasure of the object of lesser uniformity plus the pleasure of the associated pleasant thing or event override the pleasure of the object of greater uniformity. It never crossed Hutcheson's mind that the fact that the pleasure of the object of greater uniformity can be overridden and not preferred has anything to do with either the degree of beauty of the object of lesser uniformity or the degree of beauty of the more uniform object. A number of the theorists of taste who came after Hutcheson, however, give the association of ideas a central and positive role in their theories—a role, as they see it, not involving deviancy.

Alexander Gerard's theory, set forth in his *Essay on Taste* (1759), is the earlier of the two most prominent associationist accounts of the nature of taste. Gerard's *Essay* consisted originally of three parts, but in the third and final edition of 1780 he added a fourth part entitled "Of the Standard of Taste." This fourth part refers to and is clearly modeled on Hume's earlier essay of the same name, but perhaps its most striking feature is that, like Hume's essay, it makes no positive use of the association of ideas. Its only use of the association of ideas is the negative use of the kind found in Hutcheson's theory. Consequently, in this chapter, which is concerned with Gerard's associationism, I shall deal only with the first three parts of his book, as these three parts constitute a unified whole involving the association of ideas. I shall not, however, deal with the first three parts in the order that Gerard presents them because he sometimes separates points that ought to be discussed together. I shall discuss two points from Gerard's nonassociationist "Of the Standard of Taste" in Chapter 5 in connection with Hume's theory; although Gerard lacks the philosophical acumen of Hume, in two ways his essay supplements Hume's theory.

In this chapter, I shall first give an exposition of Gerard's theory and then raise a few limited questions about it. Let me note here that, even in the original three parts of his book, the notion of the association of ideas is used by Gerard in only some parts of his theory. So, Gerard's theory is in a sense only a partial associationist theory. In the next chapter I shall first discuss Archibald Alison's completely associationist theory and then attempt a full-scale evaluation of the associationisms of both Gerard and Alison as theories of taste.

Internal Sense: Nature and Number

The different uses to which the association of ideas is put are not the only important differences between Hutcheson's theory and Gerard's. For Hutcheson, the internal sense of beauty is a "black box" that reacts to uniformity amidst variety and produces pleasure. Although in his discussion of final causes, Hutcheson tells us why the sense of beauty reacts to uniformity—this part of our affective nature is aimed in the same direction that our cognitive nature is—he has nothing to say about the makeup of the sense of beauty. Gerard, in contrast, gives elaborate explanations of the internal makeup of the various internal senses he distinguishes. Also, although Gerard does not say so at the beginning of his book, he later contrasts his view of internal senses as derived and compounded with Hutcheson's view of internal senses as ultimate and original.

Another difference between the theories of Hutcheson and Gerard that is often remarked on is the fact that, while Hutcheson discusses only the sense of beauty, Gerard distinguishes and discusses seven taste senses: the senses of novelty, grandeur, beauty, imitation, harmony, ridicule, and virtue. On the question of the number of senses, however, the difference is perhaps not as great as it might at first seem. Although he does not develop his remark, Hutcheson mentions grandeur and novelty in a way that suggests that he thought that there are senses of grandeur and novelty. Also, Hutcheson treats harmony as a kind of beauty, so on the question of the number of senses the two theories are perhaps closer than they at first appear to be. Later in this chapter, I shall also show that Hutcheson thinks the moral sense can be an aspect of taste and thus that Hutcheson's moral sense is somewhat analogous to Gerard's sense of virtue.

The Coalescence and Association of Ideas

Part 1 of Gerard's book is devoted to the exposition of the natures of the seven senses of taste and their objects. He begins with a discussion of the sense of novelty. As with the accounts of the other six internal senses he

distinguishes, Gerard's discussion of novelty consists of a description of pleasure taken in a certain kind of object or objects, together with explanations
about the mental phenomena that are the source of the pleasure. Only later
in a long footnote near the beginning of Part 3 is any kind of theoretical and
technical description given of the various internal senses and the criteria that
distinguish them.

Gerard mentions seven different sources of pleasure in his discussion of
novelty. The first—and I think basic—pleasure is that which is supposed to
arise as a result of the moderate difficulty involved in conceiving of a novel
object. This mental activity puts the mind in "a lively and elevated temper"
and thereby results in "a pleasant sensation."[1] Pleasure as a result of moderate exertion of the mind is a frequent feature of other of the internal senses
as Gerard conceives of them. A little later in the discussion, Gerard adds that
even when a novel object is "so simple as to be conceived without any difficulty" (p. 6), if one is bored, the novel object will give pleasure. An example
he gives is that of wearying of one's house furnishings and changing them
just for the novelty of having new furnishings. "The pleasure of novelty is,
in this case, preferred to that which results from real beauty" (p. 7). This
pleasure of sheer novelty is not, I judge, a second source of pleasure, because
a mind "sunk into indolence and langour" will be exercised and put in "a
lively and elevated temper," which is pleasant even without any difficulty
of conception.

A second source of pleasure occurs when a novel object is agreeable in
itself. Although Gerard does not note it, the pleasure of an object agreeable
in itself is not a pleasure of novelty, and, strictly speaking, the pleasure is
irrelevant to a discussion of novelty. There are two distinct pleasures in this
case: the pleasure of novelty and the pleasure that derives from the agree-
ableness of the object.

A third source of pleasure in novelty is surprise. Gerard says that surprise "augments our delight or uneasiness, by farther enlivening the thought,
and agitating the mind" (p. 8), which sounds as if this source of pleasure is
a special case of pleasure from the exertion of the mind. So, surprise may
not really be a source of pleasure distinct from the first source.

Agreeable passion is a fourth source of pleasure.

> Any agreeable passion or emotion which a new object happens to produce, will
> run into the pleasant sentiment that naturally arises from its novelty, and will
> augment it. A new suit of cloaths gives pleasure to a child, by its being different
> from his former; it likewise excites his pride, and gives him an expectation of
> attracting the notice of his companions. (p. 9)

As with the second source of pleasure, the pleasure derived from pride,
strictly speaking, is not a pleasure of novelty and is, therefore, irrelevant to

---

1. Alexander Gerard, *An Essay on Taste.* 3d ed. of 1780, Walter J. Hipple, Jr., ed. (Delmar,
N.Y.: Scholars' Facsimiles & Reprints, 1978), p. 3. All subsequent internal page cites in this
chapter to Gerard are to this edition.

a discussion of novelty. Why does Gerard think the pleasures of agreeable objects and agreeable passions are to be thought of as pleasures of novelty?

Note that he writes in the passage just quoted that an agreeable passion produced by a novel object "will run into" the pleasure that arises naturally from novelty, that is, the pleasure that arises from moderate mental exertion. Gerard thinks that under certain conditions, when two pleasures are present in the mind at the same time, they will coalesce into a single, larger pleasure. In the present case, he thinks that the pleasure of the agreeable passion (pride in new clothes) is swallowed up by and adds to the pleasure of novelty such that the pleasure of novelty is greater than it would be without the agreeable passion. Gerard has underlying his reasoning here what I shall call *the principle of the possibility of the coalescence of ideas*. Cases such as the coalescence of an agreeable (i.e., pleasant) passion and the pleasure of novelty are supposed instances of this principle at work. As will be shown later, the notion that different pleasures (or ideas generally) can coalesce into something that is treated as a single idea is an essential feature of Gerard's associationism. So far as I know, the notion that ideas can coalesce is a genuinely new conception, appearing for the first time in the history of thought in Gerard's essay.

The fifth source of pleasure involves successful conception: "When the conception of an object is attended with very considerable difficulty, the pleasure which we feel in the exertion of mind necessary for overcoming this difficulty, is encreased by the joy with which we reflect on our success in having surmounted it" (p.10). Note that Gerard claims that the exertion pleasure itself "is encreased" by the pleasure derived from knowing we have succeeded; it is not supposed to be just an additional pleasure. He is again applying the *principle of the possibility of the coalescence of ideas* to conclude that the basic pleasure of novelty is increased in magnitude by the absorbing of another kind of pleasure.

The sixth source of pleasure also involves the use of the coalescence principle: "When objects are of such a nature that we reckon our acquaintance with them an acquisition in knowledge, the pleasure of their novelty arises in part from the satisfaction with which we reflect on our having made this acquisition" (p. 10). The satisfaction we take in having acquired knowledge, however, appears to be quite distinct from the pleasure of novelty and thus not part of the pleasure of novelty. I am not, by the way, claiming that Gerard was consciously aware of his use of the coalescence principle.

The seventh source of pleasure that he cites does not involve the supposed absorption of one pleasure by another. Gerard notes that in the case of art, when we are pleased by its novelty, we may also be pleased by the originality of the artist. He characterizes the latter as an "additional charm" (p. 10).

The notion of the association of ideas does not come up in Gerard's account of the sense of novelty, which means that the operation of the association of ideas is not a necessary conditon of an internal sense for him. The operation of the principle of the possibility of the coalescence of ideas can be inferred from what he has to say about some cases of novelty. Strictly speaking, the use of this principle is not a necessary condition of an internal sense either, but its use is vital for his treatment of some cases of novelty, sublimity, and the other taste categories, as Gerard conceives of them. The association of ideas and the alleged coalescence of ideas are different mental phenomena, but, as will be seen later, they can interact, as when Gerard thinks that certain ideas coalesce as a result of the association of ideas. In fact, Gerard's theory (and Alison's) requires the coalescence of ideas to achieve its characteristic associationist conclusions. I do not believe that the presence or the significance of the coalescence principle has been noted by earlier commentators.

There is one respect in which the object of the sense of novelty is different from the objects of the other six internal senses. Typically, an object can be novel only once for a given person.

Gerard's account of the sense of novelty is, as will be seen, similar to the accounts he gives of the other senses of taste in that they typically involve a basic pleasure produced by the workings of the cognitive faculties. As noted earlier, such a view contrasts strongly with Hutcheson's "black box" account of the sense of beauty. Hutcheson never tells us how the sense of beauty and uniformity in variety interact to produce pleasure; he just claims that they do. For all one can tell from Hutcheson's account, the sense of beauty itself is completely *affective*. Gerard, by contrast, claims that the cognitive faculties themselves are the source of the basic taste pleasures; for Gerard, the cognitive faculties operating in their *ordinary* ways are the senses of taste. In this regard, Gerard's theory resembles earlier seventeenth-century theories of beauty and in some respects resembles that of Kant's later theory of taste.

Gerard's account of sublimity is more complicated than his account of novelty because, as he treats it, the objects of the sense of sublimity are much more diverse. In the case of novelty, the only objects of concern are new objects, and that is that. He begins his discussion of sublimity as if it were as simple a matter as novelty. He writes, "Objects are sublime, which possess *quantity,* or amplitude, and *simplicity,* in conjunction" (p. 11). It turns out ultimately, however, that there are sublime things that are so without regard to quantity, and so he has to complicate his account. Nevertheless, he begins the development of his account of the sublime with a mini-theory that involves only objects of large size. Once this is done, the complication of the theory proceeds.

Gerard gives some initial examples of things that are sublime and things that are not. The Alps and the Nile are sublime, and a small hill and a rivulet are not. The first two possess amplitude (with simplicity), and the latter two do not. He then switches from the listing of sublime objects to an account of the phenomenology of the experience of such objects, focusing first on amplitude and then on simplicity. Of our experience of amplitude he writes,

We always contemplate objects and ideas with a disposition similar to their nature. When a large object is presented, the mind expands itself to the extent of that object, and is filled with one grand sensation, which totally possessing it, composes it into a solemn sedateness, and strikes it with deep silent wonder and admiration: it finds such a difficulty in spreading itself to the dimensions of its object, as enlivens and invigorates its frame: and having overcome the opposition which this occasions, it sometimes imagines itself present in every part of the scene which it contemplates; and from the sense of this immensity, feels a noble pride, and entertains a lofty conception of its own capacity. (p. 12)

I am unclear about what Gerard is saying when he writes that we contemplate objects with a disposition similar to the nature of the objects. When he speaks of the mind's difficulty in spreading itself to the dimensions of its object and of this enlivening the mind, I take him to be speaking in a metaphorical way about the difficulty of conceiving of the object and of the pleasure this mental exertion gives. He is here presumably speaking of a phenomenon that is supposed to be somewhat similar to the basic phenomenon of novelty, namely, the phenomenon of the difficulty in conceiving of an object. Also, presumably the alleged mental exertion involved in the case of the sublime also yields pleasure, although Gerard does not explicitly say so.

Having dealt with amplitude, he proceeds to simplicity. An example he gives is that of an unbroken (simple) view of the sea, which he claims is more sublime than a view of the sea that is broken by innumerable islands. The islands introduce a complexity that interferes with the perception of amplitude. The simplicity of an object allows us to "take in with ease one entire conception of . . .[an] . . . object, however large" (p. 13). Gerard is here introducing the notion of the facility of conception, which will play such a large role in his discussion of beauty. In connection with sublimity, the facility of conception made possible by simplicity is presumably thought here to aid in the production of pleasure by making amplitude conceivable.

Certain sublime objects seem to be a problem in that they do not appear to involve quantity at all, for example, heroism and magnanimity. Gerard, in effect, argues that this apparent problem arises because such things can be conceived of too narrowly. Heroism, for example, he notes is not to be conceived as "a simple emotion in the mind" but as something involving causes, objects, and effects (p. 15). When all of these are factored in, amplitude puts in an appearance. Heroism, for example, involves the domination of multitudes, vast territories, or the like.

There are, however, certain sublime objects that Gerard concedes do not involve quantity—genius, for example. In order to accommodate such objects, Gerard makes the phenomenology of the experience of the sublime *primary*—the thing that all sublime things have in common. Thus,

whatever excites in the mind a sensation or emotion similar to what is excited by vast objects, is on this account denominated sublime. . . .

Such degrees of excellence [as genius], by an original principle of the mind, excite wonder and astonishment, the same emotion which is produced by amplitude. A great degree of *quality* has here the same effect upon the mind, as vastness of *quantity,* and it produces this effect in the same manner, by stretching and elevating the mind in the conception of it. (pp. 16–17)

He also says that a storm at sea, loud thunder, and the like are sublime because they excite the same experience as vast objects. It is unclear to me why such phenomena as storms at sea cannot be treated in the same way that heroism is, and perhaps Gerard thinks that they can. In that case, he would have two ways of showing why storms at sea and the like are sublime.

Finally, halfway through his discussion of the sublime, Gerard introduces the topic of the association of ideas. Having given paradigms of the sublime—examples of vast objects—and having tried to show how some objects that are not large are nevertheless sublime, he goes on to try to show how the association of ideas can make things sublime. He begins in the following way:

> It is the nature of association, to unite different ideas so closely, that they become in a manner one. In that situation, the qualities of one part are naturally attributed to the whole, or to the other part. At least, association renders the transition of the mind from one idea to another so quick and easy, that we contemplate both with the same disposition; and are therefore similarly affected by both. Whenever, then, any object uniformly and constantly introduces into the mind the idea of another that is grand, it will, by its connection with the latter, be itself rendered grand. (pp. 18–19)

Gerard is saying here that the association of ideas can involve what I earlier called "the coalescence of ideas." In some cases of pairs of associated ideas, he is claiming that they coalesce into one idea.

As one of the examples of the association of ideas rendering something sublime, Gerard cites paintings that represent sublime natural objects or persons in the grip of sublime passions. The paintings themselves, which may even be miniatures, are sublime, Gerard claims, because of their *association* with sublime originals, that is, subject matters. What he has in mind is a case like this: A painting is a representation of, say, a particular Alpine scene, which is itself sublime. Now Gerard is claiming that because (1) the Alpine scene itself is sublime and (2) the painting regularly introduces the idea of this scene into the mind, the painting itself is thereby sublime. This occurs, he thinks, because association unites "different ideas so closely, that they become in a manner one." In this case, the two ideas are (1) the experience of the painting and (2) the idea of the sublime Alpine scene.

Directly following his claim about how association works (already cited and which I quote again next), Gerard gives an account of what makes style in language sublime.

> Whenever . . . any object uniformly and constantly introduces into the mind the idea of another that is grand, it will, by its connection with the latter, be itself rendered grand. Hence words and phrases are denominated lofty and majestic. Sublimity of style arises, not so much from the sound of the words,

though that doubtless may have some influence, as from the nature of the ideas which we are accustomed to annex to them, and the character of the persons among whom they are in most common use. (p. 19)

Consider first only word sounds and their meanings (ideas), ignoring for the moment the persons who use the words and phrases. Let it be granted for the purposes of the argument that word sounds and their meanings (ideas) are connected by the association of ideas. Let it also be granted that sublimity of linguistic style arises to a considerable degree from the ideas (meanings) involved, although some contribution may be made by the sounds themselves. If all this is granted, what it comes to is that sublimity of style has at least two sources (sounds and meanings) and that the two sources are related by the association of ideas. It is not the association of ideas, which simply relates the sources, that makes the style sublime; the sounds and the ideas themselves provide a basis for sublimity of style. Gerard, in speaking of word sounds and their associated ideas, is supposed to be presenting them as a case of something not sublime made sublime by its being related by the association of ideas to something that is sublime. The case of style as he describes it insofar as word sounds and ideas are concerned, however, is not an instance of this. By his own description, the sound itself and the associated ideas themselves are what make for sublimity of words and phrases. He concludes, from the alleged fact that the association of ideas is involved in the case of linguistic style, that *it* is what makes style sublime when it is. All he has shown, if his claim is successful, however, is that the associated items themselves are sources of the sublimity of linguistic style.

When Gerard refers at the end of the passage quoted to "the character of persons among whom they [the words and phrases] are in most common use," however, he does seem to have in view a case of something sublime (persons' characters) supposedly contributing by association to something else's sublimity (the linguistic style of the words and phrases). I shall evaluate this claim in the last section of the Alison chapter.

In the same paragraph in which he discusses sublimity of linguistic style, Gerard attributes the sublimity that, according to him, we ascribe to objects in elevated places to the association of ideas (p. 19). In justification of this conclusion, he summarizes in a long footnote what Hume has to say on the matter in the *Treatise* (pp. 19–20). The amplitude of the distance above us is transferred, Gerard maintains, by the association of ideas to the idea of the object that rests at the height of the sublime elevation; thus, the elevated object becomes sublime. There is a parallel argument about objects distant in time. Without worrying about the argument that is supposed to support the claim about the sublimity of elevated objects, consider whether it is true that we attribute sublimity to elevated objects as Gerard says we do. It is no doubt true that elevated objects are sometimes sublime, but Gerard is claiming that all objects atop sublime elevations are sublime, and this is false. A small, insignificant object atop a sublime elevation is not necessarily sublime. Once it is seen that objects atop sublime elevations are not necessarily sublime, the question of whether sublime elevation makes an object at its top sublime does not arise. Actually sublime objects that are greatly elevated are no doubt made so not by their elevation but by other of their characteristics. Of course, great elevation may befit a greatly elevated sublime object, but that is another matter. Since Gerard's conclusion about the sublimity of objects atop sublime elevations is false, there is no need to justify it by the use of the association of ideas or any other phenomena.

Gerard purports to find another way in which the association of ideas imports sublimity into literature.

> If an author's main subject is destitute of innate grandeur, it may be rendered grand, by comparing, or some way associating it with objects naturally such. By the same means the real grandeur of a subject is increased. Hence metaphor, comparison, and imagery, are often productive of sublimity. Cicero exalts Caesar's idea of clemency, by representing it as godlike. Seneca give a sublime idea of Cicero's genius, by comparing it with the majesty and extent of the Roman empire. (p. 25)

What Gerard is actually describing here is not a case of the association of ideas. The authors cited are asserting that Caesar's clemency and Cicero's genius are sublime by means of metaphorical or some other kind of assertion. Such assertion does not *render* the author's subjects sublime; it just claims that they are.

Gerard distinguishes three kinds of beauty: beauty of figure, beauty of utility, and beauty of color. A variety of different principles or mental mechanisms are supposedly involved in the production of the pleasures of these types of beauty, but what holds them together as varieties of beauty, Gerard claims, is the "similitude of their feelings" (p. 45). I take it that he is not just talking about the similarity of the various feelings of pleasure but of the whole phenomenology of the experience, but he is not explicit about this.

Gerard begins his discussion of beauty by writing, "The first species of beauty is that of *figure;* and belongs to objects possessed of *uniformity, variety,* and *proportion.* Each of these qualities pleases in some degree; but all of them united give exquisite satisfaction" (p. 29). Having said this, he immediately proceeds to explanations in terms of mental mechanisms of how the three characteristics produce pleasure. Uniformity does so by ensuring moderate facility of conception; a part in a uniform whole "suggests the whole, and [in] . . . impelling the mind to imagine the rest, produces a grateful exertion of energy" (p. 30). Uniformity alone, however, is apt to bore, and variety is needed to enliven things by giving the mind pleasant employment. Typically, uniformity and variety work together to enhance the effects of one another.

Things have proportion when the parts are not so small that they are difficult to perceive when we perceive the whole or when the parts are not so large that it interferes with the perception of the whole or the other parts. When either of these cases of disproportion obtains, our faculties fail to conceive of the whole, and this failure causes us to have a low estimation of

our faculties, which is painful. When things are proportionate, we can successfully conceive of the whole, and this success causes us to have a high
estimate of our faculties, which is pleasant.

Gerard also mentions very briefly proportion as it relates to the human
body. Any small variation in the size of a body part produces disproportion.
This sort of proportion-disproportion, I assume, applies not only to the human body but to all animal bodies, as well as other objects. Whereas the
proportion discussed in the previous paragraph is a kind of proportion having to do with the ability to perceive wholes, this kind of proportion depends upon the actual proportions of things of which we have had experience.

At the end of his discussion of beauty of figure, Gerard notes that the
uniformity, variety, and proportion that please us in works of art are indica-
tions of design *and* that we also take pleasure in conceiving of the skill of
the designing cause. There are thus, according to Gerard, two sources of
pleasure in such experiences. He then asserts that "we ascribe this pleasure
[taken in conceiving of skill] to the visible objects which led us to conceive"
of the skillful designer (p. 37). Here again is an instance of Gerard attempting to collapse into one two *distinct* pleasures: the pleasure taken in
the visible properties of an object and the pleasure taken in conceiving of a
skillful designer of that object.

Gerard identifies utility as the second kind of beauty. He is not the
first eighteenth-century philosopher to make this unlikely claim; Hume, for
example, in the *Treastise* makes a similar claim. The simple fact is, however,
that no one, except an occasional philosopher, has ever claimed that utility
is a kind of beauty.

Gerard appears to give several arguments in support of his claims about
utility. He asserts that the pleasure of regularity (beauty of figure) is destroyed by great disutility. What he is apparently trying to show is that the
lack of one kind of beauty (disutility) cancels out another kind of beauty
(beauty of figure). Although his argument shows that disutility can overbal-
ance the preference for beauty of figure, it does not really show that disutility
destroys the pleasure of beauty of figure or that utility is a kind of beauty.
The argument *assumes* that utility is a kind of beauty. He next notes that in
many natual objects utility is united with great "elegance of form" (p. 38). I
suppose he has in mind things such as the utility of the giraffe's long neck
and its elegant form. Again, this remark does not show that utility is a kind
of beauty, just that utility can exist along with beauty of fiqure.

Gerard remarks further that to be a masterpiece a work of art must
combine utility and regularity. Assuming his remark to be true, it shows
only that utility is necessary for being a masterpiece, not that it is a kind of
beauty. He writes further that "to obtain utility, forms of inferior beauty are,
for particular purposes, constantly preferred, even where beauty is far from
being neglected. The cube, not any of the more varied polygons, is chosen
for a pedestal, on account of its stability" (p. 38). What this observation
shows is that we may sometimes find it necessary to sacrifice beauty of figure

(in, for example, a pedestal) for utility; while this shows that utility is a value, it does not show that it is a kind of beauty.

In a footnote, Gerard accuses the Swiss theorist of taste Jean Pierre Crousaz of confusing utility with uniformity in his book *Traité du Beau*. Two pages later Gerard writes, "In composition, the most refined reflections, the most elaborate descriptions, the warmest pathos, displease, if they break the unity, if they do not promote, much more if they retard the main design, to which all the parts should be subordinate" (p. 39). Gerard himself here confuses the relation that exists among the elements of a work and a work's "main design"; that is, he confuses how the elements of a work fit together (unity within a work) with a work's "main design," which is its ability (utility) to realize the intention of the author. The unity of elements and a work's main design are quite distinct things, although they are usually related. He takes himself to be talking about utility, but his abstract example is clearly about unity within a work. In continuing his discussion of this point, Gerard repeats his confusion. He first writes, "In general, it is from the end and design of works of genius that their peculiar rules must be deduced . . . and by this the critic must regulate his judgment" (p. 39). Here he is clearly talking about the author's intention; a work's utility depends on how well it realizes an author's intention. He ends his discussion of utility, however, in the following confused way: "Could fitness [utility] be dispensed with, a collection of fine sentiments and figures cloathed in agreeable language, might fully gratify our taste, however unconnected they were with one another" (p. 39). He purports to be talking about utility (fitness), but, in fact, he is talking about unity within a work.

Nothing in Gerard's remarks on the topic give any support at all to his implausible contention that utility is a kind of beauty, although some of his remarks assume it to be a kind of beauty. His confusion of utility and unity may *explain,* at least in part, why he thought utility is a kind of beauty, for unity, by everyone's admission, is a beauty-making property.

The third and final kind of beauty Gerard discusses is beauty of color. This is entirely distinct from beauty of figure and utility and pleases by means of different mental mechanisms. He distinguishes three kinds of beauty of color, although his remarks about the first two species are exceedingly brief.

The first kind of beauty of color involves a physiological mechanism— color that is "less hurtful" to the eyes (p. 41). Gerard does not elaborate, but he seems to imply that all colors are hurtful to the eyes to some degree and that those that are "less hurtful" are pleasant and thus beautiful. A bit later he speaks of the greenness of fields as being "inoffensive to the eye," which suggests that it is not hurtful to the eye at all. The general idea seems to be that colors at the less hurtful or nonhurtful end of the scale are beautiful. When Gerard claims that some colors are beautiful because they are "less hurtful" or "inoffensive to the eye," he is abandoning his notion of internal sense as the cognitive faculties conceiving with facility or moderate difficulty. He is here falling back into a conception of a purely affective reaction similar to Hutcheson's notion of internal sense, although in speaking of "less hurt-ful" and "less offensive to the eye," he is offering an explanation (physiologi-cal) for the feeling of pleasure produced by color of a kind that Hutcheson never offers.

The second kind of beauty of color is what he calls "splendor." The contemplation of this lively characteristic of color produces in us a cheerful disposition, which is pleasing.

After his exceedingly brief remarks about the first two kinds of beauty of color, Gerard moves on to beauty of color produced by association. One would expect him to use a formula of a structure similar to the one he used with sublimity, namely, that something can become sublime by being associated with something else that is already sublime; that is, one expects Gerard to contend that things not beautiful in themselves can become beauti-ful by being associated with things that are already beautiful. He uses, how-ever, an even looser procedure here than he does with sublimity. He main-tains that colors acquire beauty when by association they "are connected with agreeable ideas of any sort" (p. 41). The first example he cites, given his views of utility, acutally conforms to the structure of the sublimity formula.

> The verdure of the fields is delightful, not only by being inoffensive to the eye, but chiefly by its suggesting the pleasant idea of fertility. Heath in bloom would form a carpet agreeable enough to sight, if we could separate from its appear-ance the idea of the barrenness of the mountains and wilds which it covers. (pp. 41–42)

The acquired beauty of the greenness of the fields is acquired because it is associated with fertility, which is a kind of utility that, according to Gerard, is a kind of beauty. In this case the associated agreeable idea (utility) is presumably supposed by Gerard to be beautiful. The acquired ugliness of heath in bloom is acquired because it is associated with infertility, which is a kind of disutility. In this case the associated disagreeable idea (disutility) is presumably supposed by Gerard to be ugly. His next example, however, does not follow the sublimity model. "In dress, colours are either beautiful or the contrary, according to the nature of the idea which they lead us to form of the station, sentiments, and character of the wearer" (p. 42). As an example of what he has in mind, he notes that in certain professions a partic-ular mode of dress is standard. "We come to perceive a propriety in con-forming to it; and we are displeased with the indecency of deviating remark-ably from it" (p. 42). Gerard is saying that a color is beautiful or ugly in a particular circumstance according to whether it is associated with the dress of a particular profession. In such cases, he is not even alleging that what the color is associated with is something that is beautiful; the color is associ-ated with a certain profession, and, of course, a profession itself is neither beautiful nor ugly. The idea of a profession is presumably an agreeable idea, or, perhaps, it is the idea of conforming to the standard that is the agreeable idea that the color is connected to by means of its connection to the pro-fession.

In the associationist sublimity cases, Gerard purports to conjure up sublimity for an object out of its connection with a sublime object. In some of the associationist beauty of color cases, he purports to conjure up beauty for colors out of their connection with agreeable ideas *of any sort*.

Gerard does not introduce the notion of the association of ideas into his account of beauty until he is well into his discussion of beauty of color. He clearly thinks, however, that the association of ideas has a role to play in beauty of figure as well as in the case of beauty of color. Gerard's associationism leads to the conclusion that *any visual thing* (involving figure or color) can be beautiful because anything can be associated with an agreeable idea of some sort. This spreads the notion of beauty so thinly that it threatens to become meaningless. Gerard, however, does not draw back from this conclusion. In fact, he seems to think that his account fits nicely with ordinary usage. In a passage near the end of his account of beauty, part of which is frequently quoted, he writes,

> There is perhaps no term used in a looser sense than *beauty*, which is applied to almost every thing that pleases us. Though this usage is doubtless too indefinite, we may, without a faulty diviation from precision, apply this epithet to every pleasure which is conveyed by the eye, and which has not got a proper and peculiar name; to the pleasure we receive, either when an object of sight suggests pleasant ideas of other senses, or when the ideas suggested are agreeable ones formed from the sensations of sight, or when both these circumstances concur. In all these cases, beauty is, at least in part, resolveable into association. (p. 43)

In this passage, Gerard ties beauty to the domain of visual objects, which suggests the reasonable-sounding view that there are visual objects of beauty and visual objects of the opposite sort. His associationism, however, undercuts the distinction between visual objects of beauty and visual objects of the opposite sort because it is possible for *every* object within the domain of visual objects to be associated with an agreeable object of some sort and, hence, acquire beauty. It is also possible for every object within the same domain to be associated with a disagreeable object and, hence, acquire the opposite of beauty. Thus, the visual properties of objects become irrelevant to the beauty or ugliness of those objects when it is a question of acquired beauty or ugliness. Even when the visual properties are inoffensive-to-the-eye color or splendid color, they may be canceled out or at least counteracted by negative associations. Of course, such visual properties would be added to by positive associations.

I shall at this point break off the detailed discussion of Gerard's account of the seven senses of taste. He himself devotes much less space to his treatments of the senses of imitation, harmony, ridicule, and virtue, and nothing new in terms of principles or mental mechanisms is added. Also, the notion of the association of ideas is not used in a significant way in his account of these last four senses. What is notable is that he goes beyond Hutcheson's discussions of the sense of beauty and suggestions of senses of grandeur and novelty in the "Inquiry Concerning Beauty" to add imitation, ridicule, and virtue to the list of taste categories. Gerard's discussion of the sense of harmony is not really much of an extension of Hutcheson's view, as Hutcheson treats harmony (of sound) under the category of beauty. Gerard's lengthening of the list of characteristics of nature and art in which taste takes pleasure is, I think, an important advance in the theory of taste. Hutcheson himself in his later writings begins to speak of a sense of imitation. And at about the same time that Gerard was lengthening the list of characteristics to which taste reacts, Hume was constructing more informally in "Of the Standard of Taste" an even longer list of such characteristics, but more of Hume later.

Gerard begins his account of imitation with an allusion to Hutcheson's attempt in the "Inquiry Concerning Beauty" to understand representation as a kind of unity and, hence, as a kind of beauty. He then asserts, presumably in disagreement with Hutcheson,

> We have a natural sense which is highly gratified by a designed resemblance, though there be nothing agreeable in the original. Similitude is a very powerful principle of association, which, by continually connecting the ideas in which it is found, and leading our thoughts from one of them to the other, produces in mankind a strong tendency to comparison. (p. 47)

Gerard seems to be saying here that representation is not a kind of beauty (i.e., unity); that is, he seems to be saying that we take pleasure directly in representation itself independently of any unity derived from resemblance between a representation and its subject matter. He also seems to be suggesting that representation is, at bottom, a case of the association of ideas, but he has nothing more directly to say on the topic. In any event, it seems to me to be a mistake to try to think of representation as a case of the association of ideas based on similitude. Given that there is a resemblance between a representation and what it represents, it does not seem to me that when we see, say, a portrait of Churchill that Churchill is brought to mind by the association of ideas. We *recognize* that the painting portrays Churchill; it is not just that the similitude between the portrait and Churchill brings Churchill to mind because of an association. I do not, however, want to get deeply involved in a discussion of representation.

Gerard also notes that we take pleasure in the skill involved in an artist's ability to produce representations.

The final sense of taste that Gerard discusses in Part 1 of his *Essay* is the sense of virtue or the moral sense. Given the account I gave earlier of Hutcheson's theory of taste, it may appear that Gerard is here deviating sharply from a formalist Hutchesonian tradition, but this is not really the case. Hutcheson's *An Inquiry into the Original of Our Ideas of Beauty and Virtue* consists of two treatises: the first is "An Inquiry Concerning Beauty, Order, Harmony, Design," and the second is "An Inquiry Concerning Moral Good and Evil." My earlier account of Hutcheson's theory of taste, as are most accounts, is drawn from the first treatise, which is wholly concerned with the sense of beauty, although grandeur and novelty are mentioned in passing.

Hutcheson, however, thinks that the moral sense has an application to the arts, for late in his treatise on morality he writes, "We shall find this [moral] sense to be the foundation . . . of the chief pleasures of poetry. . . . [T]he contemplation of moral objects, either of vice or virtue, affects us more strongly . . . than natural beauty. . . ."[2] So both Hutcheson and Gerard regard the moral sense as one of the senses of taste. Gerard writes that the moral sense "spreads its influence over all the most considerable works of art and genius" (p. 69). He then first says, "It claims a *joint authority* with the other principles of taste," (p. 69), but shortly afterwards he says, "Nay our moral sense claims authority *superior* to all the rest. It renders morality the chief requisite; and where this is in any degree violated, no other qualities can atone for the transgression. Particular beauties may be approved, but the work is, on the whole, condemned" (p. 69). The moral content of art, when it has such a content, has, for Gerard, an important bearing on the evaluation of art.

In his brief discussion of the sense of virtue, Gerard does not attempt any account of the principles or mental mechanisms by means of which moral approval and disapproval are produced, as he does in other cases of the senses of taste. He does not say, either, whether moral approvals or disapprovals are pleasures or pains as he does in the cases of the deliverances of the other senses of taste, but he does refer to them as sensations, sentiments, and affections (p. 71).

This concludes my exposition of Part 1. Part 2 of Gerard's *Essay* deals with standard-of-taste questions, and in the first two editions this is all there is concerning such questions. In the third edition of the *Essay,* as noted earlier, Gerard adds a Part 4 entitled "Of the Standard of Taste," modeled on the Hume essay of the same name. Logically speaking, Part 2 is the conclusion of his theory in the first two editions, and I shall discuss it last. Consequently, I move now to a consideration of Part 3 of Gerard's book.

Part 3 of the *Essay*

The material presented by Gerard in Part 3 of the *Essay* is *for the most part* either repetitious of what has already been said in Part 1 or does not really have anything new to say about his theory of taste. In this third part, from its Section 2 through its concluding Section 6, Gerard talks about the relation of taste to genius and to criticism, waxes eloquent over the abundance of beauties in art and nature, and discusses the effects of taste on character, but virtually none of these remarks tells us anything new about his theory of taste. In Section 1 of the third part, however, Gerard does have something to say of general import that helps to fill out the picture of what he takes himself to be doing in Part 1. Also in the third part, in Section 3, which is devoted to the relation of taste to criticism, Gerard makes some remarks

2. Francis Hutcheson, *An Inquiry into the Original of Our Ideas of Beauty and Virtue,* 2d ed. (London: 1726), p. 261.

concerning the methodology that he presumably used in arriving at the conclusions he draws in Part 1. So, there are two places in Part 3 that require attention.

Gerard begins the first section of Part 3 with a discussion of how taste
arises from what he calls "the general laws of sensation" and "certain operations of the imagination" (p. 144). The only law of sensation that he mentions in this first section involves descriptions, familiar from Part 1, of how
difficulty in comprehending an object exerts the mind and produces pleasure
and the like. What he has to say in this section about the operations of the
imagination is also a repetition of what he said in Part 1. He, however,
interrupts his repetitious discussion with what may well be the longest footnote in the philosophical literature, in which he explains the criteria of being
a sense and related matters. The footnote, unlike the other material in this
first section, does help give a better picture of Gerard's theory by giving a
more general account of his conception of the nature of the internal senses.
Gerard begins his footnote by asserting that Hutcheson's conception of a
sense assumes that a sense is "ultimate and original" (p. 145), by which
Gerard means uncompounded and innate. He notes that, according to
Hutcheson's notion of what a sense is, "the powers of taste [as he, Gerard,
conceives of them] would not be senses" (p. 145). Gerard believes himself
to have shown in Part 1 that the powers of taste are compounded and,
hence, not innate. Of course, the elements (the cognitive powers) out of
which the powers of taste are compounded are innate or original, but the
various senses of taste themselves are not innate in their compounded form.
Gerard is determined to call the powers of taste internal senses, although he
has no real theoretical need to do so. He spells out in the footnote the
criteria of being a sense. The criteria are identical with those of Hutcheson
except Gerard omits Hutcheson's criterion of innateness. The justification for
the exclusion of innateness, at least in part, is that it is not apparent in our
experience. Gerard writes, "We are directed by the *phaenomena* of our faculties" (p. 145) in classifying senses and in arriving at conclusions about criteria of being a sense. He continues,

> The obvious phaenomena of *a sense* are these. It is a power which supplies us
> with such *simple* perceptions, as cannot be conveyed by any other channel to
> those who are destitute of that sense. It is a power which receives its perception
> *immediately,* as soon as its object is exhibited, previous to any reasoning con-
> cerning the qualities of the object, or the causes of the perception. It is a power
> which exerts itself *independent of volition;* so that, while we remain in proper
> circumstances, we cannot, by any act of the will, prevent our receiving certain
> sensations, nor alter them at pleasure. . . . (pp. 145–46)

Gerard notes that his three criteria are satisfied by the external senses;
he illustrates his point by discussing vision. He then illustrates how the three
criteria are met by the sense of harmony and the sense of beauty. On hearing
a musical passage, one *immediately* and *involuntarily* perceives the *simple* perception of harmony, if one has a musical ear (i.e., a sense of harmony). On
seeing an object that has uniformity and variety or proportion, one *immedi-*

ately and *involuntarily* perceives the *simple* perception of pleasure. Note that the sense of harmony perceives *harmony,* which makes it essentially cognitive, and that the sense of beauty perceives pleasure, which makes it essentially affective. Gerard does not appear to notice this lack of parallelism in his accounts of the two different powers of taste. What he is focused on showing is that although the mental machinery of the internal senses in both cases are complex, the perceptions produced by the mental machinery are simple. In the case of the sense of harmony, he writes that "harmony . . . is a simple perception" (p. 146). In the case of the sense of beauty, he writes, "This sentiment [pleasure] is . . . perfectly simple in its *feeling*" (p. 147). What Gerard says about the criteria of immediacy and involuntariness fits both cases. What he says about the sense of harmony fits what he says about the criterion of simplicity, for he writes, "It is a power which supplies us with such *simple* perceptions, as cannot be conveyed by any other channel to those who are destitute of that sense" (pp. 145–46). A perception of harmony can be had only by someone with a sense of harmony. What he says about the sense of beauty, however, does not fit what he says about the criterion of simplicity with its "no other channel" qualification, for he says that the sense of beauty's perception is pleasure, and pleasure can be felt by persons destitute of a sense of beauty. Pleasure, unlike harmony, can derive from a great variety of sources (channels). Gerard must drop part of his simplicity criterion—the part that specifies "as cannot be conveyed by any other channel to those who are destitute of that sense"—because in the bulk of his accounts of the senses of taste, pleasure is the thing perceived by a sense of taste. He also has the problem that his account of the sense of harmony is not parallel to his accounts of the other senses of taste. What has perhaps confused Gerard is that, in the case of the sense of harmony, (1) perceived harmony and (2) the pleasure it causes are *both* simple. Thus, in looking for something simple to cite, Gerard cites harmony and thereby gives an account of the sense of harmony that conforms to the "no other channel" requirement but deviates from the pattern of his accounts of the other senses of taste. In the case of the sense of beauty, perceived uniformity, variety, and proportion are each complex, and only the pleasure they cause is simple. In this case, Gerard does not have a choice between two simple things to confuse him. The sense-of-beauty case does not conform to the "no other channel" requirement, but Gerard's discussion of this case is more removed in his text from his statement of his criteria than the sense-of-harmony case, and this perhaps caused him not to notice the problem.

Gerard's long footnote gives a general and concise summary account of his notion of what a sense of taste is. It also reveals a difference in the way the sense of harmony supposedly works as compared to the other senses of taste, although Gerard does not appear to realize this.

Before leaving Section 1, I want to take note of a puzzling passage. At one point, after claiming that the external senses are innate and simple, Gerard, by way of contrast, writes that "taste, in most of its forms at least [is]. . . a derivative and secondary power" (p. 151). Throughout the *Essay,* Gerard has maintained that the senses of taste are compounded and derivative, but here he makes the qualification that taste is derivative in *most* of its forms. Perhaps he has in mind cases of color that please by being "less hurtful to the eye" or by their splendor that do not seem to involve the kind of "law of sensation" he cites or the association of ideas. Gerard does not follow up on his remark in any way!

I shall now focus on the second place in Part 3 where Gerard supplies new information about his theory. In the middle of his remarks in Section 3 on the relation of taste to criticism, Gerard launches into an account of the *inductive* procedure that good critics must use in determining "the general rules" to be used in criticism (p. 171). This procedure is without doubt the one that Gerard takes himself to have used to discover the characteristics of things that affect the senses of taste. He presented his list of these characteristics (novelty, quantity, uniformity, etc.) in Part 1, although he nowhere presents the actual detailed inductive argumentation that was supposedly used to arrive at his conclusions. He writes of the procedure,

> It is not enough to discover that we are pleased or displeased [by characteristics]; we must ascertain the precise species of either [that please or displease]. . . .
>
> The qualities common to the lower classes [of characteristics] will naturally be determined first, by regular induction. But the true critic will not rest satisfied with them. By renewing the induction, and pushing it to a greater degree of subtilty, he will ascertain the less conspicuous properties, which unite several inferior species under the same genus; and will carry on his analysis, till he discovers the highest kinds, and prescribes the most extensive laws of art, and thus arrives at the most universal distinctions that can be made, without falling into the uninstructive affirmation of mere excellence or faultiness in general. (pp. 172–73)

He then goes on to say the process is to be completed by discovering the mechanisms by means of which the pleasure or displeasure is produced.

Part 2 of the *Essay*

Gerard concludes Part 1, which is concerned with the individual senses and their objects, with a summary that serves as a preamble to Part 2.

> There are qualities in things, determinate and stable, independent of humour or caprice, that are fit to operate on mental principles common to all men, and, by operating on them, are naturally productive of the sentiments of taste in all its forms. If, in any particular instance, they prove ineffectual, it is to be ascribed to some weakness or disorder in the person who remains unmoved when these qualities are exhibited to his view. Men are, with *few* exceptions, affected by the qualities we have investigated: but these qualities themselves are, without *any* exceptions, the constituents of excellence or faultiness of the several kinds. What is necessary for perceiving them with perfect relish, we shall next examine. (p. 72)

There are several things to note about this summary of Part 1. First, there is no mention here of the association of ideas, as there should be in a summary of an account in which this notion plays such a prominent role. Second, it is a clear rejection of any kind of relativism; there are, he says, specific qualities of objects to which normal persons, who are an overwhelming majority, react, and these qualities constitute the goodness or badness of objects of taste. Third, it is implied that in Part 2 an explanation will be given of the conditions under which normal persons discriminate and take pleasure in taste qualities and of the ways in which (a few) persons can deviate from this norm. Fourth, it is strongly suggested that the characteristics cited in Part 1—novelty, quantity, simplicity, uniformity, variety, proportion, utility, color less hurtful to the eye, splendor of color, harmony, imitation, incongruity, and virtue—constitute a complete list of the qualities that affect the internal senses directly.

The whole of Part 2 is devoted to the task of determining what constitutes "taste in its just extent, that is, to establishing a standard of taste" (p. 73). The most surprising thing about Part 2, portended by the summary at the end of Part 1, is Gerard's single, perfunctory mention of the association of ideas. His ignoring of his own doctrines of the association of ideas and the coalescence of ideas results in a failure to integrate them with his account of the standard of taste and causes him to miss the relativistic implications of his use of these two notions. If the association and coalescence of ideas can cause virtually *anything* to acquire *any* taste property for some person or persons, then the notion that there are standards that can adjudicate between differing tastes of persons does not make much sense. As will be noted in the next chapter, Alison, who makes even greater use of the notions of the association and coalescence of ideas, does not even raise the question of a standard of taste, presumably because he saw the futility of doing so within the kind of associationist views Gerard and he had developed.

I shall now examine Gerard's attempt in Part 2 to defend a standard of taste, ignoring, as does Gerard, the fact that his theory is the kind of associationist theory that it is; that is, I will examine and evaluate Gerard's attempt at establishing a standard of taste as if he were trying to do this for a nonassociationist, nonrelativist theory of a kind that conforms to the summary at the end of Part 1. Leaving aside his associationism, then, Gerard's attempt at establishing a standard of taste is an attempt to show that novelty, quantity, simplicity, uniformity, variety, proportion, utility, color less hurtful to the eye, splendor of color, harmony, imitation, incongruity, and virtue are the qualities in things that are productive of the sentiments of taste in normal persons.

The first section of Part 2 is devoted in part to a topic that does not arise for Hutcheson, because Hutcheson in his actual treatment confines his discussion of taste entirely to a consideration of the sense of beauty. Gerard, however, explicitly and in detail, discusses *seven* different internal senses of taste. Consequently, unlike Hutcheson, he feels he must raise the topic of what he calls "the union" of the seven senses (p. 73).

The objects of taste, whether of art or nature, are, Gerard notes, frequently complex in that they exhibit a variety of characteristics that affect the various senses of taste. Consequently, all seven of the internal senses "must at once be vigorous, in order to constitute taste in its just extent" (p. 73). This simultaneous vigor of the seven senses is what Gerard calls "the union" of the internal senses. These senses and their objects are not simply additive in the pleasure they can produce. Gerard claims that they can interact to produce greater pleasure than the sum of what each produces; he notes, for example, that novelty makes the pleasure of sublimity more intense.

Gerard notes also that, in given persons, particular internal senses may be weak or nonexistent and that this fact will cause persons to react differently to the same objects of taste. A weakness of or lack of a particular internal sense is, of course, a defect and can explain both a deviant reaction to a particular work of art and a deviant judgment of its merit.

In addition to weakness or lack of particular internal senses, Gerard discusses two affective factors that cause persons to react differently to objects of taste. First, a person's differing moods may cause him to react one way at one time and another way at another time. Second, different persons have different permanent dispositions; he mentions specifically hard-heartedness and soft-heartedness, although he has all the "passions," as he calls them, in mind. Hard-hearted persons "will be little affected by the most moving tragedy," and soft-hearted persons will be moved by "a very indifferent one." Such temperamental differences may produce a diversity of reactions to works of art and disagreement in the judgment of their merits (p. 80). Although he does not say so explicitly, it is clear that Gerard regards both hard-heartedness and soft-heartedness as defects that can cause deviant reactions and incorrect judgments regarding works of art. No doubt he thinks of the other passions as having opposite and defective extremes. The generalized nondefective disposition, which I think he conceives of as a golden mean between the various pairs of defective dispositions, is called by him "delicacy of passion." Gerard regards the aspects of art that exercise the passions as very important: "A very great part of the merit of most works of genius arises from their fitness to agitate the heart with a variety of passions" (p. 80).

The passions are different from and independent of the internal senses, and where works of art are concerned, delicacy of passion is, Gerard believes, even more important than the internal senses. He writes, "If a person possessed all the internal senses in perfection, without delicacy of passion, he could estimate the principal works of genius, only by their inferior qualities. . . . Delicacy of passion must be united with vigorous internal senses, in order to give taste its just extent" (pp. 81–82). Gerard has presumably realized that his senses of taste do not exhaust and account for all the value we find in art. Thus, he adds his notion of "delicacy of passion," that relates to other valuable aspects of works of art. So, in this first section of Part 2, Gerard has two unions in mind: first, the union of the seven internal senses themselves and, second, the union of the delicacy of passion with the united internal senses. After having made this point about delicacy of passion and its very great importance, Gerard seems to forget about it and talks only of the internal senses in the remainder of Part 2. Delicacy of passion, however, should occupy a place at least on a par with the seven senses, and I have inserted mention of it at appropriate points.

The general topic of Part 2, as noted earlier, is the determination of nature of taste "in its just extent." In the second section of Part 2, Gerard addresses the question of the role of judgment in this determination. By *judgment* he means the ability to acquire knowledge (determine the facts) about the objects of taste. He writes, "It is *sense* which is pleased or displeased when these things are determined: but *judgment* alone can determine them, and present to sense the object of its perception" (pp. 86–87). What Gerard is claiming here seems unobjectionable. One must have a perception of or an understanding of an object of taste before one can be pleased or displeased by it; judgment is a necessary condition for taste, and good judgment is a necessary condition for taste "in its just extent." He also adds that judgment is employed in "comparing and weighing" the deliverancies of the internal senses (p. 88). At the end of this section, however, Gerard makes the following claim about taste in persons.

> In some [persons], the acuteness of the *senses;* in others, the accuracy of the *judgment,* is the predominant quality. Both will determine justly: but they are guided by different lights; the former, by the perception of sense; the latter, by the conviction of the understanding. One *feels* what pleases or displeases; the other *knows* what ought to gratify or disgust. (p. 88)

It seems to me that with this last remark Gerard has wandered into confusion about what his actual view can be. Given what he has already said, he should say that both acuteness of the internal senses and accuracy of judgment are necessary conditions to "determine justly." Any imperfection of either internal sense or judgment will result in something less than a just determination of taste. In any event, the important point of this section on judgment is that judgment is a necessary condition of taste in its just extent.

There is the additional puzzle of how an internal sense could be weak when judgment is strong, since both internal sense and judgment involve the same cognitive faculties for Gerard. Cognitive faculties function as judgment when they enable a person to comprehend the facts of a situation; they function as internal sense when their comprehendings produce pleasure. Presumably, although he does not say this, Gerard's position would have to be that internal sense is weak or deficient when judgement is strong in the case that a comprehension is achieved but pleasure does not result. How judgment could be weak and internal sense stong, however, is a real mystery because the proper functioning of comprehension is a necessary and prior condition for the functioning of internal sense.

In the first two sections of Part 2, Gerard states what he takes to be taste "in its just extent," namely, all the elements of taste at their highest development. These elements are (1) the union of the seven internal senses, (2) that union united with delicacy of passion, and (3) this two-layered union supported by good judgment. Presumably, if everyone had taste "in its just ex-

tent" there would be no disagreements over objects of taste. There are, however, such disagreements, and the remainder of Part 2 is devoted to trying
to show how taste can be improved when it occurs in less than "its just
extent" and, hence, how disagreements can be reduced.

"*Goodness* of taste," Gerard writes, "lies in its maturity and perfection. It
consists in certain *excellences* of our original powers of judgment and imagination combined. These may be reduced to four; *sensibility, refinement, correctness,* and the *proportion* or *comparative adjustment of its separate principles*"
(p. 95). I turn now to Gerard's accounts of the four excellences that perfect
taste. In his discussions of the first three of these four—sensibility, refinement, and correctness—Gerard is concerned with taste as it relates to single
properties such as uniformity and not as it relates to whole objects of taste.

Gerard begins his section on *sensibility* of taste by remarking on the great
range of difference among persons in their sensibilities, by which he means
the power to feel pleasure or pain from objects of taste. He then claims that
sensibility is less improvable by use than the other elements of taste because
it derives so greatly from "the original construction of the mind" (p. 97).
Having noted the great variability of sensibility and the difficulty of improving it, instead of trying to counteract the relativism threatened by these two
factors, Gerard changes the subject and launches into a discussion of a supposed paradox involved in the functioning of sensibility.

The supposed paradox runs like this: Frequent experience of an object
should cause us to receive decreasing pleasure because such experience
makes the conception of the object easier and easier until it gives no exercise
at all to the mind and, hence, no pleasure. On the contrary, however, frequent experience in fact heightens our relish of objects of taste. The resolu-
tion of the paradox is that the frequent experience of objects of taste continues to reveal new and more perfect aspects of these objects because "the
objects of taste are infinitely various" (p. 98). Gerard's solution is not a complete one because some objects of taste are quite simple and all their characteristics are soon discovered. Gerard continues his point about discovery in
a somewhat different vein: "A person unskilled in poetry and painting will
survey a work with perfect indifference, because he does not really see its
beauties, or its blemishes. But let these be pointed out to him by one more
known in the art, immediately he begins to approve, or disapprove" (pp.
99–100). Interestingly, this last quoted point does tend to counteract relativism. It shows how *judgment* can be improved *and* known to be improved by
the person whose taste is improved; that is, a person knows that his taste
has been improved because he knows that he can discriminate a taste quality
that he could not discriminate before it was pointed out to him. This point,
however, does nothing to counteract the threat of relativism that arises from
the variability of sensibility, that is, the variability of *the reaction* to what is
discriminated, which is the topic of the section.

Gerard does return to a discussion of sensibility. He claims that it involves faculties of a kind involving mental actions (conceiving of objects and
receiving pleasure from it); consequently, use strengthens such faculties and

the sensations thereby produced. Gerard is here still trying to show how frequent experience of objects of taste can increase our relish for them despite the tendency of frequency experience to diminish our pleasure. He is still pursuing his paradox rather than combating sensibility relativism.

In the last paragraph of the section on sensibility, Gerard finally raises again the problem of sensibility relativism. He writes,

> Sensibility of taste arises chiefly from the structure of our internal senses, and is but indirectly and remotely connected with the soundness or improvement of judgment. Insensibility is *one* ingredient in many sorts of false taste; but does not alone constitute so much one species of *wrong* taste, as a total *deficience* or great *weakness* of taste. Sensibility may sometimes become *excessive;* and render us extravagant both in liking and disliking, in commending and blaming. (pp. 102–3)

Gerard presumably thinks that proper sensibility is a mean between deficiency or weakness of sensibility and excessive sensibility, but he does not say so or even say anything more on the topic. Instead, he again reverts to the topic of judgment, specifically, to cases of judgment's inability to distinguish properly characteristics of objects of taste. This cognitive inability, he claims, results in persons who are unable to give specific reasons why they are pleased or displeased and results also in their being able to express their pleasure or displeasure only in very general terms. This is an extremely interesting point, but it is no part of a solution to the problem of sensibility relativism.

The second category under which Gerard thinks taste can be improved is that of *refinement.* As he conceives of it, the refinement of taste depends on comparisons. A low degree of "real excellence"—by which I assume he means quantity, uniformity, and the like—will please an unimproved taste when that is all that is known. When, however, this low degree of excellence is compared to a higher degree of the same quality, the higher degree will please and the lower degree will cease to please or please less (pp. 105–6). By noting the highest degrees of quantity, uniformity, and the like that we experience in the comparison of a wide variety of objects of taste, we can "form in our minds a model of perfection" (p. 113). This model would have to be, I take it, the collection of remembered instances of the highest degrees of each of the taste properties—quantity, uniformity, and so on—that one has experienced in objects of taste. There would no doubt be a companion model involving taste properties of the lowest degree, although Gerard does not mention it. Such a model, he is saying, is constructible by each person, and, he is implying, every person will know that the model is a movement in the direction of the improvement of that person's taste if it is assumed that higher degrees of uniformity and the like are better. He does not note, however, that each person's model(s) will be relative to his own experience, and it is possible that no two models will be the same.

Gerard does, however, specify a nonrelativistic account of refinement: "Refinement of taste exists only where to an original delicacy of imagination, and natural acuteness of judgment, is superadded a long and intimate acquaintance with the best performances of every kind" (p. 114). Gerard is saying that comparisons refine both judgment and internal sense. Judgment is refined by discovering greater (and lesser) degrees of the taste properties in its objects, thereby expanding its discriminatory scope. Internal sense is refined by having its exertions coming to produce greater (and lesser) pleasures, thereby expanding its reactive scope.

It seems to me that what Gerard says about the antirelativistic results of refinement—that is, comparisons—is exactly right. Comparisons do enable persons to increase the range of their cognitive discriminations and the scope of their affective reactions. Of course, there may still be limits on the expansion (i.e., normalizing) of these cognitive and affective aspects in individual persons, so there may still be relativistic problems.

A great deal of space in Gerard's section on *correctness* of taste is taken up with examples of the confusion of merits with blemishes; merits, he claims, are always a mean between two blemish extremes, one of which resembles the merit. The task of the section is the improvement of taste such that these kinds of confusions can be avoided.

Confusions of merits with blemishes can, Gerard asserts, derive from either "the dulness of our internal *senses*" or "the debility of *judgment*" (p. 128). As far as I can see, however, everything that Gerard says in this section is directed at the correcting of judgment. What he says, at rather great length, amounts to advising the careful study of objects of taste so that through practice we can become aware of their smallest details. This study, he thinks, will enable us to distinguish not only the kinds of merits and blemishes but the degrees of them as well. He sums up the procedure he has in mind as follows:

> These corruptions of taste can be avoided only by establishing within ourselves an exact standard of intrinsic excellence, by which we may try whatever is presented to us. This standard will be established by the careful study of the most correct performances of every kind, which are generally indeed the most excellent. (p. 131)

Again, as with his discussion of sensibility, Gerard's remarks under the heading of correctness are devoted entirely to the improvement of judgment, so that even if his remarks are completely successful, they do nothing to counteract the threat of relativism that derives from the variability of sensibility, that is, from the variability of the affective side of persons.

Sensibility, refinement, and correctness are discussed with regard to specific, individual properties of objects, but *due proportion* is "not confined to the parts of objects, but extended to the whole" (p. 133). What Gerard has in mind concerning due proportion is that (1) each of the seven internal senses is vigorous but none crowds out any other sense, (2) delicacy of passion obtains (although it is not specifically mentioned), and (3) good judgment obtains. When this is the case, every valuable property of every object of taste can be experienced and relished. But strictly speaking, due proportion as such does not deal with the whole, as Gerard asserts, but with each part of the whole. (The judgment of the whole of an object of taste is an additional matter, and Gerard has something to say about the judgment of the whole object of taste at the end of this section.)

Gerard maintains that a small disproportion among the internal senses is natural and inevitable and, therefore, blameless. When, however, the disproportion becomes larger such that, for example, the relish for sublimity crowds out the relish for beauty, the bounds of due proportion are breached. Gerard advises two ways to improve proportion. The first is achievement of an ability to comprehend all aspects of an object of taste and not to focus narrowly on one or a few. Such an ability presumably can be achieved by practice, which improves judgment. The second way of improving proportion is to exercise the internal senses equally! "If. . . any of them has fallen below its proper tone, it must, by particular attention, be again wound up to it" (p. 137).

In the last few pages of this section, which is the last section of Part 2, Gerard turns to the problem of the overall judgment of an object of taste. He begins by warning that all the merits and blemishes of an object are to be taken into account. Furthermore, one should not be unduly put off by the presence of a blemish or overly impressed by a merit. "But a person of true taste forms his judgment only from the surplus of merit" (p. 139). And he quickly adds that the best critics focus not on the number of merits but on the merits of higher rank. Since Gerard has not argued for or sought to establish an ordering of merit among the taste properties, it is not clear what he can mean by his claim about merits of higher rank.

At the very end of the section, Gerard summarizes his account of the improvement of taste. He cites all the elements of taste: judgment, the internal senses, and (delicacy of passion) improved in sensibility, refinement, correctness, and due proportion. And then, in a remark that anticipates Hume's later, well-known view,[3] he writes, "Could any critic unite them [the elements of taste] all in a great degree, to his sentiments we might appeal, as to an unerring standard of merit, in all the productions of the fine art" (p. 141).

The question is, as Hume says in a similar situation, how are such critics to be found and how are they to be distinguished from pretenders? Gerard's answer to this question, if he has one, has to be contained in his remarks about the improvement of the elements of taste in Part 2, an account of which I have just finished giving. I shall now reflect on and evaluate Gerard's remarks as an answer to the problem of how good critics are to be produced and identified.

Gerard has cited four factors that are relevant to the improvement of the elements of taste when in a given person taste occurs in less than "its just

3. Although Gerard's *An Essay on Taste* was published in 1759, it was submitted to the Edinburgh Society for a prize in 1756. Thus, Gerard's *Essay* was written before the 1757 publication of Hume's "Of the Standard of Taste."

extent." The factors, in the order he cites and discusses them, are sensibility, refinement, correctness, and the due proportion or comparative adjustment of the separate principles of taste. If a consideration of these factors results in the improvement of people's tastes, then theoretically virtually anyone could become a critic of the kind Gerard envisages, and the problem of disagreements of taste would be theoretically dissolvable.

Gerard's remarks about *due proportion* amount to a kind of tidying up, given that all the problems involved in the other three factors have been dealt with satisfactorily.

Gerard's remarks about *refinement* (comparisons) involve important and useful things. The comparing of objects of taste does expand the scope of both the cognitive ability to discriminate and the affective ability to react with pleasure or pain. But while the expansion of the scope of the cognitive ability to discriminate fosters agreement in judgment, the expansion of the scope of the affective ability to feel pleasure or pain does not foster agreement about how much pleasure or pain is felt in individual cases or agreement about whether one feels pleasure or pain in an individual case. So, comparisons do not relieve the threat of relativism insofar as affective considerations are concerned.

Gerard's remarks under the heading of *correctness* are directed to the improvement of judgment (cognitive discrimination) and, even if they are successful, they do not resolve the threat of relativism posed by disagreements resulting from the affective side of persons (sensibility). So, the justification of Gerard's notion of a standard of taste comes down to what he has to say under the heading of sensibility.

Gerard begins his discusssion of *sensibility* (the power to feel pleasure and pain from objects of taste) by noting the great range of differences among persons in their sensibilities and how much less improvable sensibility is than judgment. He attributes these two facts about sensibility to its deriving so much from "the original construction of the mind." Thus, sensibility is the greatest source of the threat of relativism for Gerard. In the part of his text devoted to the discussion of sensibility, however, he does not have anything at all to say that addresses the threat of sensibility he poses at the beginning of this part of the text. His remarks are devoted either to the improvement of judgment or to the alleged paradox that we continue to delight in objects of taste despite our familiarity with them. It must be concluded that Gerard fails to show how his suggestion about the possibility of an improvement of taste that can result in the production of critics who are "an unerring standard of taste" is to be realized.

3

Complete Associationism: Archibald Alison

I shall begin my discussion of Archibald Alison's complicated and elaborately presented theory with a summary description of his account of the experience of taste. I hope this characterization will help the reader get a clear idea of a theory of heroic, Rube Goldbergian intricacy. In presenting this abbreviated account, I shall be following Alison, who summarizes his theory in a brief introduction to his *Essays on the Nature and Principles of Taste* (1790).[1] He understands experiences of taste to be either experiences of beauty or experiences of sublimity.

Alison's theory of taste is developed, as are Hutcheson's and Gerard's, within the framework of Locke's scheme of mind and perception. According to the Lockean account, characteristics of the external world cause ideas (objects of perception) to occur in a person's experience (in the mind). Experience is conceived of as a collection of ideas. According to Alison, in an experience of *taste,* an object of perception produces a twofold result in the mind. Each of the results is necessary, and both are jointly sufficient for an experience of taste. The first result of a perceived object of taste is a simple emotion such as cheerfulness, which initiates the whole affective aspect of a taste experience. Such a simple emotion in an experience of taste, Alison holds, is pleasant. The perceived object's second result is the initiation of an exercise of the imagination—a chain of associated ideas or images. Each member of such a chain of associated images in turn produces a simple emotion that is pleasant. The chain of images in an experience of taste is unified by an overall character of gaiety, melancholy, or the like. The *exercise* of the imagination is itself productive of an additional pleasure. The collec-

1. Archibald Alison, *Essays on the Nature and Principles of Taste,* 5th ed. (London: Ward, Lock, and Co., 1817). All subsequent internal page cites in this chapter to Alison are to this edition.

tion of pleasures—the pleasure of the initial simple emotion, the pleasures of each of the simple emotions connected to each of the associated images in the chain of images, plus the pleasure of the exercise of the imagination—is called "delight" by Alison. The collection of all affective elements in the experience—emotions and pleasures—he calls "the emotion of taste." Alison contrasts the *complex* emotion of taste with the *simple* emotions that in part make it up.

Of course, not every object of perception produces an experience of taste. Alison claims that experiences of taste can be produced only by those characteristics of the material world that are taken to be signs of qualities or expressive of qualities innately fitted to produce emotion. It then turns out on his view that the only characteristics innately fitted to produce emotion are *qualities of mind*. Thus, according to Alison, only characteristics of the material world that are taken to be signs of or expressive of qualities of mind can produce emotion and thereby initiate experiences of taste. Since the perception of characteristics of the material world that are *not* taken to be signs of or expressive of qualities of mind cannot produce emotion, they cannot initiate experiences of taste. By the way, Alison also thinks that experiences that contain chains of associations but that are *not* experiences of taste are not because they lack chains of associated images *with a unified overall character*.

Something's either being a sign of or being expressive of some other thing is based upon the association of ideas, according to Alison. In his theory, there is then a twofold and related use of the association of ideas. First, there is the association of ideas that derives from the perceived object and that produces in the mind the chain of associated images, with their connected emotions and pleasures. The second kind of association of ideas relates the perceived object to what the perceiver takes to be a quality of mind. I shall call the second kind of association "inferential association," although in some cases the existence of an actual quality of mind cannot be inferred.

With the advent of Alison's account of the experience of beauty or sublimity, a *fully* associationist theory of taste has come into being. This is so because he holds, unlike Gerard, that the association of ideas is a necessary component of every taste experience. Indeed, as just noted, Alison maintains that two different kinds of the association of ideas are required for every taste experience—one that produces trains of associated images and one that is involved in inferring qualities of mind. I shall not, by the way, attempt any analysis or criticism of Alison's notion of expression. He uses this notion more loosely than a present-day thinker would, but it is unnecessary for the understanding and criticism of his theory to raise the issue of whether his account of expression is adequate.

Alison conceives of his theory as having two basic parts: (1) an account of the complex *emotion* of taste, together with its complex cognitive accompaniments, and (2) an account of the complex *cause* of this emotion. The first part generates the task of describing the emotion of taste. The second part that concerns the *cause* of the emotion of taste divides into two subparts and generates two subtasks: (1) the determination of the nature of the faculty(ies) of the mind that is (are) triggered and caused to produce the emotion of taste and (2) the determination of which qualities in the material world trigger (cause) this complex emotion.

How does Alison arrive at and try to justify his theory? He at first focuses introspectively on what he calls "the emotion of taste." This emotion, which is either of sublimity or beauty, is, he claims, "very distinguishable from every other pleasure" (p. 63). Since we can distinguish and focus on this emotion, we can analyze and describe it. From this analysis and description, one can move in two different directions: inwardly into the depths of the mind to its faculties, and outwardly into the material world; that is, we can determine the faculty or faculties in the mind that underlie the production of the emotion, and we can discover the causes of the emotion of taste in the material world. Thus, we can just introspectively "see" what the emotion of taste is like, and the "seeing" of this emotion is the Cartesian-like peg from which the rest of his theory is suspended. It is thus that Alison can "see" that the emotion of taste is complex and reject Hutcheson's claim that the affective aspect of taste is simple and, hence, derived from a sense. "It seemed to me," Alison writes, "that the simplicity of the emotion of taste, was a principle much too hastily adopted. . ." (p. 66). Hutcheson, Alison is claiming, adopted the wrong theory because he did not peer carefully enough into his own mind at the affective aspect of experiences of taste. Hutcheson, by the way, does not speak of an *emotion* of taste; he speaks simply of pleasure.

Gerard's theory advanced the theory of taste in that he expanded to thirteen the number of characteristics that interact with taste. Of course, Hutcheson *mentions* grandeur, novelty, and moral content, in addition to the account of beauty he developed. Alison's development of his theory entirely in terms of beauty and sublimity thus seems like a backward step. However, he mentions innumerable instances of what we would now call aesthetic characteristics such as delicacy, cheerfulness, and the like, which he conceives of as contributing to beauty and sublimity. Thus, in its own way, Alison's theory continues the multiplication of taste characteristics.

The Emotion of Taste

Alison's book is divided into two long essays: "Essay 1" sets forth his account of the very complicated emotion of taste, and "Essay 2" is his account of the beauty and sublimity in the material world that evoke the emotion of taste. Alison begins the justification for his view of the nature of the emotion of taste in the very first section of his first essay proper. He claims that it is universally acknowledged that taste is a matter of the imagination. He claims, moreover, that the fine arts are addressed to the imagination and that the pleasures of the fine arts are deemed the pleasures of the imagination. He then writes,

When any object, either of sublimity or beauty, is presented to the mind, I believe every man is conscious of a train of thought being immediately awakened in his imagination, analogous to the character or expression of the original object. The simple perception of the object, we frequently find, is insufficient to excite these emotions, unless it is accompanied with this operation of mind,—unless, according to common expression, our imagination is seized, and our fancy busied in the pursuit of all those trains of thought which are allied to this character or expression. (p. 69)

It is puzzling that in the second sentence of this passage Alison writes that "we frequently find" that the simple perception (that is, without associations) of an object of taste is insufficient to excite the emotion of taste. It seems to me his view is that we *always* find that the simple perception of an object of taste is insufficient to excite the emotion of taste, and I shall assume this to have been his intended meaning. Alison's view is that we find a neat, associational parallelism between the affective and cognitive aspects of the experiences of beauty and sublimity; on the one hand, there is the emotion of taste in the mind with its trains of associations, and, on the other hand, there is the perceived object of taste in the material world with the associations that are involved in inferentially relating it to what it expresses or signifies.

In the passage just quoted, Alison assumes without argument that we can identify objects of taste—of sublimity and of beauty. The method of argument he then uses is an appeal to the introspection of these experiences of taste, an appeal to noting what is always the case in experiences of sublimity and beauty. His first major introspective conclusion is that emotions of taste always include trains of associations. Notice that, in concluding that the emotion of taste is always involved with trains of associations, Alison is also concluding that the imagination, which is the faculty that produces associations, is at least an aspect of the *faculty* of taste.

Alison follows the quoted passage with a series of examples of experiences of taste from both nature and art in which it is supposedly revealed that trains of associated images are present within the emotion of taste in each case. For example, he writes,

When we feel either the beauty or sublimity of natural scenery,—the gay lustre of a morning in spring [and the like] . . . we are conscious of a variety of images in our minds, very different from those which the objects themselves can present to the eye. Trains of pleasing or of solemn thought arise spontaneously within our minds; our hearts swell with emotions, of which the objects before us seem to afford no adequate cause. (pp. 69–70)

Alison makes parallel remarks about the presence of associations in the experiences of works of art. But even if it is true that the dozen or so examples of experiences of sublimity and beauty he cites involve trains of associated images, he has not shown that all experiences of taste involve such trains. His appeal to the consciousness of the reader (introspection) assumes that everyone will *always* find that experiences of taste involve a complex emotion within which there are trains of associated images. It will take only one instance to upset Alison's theory. In any event, Alison turns to the task of trying to show that, unless the imagination is exercised, the emotion of taste is not felt. His argument notes that under certain conditions the emotions of beauty and sublimity are not felt and that the same conditions prevent the exercise of the imagination. He concludes from this that it is the nonoccurrence of the exercise of the imagination that prevents the occurrence of the emotion of taste. He cites instances of being in pain, grieving, and the like that make us oblivious to the beauties of nature and art. He claims that these same conditions prevent the exercise of the imagination and thereby prevent the occurrence of the emotion of taste.

Alison, then, in an often quoted passage, offers what he takes to be further evidence of the connection of taste and the imagination by claiming that the conditions that most favor the exercise of the imagination also most favor the occurrence of the emotion of taste.

> That state of mind, every man must have felt, is most favourable to the emotions of taste, in which the imagination is free and unembarrassed, or, in which the attention is so little occupied by any private or particular object of thought, as to leave us open to all the impressions which the objects that are before us can produce. It is upon the vacant and the unemployed, accordingly, that the objects of taste make the strongest impression. (p. 71)

What Alison's argument overlooks is that the conditions that prevent or promote the exercise of the imagination may also prevent or promote the exercise of some other aspect or aspects of mind that may underlie the experiences of taste, say, Hutchesonian senses of beauty and grandeur. Of course, Alison thinks he has introspective evidence that rules out Hutcheson's solution, but his argument does not rule out the possibility that *some* aspect of mind other than the imagination might underlie experiences of taste.

Alison now turns to the task of sorting out which trains of associations are involved with the emotion of taste and which are not. Again, as always, his method is introspection—in this case the introspection of trains of associations involved with objects of taste and trains involved with objects that are not objects of taste. It is revealed that ordinary trains of associations "excite no emotions either of pleasure or pain" (p. 92) and that trains started by objects of beauty or sublimity are composed of "ideas capable of exciting some affection or emotion" (p. 93). Furthermore, the latter trains of associations are revealed to always have "some general principle of connection which pervades the whole, and gives them some certain and definite character" (p. 94). This connectedness or character of the emotion of taste parallels and is caused by the expression of the perceived object of beauty or sublimity in the material world.

In addition to the variety of pleasures that derive from the many emotions within the emotion of taste, Alison also believes that pleasure is derived from the *exercise* of the imagination. He makes no attempt to justify this view about the exercise of the imagination and pleasure. He takes it more or less as a given, as something that is already believed by everyone. And, indeed, it was widely believed by earlier theorists of taste that the exercise of the imagination produces pleasure.

The second and last major element of the emotion of taste that Alison attempts to justify introspectively is the simple emotion that an object of taste is alleged to cause before or as that object initiates a train of associations and its connected simple emotions and pleasures. In addition to the presumably introspective obviousness of the necessity of this simple emotion, Alison has two more things to say in justification of its requiredness.

> If any man were to assert, that some object, though positively indifferent or uninteresting, was yet beautiful or sublime, every one would consider it as asserting an absurdity. If, on the other hand, he were to assert, that the object had neither beauty or sublimity to him, because there was no quality in it which could give him any emotion, I apprehend we should not only clearly understand his meaning, but very readily allow his reason. (p. 95)

In the second part of his remark, he just explicitly asserts that the evocation of an emotion is a necessary condition for experiences of taste. In the first part of his remark, he presents a reductio ad absurdum argument that is supposed to establish the same point, but here, instead of talking about emotion, he speaks of interestingness; that is, he is equating the interesting with emotion arousing and the uninteresting with failure to arouse emotion. This means that Alison can use "emotion" in a very weak sense. I shall return to the topic of his use of "emotion" later.

Alison's view of the nature of the emotion of taste and his justification for his view are now clear. His view of the nature of the faculty of taste is also now clear, although he does not have an explicit discussion of this in his essay. The faculty of taste is the combination of the imagination and that disposition of the mind that produces simple emotion in response to the perception of some feature of the world. At one point, Alison calls this mental disposition "sensibility." Of course, not every exertion of sensibility and the imagination counts as a functioning of the faculty of taste, only those cases in which sensibility produces a simple emotion and the imagination produces trains of images with a unified character, which in turn produces simple emotions and pleasures. Strictly speaking, the faculty of taste is the combination of sensibility and the imagination when it succeeds in producing this special kind of mental phenomenon; the faculty of taste is the combination of sensibility and imagination.

During his discussion of the imagination, Alison claims that, if what he says about trains of associations in experiences of taste is true, then we ought to find that experiences with such unified trains of associations can be caused only by objects that themselves have a unified character. He then goes on to give examples of natural objects and works of art that lack or have little unified character and fail to produce the emotion of taste or produce only a diminished one, as well as examples of such objects that have a unified character and succeed in producing the emotion of taste. This conclusion about the nature of objects that cause the emotion of taste is of some interest. Even if this conclusion is true, however, it is something of a side issue without direct relevance to the two central claims of his first essay, which concern (1) the nature of the emotion of taste and (2) the nature of the faculty of taste. His main concern with this argument seems to be to justify the point that the unified character of an object is a value-making property.

Also during his discussion of the imagination, Alison introduces the claim that there are certain examples that further illustrate his claim about the imagination and the emotions of taste, but in fact he uses the examples to try to make another, very different point, namely, that associations *create* beauty or sublimity in objects by means of the coalescence of ideas. For example, he speaks of seeing the residences of persons we admire.

> The scenes themselves may be little beautiful; but the delight with which we recollect the traces of their lives, blends itself insensibly with the emotions which the scenery excites; and the admiration which these recollections afford, seems to give a kind of sanctity to the place where they dwelt, and *converts everything into beauty* which appears to have been connected with them. (pp. 75–76; italics mine)

In this case, it is claimed that the delight of the associations *blends with* the emotions generated by the little or no beauty that the scene possesses to create a beauty or a greater beauty.

In similar vein of sublimity, he writes

> No man, acquainted with English history, could behold the field of Agincourt, without some emotion of this kind. The additional conceptions which this association produces, and which fill the mind of the spectator on the prospect of that memorable field, diffuse themselves in some measure over the scene, and *give it a sublimity* which does not naturally belong to it. (p. 76; italics mine)

In this case, it is claimed that the sublime historical associations diffuse over the scene and generate sublimity for the scene, which in and of itself is not sublime.

In the residences case, Alison seems to be claiming that beauty is being *generated* for a scene by historical associations that apparently do not involve beauty at all coalescing with a scene of little or no beauty. In the Agincourt case, Alison seems to be claiming that sublimity is being *generated* for a scene by the historical associations of a sublime military event coalescing with the nonsublime scene. It seems to me that there is a very important difficulty involved in Alison's notion of the creation of beauty or sublimity by means of coalescences of ideas, but I shall wait until the general criticism of the theory to raise the matter.

Sublimity and Beauty of the Material World

Alison turns in "Essay 2" of his book to an investigation of those objects in the material world that trigger the emotion of taste. "What is the source of the sublimity and beauty of the material world?" he asks (p. 124). He devotes two hundred, small-print pages to this topic. His exhausting treatment consists of applying the same arguments over and over again to different characteristics of the material world and drawing the same kind of conclusion. He wants to show that *every* instance of beauty or sublimity involves inferential association and that qualities of the material world by themselves and unassociated with nonmaterial things are not beautiful or sublime.

Alison sets up the repetitious procedure of the second essay by showing in its short introduction how his views about the beauty and sublimity of the material world depend on his conclusions from "Essay 1" about the emotion of taste. More specifically, he sets up his procedure by showing how his views about the beauty and sublimity of the material world depend on *one* earlier conclusion, namely, that the emotion of taste always begins with the evoking of a *simple emotion*. He will subsequently maintain that such a simple emotion can be evoked by a quality of matter only as a result of an inferential association between a quality of matter and a nonmaterial characteristic. Alison does not need to mention trains of unified associations, which he alleges always accompany the emotion of taste, because all he is trying to show in the present argument is that the presence of a simple emotion alone rules in certain kinds of characteristics as candidates for beauty or sublimity and rules out others. Of course, according to Alison's theory, *both* an initial simple emotion and a train of unified associations are required as constituents of an experience of taste.

Alison's first step in the introduction to "Essay 2" is to assert that many objects in the material world are beautiful or sublime. Everyone will agree with this assertion. This means *for Alison,* however, that these objects are invariably capable of producing an emotion of taste, with its initiating simple emotion. Everyone may not agree with this claim.

If, according to Alison, beautiful and sublime objects are always connected to the production of a simple emotion, then only those objects in the material world that can provoke emotion can be beautiful or sublime. The task is then to seek out those characteristics that provoke emotion and see what they are like.

Alison's next step is a preemptive one with which he tries to rule out with a stroke a large class of objects as candidates for beauty or sublimity because they cannot evoke emotion. As usual, he relies on introspection.

> I think it must be allowed that matter in itself is unfitted to produce any kind of emotion. The various qualities of matter are known to us only by means of our external senses; but all that such powers of our nature convey is sensation and perception; and whoever will take the trouble of attending to the effect which such qualities, when simple and unassociated, produce upon his mind, will be satisfied that in no case do they produce emotion, or the exercise of any of his affections. (p. 125)

This claim is Alison's basis for concluding that material objects as such cannot be beautiful or sublime: They cannot be objects of taste because they cannot evoke emotion. Alison cites as examples of simple and unassociated material qualities "the smell of a rose, the colour of scarlet, the taste of pine-apple," concluding that since they can produce only agreeable sensations and not agreeable emotions, they cannot be beautiful or sublime (p. 125).

Many material objects are obviously beautiful or sublime. Because, however, he thinks that characteristics of matter as such cannot be responsible for this fact, Alison concludes that beautiful and sublime material objects must be associated with "such qualities as are fitted by the constitution of our nature to produce emotion" (p. 125). Alison then finishes off the introductory remarks to "Essay 2" by mentioning seven classes of qualities that our constitution responds to with emotion and that can be associated with material objects, thereby supplying a basis for the beauty or sublimity of material objects. The material objects in these cases, he says, are either signs of or expressive of the qualities that evoke emotion.

The members of Alison's first class of emotion-evoking qualities are *utility, convenience,* and *pleasure.* Material objects that are expressive of these qualities are candidates for beauty or sublimity. (To be *successful* candidates, material objects would also have to evoke trains of unified associations and their accompanying emotions and pleasures.) He mentions a plow and a printing press as examples of the sort of thing he has in mind. He then writes that "in this manner, the utilities or pleasures of all external objects are expressed to us by their signs of colour and of form" (p. 126). Thus, do plows, printing presses, and the like fulfill one of the necessary conditions of beauty or sublimity.

The members of the second class of emotion-evoking qualities he mentions are *design, wisdom,* and *skill,* and the members of the third class are "power, strength, wisdom, fortitude, justice, benevolence, magnanimity, gentleness, love, etc." (p. 126). There is explicit overlap (wisdom) in the membership of the second and third classes, and Alison's "etc." indicates that his third list is not supposed to be a complete one. It is not clear to me that there is any reason to separate the qualities on the these two lists into two classes; these qualities are all what he will call in the summary at the end of "Essay 2" *active* qualities of mind.

Alison begins his discussion of the fourth class of characteristics by saying, "Besides these immediate expressions of qualities of mind by material signs, there are others which arise from resemblance, in which the qualities of matter become significant to us of some affecting or interesting quality of mind" (p. 127). This is the first time that Alison has indicated that he believes the emotion-evoking characteristics he has been listing are qualities of mind. Ultimately, he wishes to conclude that only qualities of mind can evoke emotion and thereby qualify something as a candidate for beauty or sublimity. He has already concluded that qualities of matter as such cannot evoke emotion, and, if it is assumed that a characteristic is either material or mental, then his desired conclusion would seem to follow. He does not, however, make this argument here.

The official point of the discussion of the fourth class of qualities is to introduce a new kind of consideration—an explanation of how inanimate matter can be beautiful or sublime *by means of resemblance*. When, Alison says, aspects of inanimate matter *resemble* those of an animate material thing that expresses a quality of mind, then "we are disposed to consider them [the aspects of inanimate matter] as expressive of the same qualities [that the aspects of the animate matter are expressive of], and to regard them with similar emotions" (p. 127). He mentions, among other examples of expressiveness, the strength of the oak and the delicacy of the myrtle, claiming that, literally speaking, strength and delicacy are qualities of mind. What he means in cases such as these is that, for example, the configurations of myrtle can be expressive of delicacy and thereby be a candidate for beauty.

The fifth class of objects also involves the notion of resemblance. Objects, Alison says, that produce sensations that *resemble* emotions can thereby become expressive of the qualities of mind that produce the emotion. He gives a number of examples. The sensation of gradual ascent resembles "the emotion of ambition," and the cause of the sensation can thereby express ambition. The sensation of darkness resembles "the dispiriting emotion of sorrow," and, he claims, the cause of the sensation can thus express sorrow (p. 127).

Without giving any examples of the sixth class of objects, Alison just remarks that the many resemblances between qualities of mind and qualities of matter provide a basis for the association, which allows for expression by qualities of matter sufficient for the evocation of emotion.

Finally, Alison's seventh class of objects are said to evoke emotion merely on the basis of accidental association, which means that not even resemblance is required. Thus, by being "accidentally" associated with some quality of mind could the smell of a rose, the color of scarlet, or the taste of pineapple become capable of evoking emotion and thereby become beautiful or sublime, if it could also evoke trains of unified associations with their attendant emotions and pleasures. Thus, in fact, *any* given thing in the material world could become beautiful or sublime, or *both* beautiful and sublime for that matter.

Having concluded his introductory remarks, Alison moves on to a step-by-step discussion of a very large variety of objects of taste. I need to discuss only a few of his cases in order to get all of his arguments set out and to show his typical conclusions. What Alison is trying to do in this extended step-by-step procedure is to confirm by arguments the generalized conclusions about the beauty and sublimity of the material world he has already come to in his introduction to "Essay 2" on the basis of introspection.

I shall begin my discussion with Alison's account of the sublimity of sound. Sounds, in general, are sublime, Alison asserts, when associated with ideas of danger, great power, or majesty (or any other strong emotion). Alison first attempts to show that sounds in themselves are not sublime because the *nature* of the sublimity of a given kind of sound—say, thunder—varies from case to case. The nature of the sublimity of a given kind of sound depends, Alison claims, upon the kind of emotion evoked by the thing associated with the sound. Thus, on his view, the nature of a sound's sublimity varies when the emotion associated with it varies. As an example of this, he says that thunder is generally sublime because of its association with awe and terror, but "how different is the emotion which it gives to the peasant who sees at last, after a long drought, the consent of heaven to his prayers for rain" (p. 130). Different associations that produce different emotions are alleged to produce different kinds of sublimity for the same sound.

Alison's second argument against the sublimity of sound itself is the claim that, if sound independent of associations were sublime, "it seems impossible that sounds of a contrary kind" could be sublime (p. 131). He contends, however, that, for example, both loud and soft sounds can be sublime, and he thinks that this phenomenon can be attributed only to the fact that both loud and soft sounds can have associations that produce the same kind of emotion.

His third argument against the sublimity of sound itself is that a given sound may or may not be sublime. A sound taken to be thunder and there- fore associated with danger is sublime; the same sound taken to be the rum- bling of a cart and thus not associated with danger is not sublime. Thus, the sublimity and lack of sublimity of a given sound are accounted for by varia- tion in association.

Alison moves from simple sounds to the complex, composed sounds of music. He begins his discussion of the beauty and sublimity of music with a long account of musical expressiveness, which is interesting and unobjec- tionable. He contends—and I think everyone will agree—that the expressive qualities of music are important for the beauty and sublimity of music. Then he begins his argument that expressive qualities, which function by means of inferential association, are the only things important for the beauty or sublimity of music.

Alison maintains that musical compositions' capacity to cause the emo- tions of beauty or sublimity (and, hence, be beautiful or sublime) must de- rive from one or more of three sources: (1) the individual sounds of the music, (2) the regular composition of the sounds, or (3) the qualities it expresses by means of association. First, he thinks the individual sounds are ruled out as a source by the kinds of arguments he uses against thunder in itself being sublime. Regular composition, he believes, can also be ruled out. If, he says, regular composition were the source, then all music would be beautiful, since all music has regular composition, but he concludes that "there is a very wide distinction between music, and beautiful music" (p. 156). Only the third possibility remains, and Alison adds as a clincher that, if a musical composition lacks expressive qualities, then no one will find it beautiful. He concludes,

> As there is therefore a very evident distinction between the mechanical pleasure which we receive from mere music [regular composition], and the delight which we feel from music when beautiful or sublime, it is obvious, that the mere regular composition of related sounds, is not the cause of the emotions either of sublimity or beauty. (p. 156)

Notice that Alison begins this particular argument by asking what can produce the *emotion* of taste. He thinks he can safely set aside the "mechanical" pleasure of the succession of related sounds because such pleasure is not emotional in nature. Such "mechanical" pleasure, Alison believes, is a matter of sensation only and is, therefore, quite different from the pleasure that accompanies emotion and, he thinks, is the source of beauty and sublimity.

Alison's next and second argument against regular composition and in favor of expressive qualities as the source of the emotion of taste is his contention that no one ever cites characteristics of regular composition as a reason for music's beauty or sublimity and that expressive qualities or such characteristics as the learning or inventiveness of the composer are the kinds of things cited as reason for beauty or sublimity. While it is certainly true that expressive qualities are frequently cited as reasons for music's value, Alison's contention that characteristics of the music that derive solely from the compositional aspect and are nonexpressive are never cited as reasons is not obviously true.

Some of the possible difficulties of Alison's view come out clearly in his third argument.

> If the beauty or sublimity of music depended *solely* upon the nature of its composition, and was independent of the qualities of which it is expressive, it would necessarily happen, that the same compositions must always be beautiful or sublime, which once were so; and that in every situation they must produce the same emotion, in the same manner as every other object of sense uniformily produces its correspondent sensation. (pp. 157–58; italics mine)

Alison assumes here that the beauty or sublimity of music must depend *solely* on regular composition or *solely* on its expressive qualities. Although perhaps some formalists might contend that the beauty of music depends solely on its regularity of composition, few will maintain that music's expressive qualities are not involved in its beauty or sublimity. Furthermore, it does not follow that, if in a given case beauty does depend solely on regularity of composition, it would produce the same emotion in every situation. A grieving person might be totally unaffected by the beauty of a piece of music or notice its beauty and not be moved by it. The same person in different circumstances might be strongly moved by the music. The *basis* (regular composition or expressive qualities) for a piece of music's beauty is irrelevant as to whether in a given instance it will produce a given emotion or any emotion at all.

Alison's fourth argument against regular composition as the basis for beauty of music is that a person with no musical ear—who thus cannot attend to the compositional aspects of music—can nevertheless to a degree be aware of the gaiety, plaintiveness, and the like of music and can therefore appreciate its beauty. Alison concludes, "If the sublimity or beauty of music arose from the discernment of such relations as constitute the laws of composition, it is obvious that they who are incapable of discerning such relations, would be incapable, at the same time, of discovering either its sublimity or beauty" (p. 159).

Here, as earlier, Alison is assuming that regular composition can give rise only to mechanical pleasure and, hence, cannot contribute to beauty or sublimity. He is, I think, again assuming his envisaged opponent to be claiming that beauty and sublimity arise *solely* from regular composition.

Alison begins his discussion of the beauty of color with the conviction that such beauty derives from the expressiveness of color, which depends on inferential association. He specifies the three kinds of association that support the expressiveness of color.

First, there is the expressiveness that depends on the permanent color of the objects that excite emotion. "White, as it is the colour of day, is expressive to us of the cheerfulness or gaiety which the return of day brings" (p. 162). Presumably, fire engine red would express the emotion of excitement, which the designed activity of fire engines brings. Second, there is the expressiveness that depends on the resemblance between colors and qualities of the human mind. For example, a color is cheerful because it resembles a cheerful quality of mind. Third and finally, there is the expressiveness that derives from accidental association. For example, purple is associated with royalty and thus evokes the emotions evoked by royalty and thereby expresses dignity. Of course, accidental association does not have to be an association shared by all or even a large number of people in order to provide a basis for expressiveness; the accidental associations of a single person can suffice to support expression *for that person.*

Alison concedes that colors by themselves can produce agreeable and disagreeable *sensations,* but, just as with the "mechanical" pleasure of the regular composition of music, he maintains that this has nothing to do with beauty.

The first argument Alison gives against the beauty of color in itself is that the beauty of color varies from country to country, and he attributes the variation to different associations in different countries. For example, for Westerners, white is alleged to be beautiful because it expresses innocence and cheerfulness, but in China it is not beautiful because it is the color of mourning.

Alison's second argument that colors in themselves cannot be beautiful begins by asserting that beautiful colors are always expressive of pleasing or interesting qualities. He believes this constant conjunction is not just a coincidence but a causal one. He claims that the common colors of earth, stone, and the dress of common people do not have interesting associations and are not beautiful, whereas the colors of such things as the dress of the great are beautiful. Similarly, he argues that when a new color appears it is never beautiful, and he attributes this alleged fact to the new color's lack of association. "As soon as it [the new color] is generally adopted by those who lead the public taste, and has become of consequence the mark of rank and elegance, it immediately becomes beautiful" (pp. 164–65). Even a color disagreeable in itself, he says, can thus become beautiful.

Alison continues his argument against the inherent beauty of colors by claiming that when a color's associations are destroyed, its beauty is destroyed; for example, he says that objects manufactured to serve the conveniences of life may have a characteristic color. "This colour becomes accordingly in some degree beautiful, from its being the sign of such qualities [conveniences of life]" (p. 165). If, he claims, the association is destroyed, the color loses its beauty. In another version of this argument, Alison notes that the members of some professions dress in a characteristic color. When a member of such a profession "is in this dress, we conceive that there is a propriety and beauty in such a colour. Change the colours of these several dresses, and all this species of beauty is destroyed" (p. 166).

Alison's final argument against the beauty of color inhering in the perceptible aspects of color is his claim that blind persons such as Dr. Blacklock, a Scottish poet who had been blind since early infancy, can "receive the same delight, from the ideas which they associate with colours, that they do who see" (pp. 166–67). It is alleged—and I do not wish to contest it—that Blacklock used color words correctly in his poetry and that he had formed all the usual associations with colors. Despite the fact that blind persons such as Blacklock cannot see color, Alison is maintaining that there is no difference between the beauty aspect of beauty-of-color experiences of blind persons such as Blacklock and of sighted persons. If Alison's theory of beauty of color is true and beauty of color does not depend on the perceptible aspects of color, then he is right: Blind persons such as Blacklock can have the same experience of the *beauty* of color that a sighted person can, despite the fact that they cannot see!

Alison goes on for another 150 pages or so discussing the beauty and sublimity of forms, motion, the human countenance, the human form, and gesture, but no new considerations or arguments emerge. Thus, I will end my exposition of his theory here.

But before moving to the critical examination of associationism, I wish to note a curious and striking fact about the very different summaries Alison appended to the end of "Essay 2" in the fifth edition and in the first edition. The gist of the summary of the fifth edition is caught by the following unsurprising passage:

> The conclusion, therefore, in which I wish to rest is, that the beauty and sublimity which is felt in the various appearances of matter, are finally to be ascribed to their *expressions of mind;* or to their being, either directly or indirectly, the signs of those *qualities of mind* which are fitted, by the constitution of our nature, to affect us with pleasing or interesting emotion. (p. 317)

In the parallel summary in the first edition, Alison introduced an argument that prevented him from drawing the highly unified conclusion of the fifth edition.

> That the only subjects of our knowledge are matter and mind, cannot be denied; but it does not follow, that all the qualities with which we are acquainted, must be the proper qualities either of body or of mind. There are a number of qualities which arise from relation; from the relation of different bodies or parts of bodies to each other; from the relation of body to mind; and from the relation of different qualities of mind to each other, that are as much the objects of our

knowledge, and as frequently the objects of our attention, as any of the proper qualities either of body or mind. Many qualities also of this kind, are productive of emotion.[2]

He mentions novelty, harmony, fitness, and utility as examples of qualities that arise from relation and that are not qualities of mind. This argument and its conclusion are inconsistent with the general doctrine of both the first and fifth editions, and no doubt with that of all the editions in between. Nevertheless, Alison, following the implication of his relation argument, ends the first edition with this passage:

> Instead therefore of concluding, that the beauty and sublimity of matter arises from the expression of the qualities of mind, we shall rest, in a more humble, but, as I apprehend, a more definite conclusion, that the beauty and sublimity of the qualities of matter, arise from their being the signs or expressions of such qualities as are fitted by the constitution of our nature, to produce emotion.[3]

Thus, the conclusion of the first edition clearly allows, for example, for harmony unassociated with any quality of mind to be beautiful or to be a beauty-making property. Somewhere between the first edition and the fifth edition, Alison dropped his relation argument and drew the highly unified conclusion that he had wanted to draw all along, namely, that the beauty and sublimity of matter derive solely from the expression of qualities of mind. It is not clear to me that he was justified in suppressing the relation argument.

Evaluation of Associationism

A number of minor evaluative criticisms of various aspects of associationism have already been made in this chapter and the previous one. In this section, I shall examine what I consider to be major difficulties in associationism.

Before launching into criticism of them, it will be useful to make a brief comparison of Gerard's and Alison's theories. Both theories involve the association of ideas, but Gerard's version is only a partial associationism, whereas Alison's is a complete associationism. Gerard's version is partial because the notion of association is not involved in his accounts of novelty and in some of the cases of sublimity and beauty he describes. The association of ideas, therefore, is not, for Gerard, a universal or necessary feature of a taste experience. It can be noted then that on Gerard's theory the association of ideas is not an aspect of his notion of the faculty of taste (internal sense) but merely a phenomenon that sometimes functions together with internal sense. Alison's version of the theory of taste is a complete associationism because he maintains that the association of ideas is a feature of every taste

---

2. Archibald Alison, *Essays on the Nature and Principles of Taste*, 1st ed. (London: J.J.G. and G. Robinson; Edinburgh: Bell and Bradfute, 1790), p. 412.

3. Alison, *Essays on the Nature and Principles of Taste*, p. 413.

experience. In fact, as noted earlier, he claims that every taste experience involves two different instances of the association of ideas.

There are a number of other differences between Gerard's and Alison's theories. Gerard uses the language of internal sense, although his notion of an internal sense, as he usually conceives of it, is very different from the "black box" version of Hutcheson. In Alison's theory, even the language of internal sense has disappeared, and the faculty of taste is conceived of as the combination of sensibility and imagination. One might be tempted to think that in the notion of sensibility there is at least a trace of a Hutchesonian internal sense, but on Alison's view sensibility reacts to a wide variety of features of the world (those which produce emotion, even garden variety emotions such as joy and pity) and not to a specific, "aesthetic" feature such as uniformity in variety. Alison's notion of sensibility is thus very different from Hutcheson's conception of an internal sense that supposedly is innately attuned to one specific feature of the world. His notion of sensibility is also quite different from Gerard's notion of internal senses as the cognitive faculties functioning in ordinary ways, for example, conceiving of things with moderate difficulty.

Another important difference between the two associationist theories is that characteristics of the material world have real significance for the faculty of taste on Gerard's view but not on Alison's. For Gerard, on the one hand, some of the characteristics of the material world, such as amplitude, simplicity, and inoffensive color, interact with internal senses to produce pleasure *because of their perceptible qualities*. On the other hand, for Gerard, there are characteristics of the material world that "acquire" sublimity or beauty by means of the association of ideas independently of or even in spite of their appearances. In the case of such "acquired" sublimity and beauty, the fact that the sublime or beautiful object is a material object with its particular perceptible qualities is deprived of significance. There are, however, for Gerard, at least some cases of beauty and sublimity that arise from the perceptible qualities of material objects. For Alison, the sublimity and beauty of the material world are in all cases "acquired," and the actual perceptible qualities of objects are irrelevant to their sublimity or beauty. Furthermore, for Alison, the acquisition of sublimity or beauty by material objects derives in every case from its associated relation to *qualities of mind,* so that even *being* a material object is in a sense irrelevant to an object's sublimity or beauty.

The notion of emotion comes up only incidentally in Gerard's account of taste experience. He mentions, for example, that an agreeable passion may occur within an experience of novelty, but emotion is not for him a necessary or even a frequently mentioned component of a taste experience. For Alison, on the contrary, every taste experience is initiated by a simple emotion and is replete with additional emotions. He introduces the conception of "the emotion of taste" as a necessary feature of taste experiences in the second sentence of his book. Alison is insistent on the necessity of emotion in the first part of his book because in the second part of the book he is going to argue that the qualities of the material world cannot by themselves evoke the emotion *necessary* for beauty or sublimity and therefore by themselves cannot be beautiful or sublime; only qualities of mind, he will argue in the second part, can evoke the necessary emotion and thereby make associated material objects sublime or beautiful. From the beginning, Gerard makes a sustained effort to establish a standard of taste. The addition of the chapter entitled "Of the Standard of Taste" in the third edition of 1780 is a supplement rather than the raising of a new topic. Alison, however, makes no attempt at all in his long book to justify a standard of taste; he no doubt realized that the notion of a standard of taste has no significance for a theory that holds that the perceptible characteristics of the material world are irrelevant to its sublimity and beauty and that *anything* in the material world can acquire sublimity or beauty.

There are important similarities between the two theories. Both Gerard and Alison regard utility as a kind of beauty. This curious view is not a result of their associationism and is a view shared with some nonassociationist theorists.

During my discussion of Gerard's theory, I identified what I called his "principle of the possibility of the coalescence of ideas." This principle is absolutely essential to an associationist theory of taste because it is the foundation for the central and distinctive conclusions of the theory. The principle makes possible Gerard's conclusion that certain pleasures coalesce with other pleasures to create a greater pleasure. More important, the principle makes possible the distinctive conclusions of the associationist theory of taste, namely, that the association of ideas is involved in causing things to possess taste properties such as sublimity and beauty. In Gerard's version of the theory, the coalescence of ideas is *sometimes* involved in taste experiences, but, in Alison's version, it is *always* involved.

Gerard is very explicit about how the association of ideas coalesces ideas. In a passage cited earlier, he writes,

> It is the nature of association, to unite different ideas so closely, that they become in a manner one. In that situation, the qualities of one part are naturally attributed to the whole, or to the other part. . . . Whenever, then, any object uniformly and constantly introduces into the mind the idea of another that is grand, it will, by its connection with the latter, be itself rendered grand.[4]

The kind of case that Gerard has in mind here is, for example, that of an experience of a not-in-itself-sublime painting (a complex idea) and the associated idea of the sublime scene represented by the painting. According to Gerard, these two ideas coalesce into one idea, thereby rendering sublime the painting in the experience. Another example of the kind of thing he has in mind is the case he cites of the idea that is the experience of a green field made beautiful by its association with the idea of fertility (fertility being a kind of utility, which is, of course, thought to be a kind of beauty). In the

---

4. Alexander Gerard, *An Essay on Taste*. 3d ed. of 1780, Walter J. Hipple, Jr., ed. (Delmar, N.Y.: Scholars' Facsimiles & Reprints, 1978), pp.18–19.

two cases just mentioned, a taste property is acquired by an object when an idea of it coalesces with the idea of an object that already has that property.

There is an additional kind of case described by Gerard in which it is alleged that beauty is acquired by a color when the color is associated with an agreeable idea "of any sort." In this kind of case, a taste property is alleged to be generated by the coalescence of two ideas, neither of which has the taste property itself!

I shall now begin my general critique of associationism. First, I shall evaluate the features of Alison's theory that are not shared by Gerard's. Next, I shall critically examine the core of associationism—shared by Alison's and Gerard's theories—the doctrine of the coalescence of ideas. Finally, I shall critically evaluate those features of Gerard's theory not shared with Alison's.

The respect in which Alison differs most strikingly from Gerard, and indeed from Hutcheson and almost every other taste theorist, is his view concerning the place and function of emotion in experiences of taste. Alison asserts on the very first page of his book that such experiences always contain an emotion of taste, which he subsequently describes as a complex of emotions and pleasures derived from trains of unified associations. In addition, he asserts that every taste experience is initiated by a simple emotion such as cheerfulness, melancholy, terror, or the like and that "no objects, or qualities in objects, are, in fact, felt either as beautiful or sublime, but such as are productive of some simple emotion" (p. 95). I shall focus first on Alison's view of the initiating simple emotion. He thinks his thesis about the necessity of such an emotion is introspectively obvious, but he does give an argument in support of it. He claims it is an absurdity to assert both that an object is sublime or beautiful and that one is "positively indifferent [to it] or [finds it] uninteresting" (p. 95). This argument, in effect, merely *asserts* that beauty or sublimity is always interesting, and it *assumes* that an interesting object always evokes emotion. The argument's assumption is unwarranted; it is perfectly possible to find something interesting without feeling any emotion. I might peer with some interest at a leaf without feeling any emotion at all. There is just no necessary connection between being interested in something and feeling emotion. So, even if a beautiful or sublime object is always interesting, this fact would not provide a basis for the view that objects of taste always evoke emotion. Alison's claim that sublime or beautiful objects must always evoke emotion is undermined because his assumption about the link between interest and emotion just does not obtain.

Although Alison's argument gives no support at all to his claim, it still might be the case that every taste experience is initiated by a simple emotion. He does not give an example of the phenomenon he has in mind, but his thesis can be illustrated with an example he gives elsewhere. Consider the beauty of "the gay lustre of a morning in spring" (p. 69). Alison would claim that for someone to experience the beauty of such a scene, the scene must produce in that person an emotion such as gaiety or cheerfulness. There are, in the experience as envisioned here, two references to emotive entities: (1) the gaiety of the morning and (2) the gaiety or cheerfulness of the emotional response to it. Of course, one may respond to the beauty of the the gay luster of a spring morning with an emotion of cheerfulness, but one may also experience the beauty of the gay luster of morning and experience depression or experience no emotion at all. There is just no necessary connection between the experiencing of such things as the beauty of the "gay lustre" of morning and the feeling of an "appropiate" emotion such as cheerfulness or any other emotion. One may even go so far as to say that *typically* one responds to beauty with an emotion such as cheerfulness or joy and to sublimity with an emotion such as awe. It can even be said that such responses are appropriate. Nevertheless, reflection just will not support the view that a simple emotion must be felt as a response to experiences of beauty and sublimity. Of course, Alison's actual position is that a simple emotion must be felt as a *precondition* of experiences of beauty or sublimity, and this claim is even less plausible than the view that a simple emotion must be felt as a response to experiences of beauty or sublimity. When, in fact, one does feel an emotion of the kind Alison has in mind in such experiences, it is *in response* to first having had an experience of sublimity or beauty; that is, the emotion is felt *after* experiencing a sublime or beautiful object, not *before* and as a condition of such an experience.

Alison's claim about the necessity of a *simple* emotion for the initiation of an experience of taste is not just false, it is completely devoid of plausibility. This conclusion is sufficient to refute Alison's view about the *content* of taste experiences, but I shall continue examining his other views about the contents of such experiences. The alleged necessity of the *complex* emotion of taste is just as suspect as the necessity of the simple emotion it supposedly follows. Even in a case in which one *responds* to an object of taste with a simple emotion—say, awe at the sight of the Grand Canyon—it is certainly not typical that a whole set of unified emotions with attendant pleasures is set in motion. In fact, it would be a rare case in which the sight of something like the Grand Canyon would produce a *series* of emotions and pleasures. Typically, on seeing the Grand Canyon or any other sublime object, one remains for a time transfixed in the initial awe it evokes. Similarly, in a paradigmatic case of an experience of beauty such as that of a vivid sunset, a *series* of emotions and pleasures is not typically evoked. Typically, a *single* emotion is evoked by such an experience—an emotion of the kind that goes with sincere utterances of expressions such as "What a gorgeous sight!" Furthermore, in the case of this emotion or the awe felt in connection with a sublime object, the emotion is felt *in response* to an object already experienced as beautiful or sublime; the emotion is not experienced, as Alison also maintains of "the emotion of taste," as a necessary *condition* of an experience of sublimity or beauty.

The only kind of Alisonian *content* of experiences of taste that remain to be discussed is unified trains of associations. It is these unified trains of associations that are alleged to call up all the emotions of experiences of taste except for the *initial* simple emotion. Since it is false that experiences of taste always or even frequently have the welters of emotions that Alison's theory envisions, it is unnecessary to think that swarms of associations are required to call them forth. Of course, it might still be the case that every taste experience contains a train of unified associations even if every such experience does not contain a series of emotions.

There are, however, numerous taste experiences of great simplicity—views of sunsets, of vast landscapes, and the like—that do not typically contain any associations at all and that serve as counterexamples to Alison's theory. Associations may occasionally be evoked by such experiences, but this fact does not aid Alison's theory. Suppose even that the beauty of a sunset and the associations it evokes become parts of a larger whole, which is itself an object of beauty. Even in this case, associations, which have become elements in the beautiful larger whole, are irrelevant to the beauty of the sunset and are unnecessary for experiencing the beauty of the sunset.

There are, nevertheless, taste experiences of great complexity—for example, that of a play—and one might be tempted to think that experiences of this sort would be instances of taste experiences containing trains of associations that would, therefore, give a kind of comfort to Alison's theory. The complexities of the actual experience of a play, however, are very different from the complexities of an experience of taste as envisioned by Alison's theory. The elements of a play do not typically evoke associations, and they certainly do not typically evoke *trains* of associations. If a train of associations were evoked during a play, it would surely distract the spectator from the swiftly moving elements of the play. Even associations that do not initiate trains of associations might interfere with the spectator's experience of the play, although they might not. Clearly, trains of associations can have very little role in the taste experiences of temporal arts such as plays.

Trains of association play very little role in the taste experiences of the nontemporal arts as well. When, for example, one looks at a painting properly, one does not have and focus on distracting *trains* of associations that would lead one's attention away from the painting. Associations may occasionally pop into one's mind as one contemplates a painting, but they are harmless unless they start other associations and distract one's attention from the work of art. I am not counting such things as the recognition that a design is a representation of a human being or of space as instances of association, although perhaps Alison would. In any event, such recognition phenomena are not the sort of thing Alison has in mind when he speaks of objects of taste producing trains of associations.

I have devoted more space that one might think necessary to the refutation of Alison's views on the content of taste experiences. I have done so for two reasons. First, writers with whom I am familiar have contented themselves merely with an exposition of Alison's account of the content of taste experiences, and this leaves the impression that they thought this aspect of his theory is satisfactory. And perhaps they did, or perhaps they were so fascinated by or caught up in the complex details of this aspect of his theory that they just never got around to a criticism of it. Second, it seems to me that Alison's view about the necessity of emotions and trains of associations is not just wrong in some marginal way, but that it is massively wrongheaded and constitutes a dead end from which virtually nothing can be salvaged.

I move now to a consideration of another of Alison's conclusions that is not shared with Gerard, namely, the view that the causes of taste experiences *always* involve qualities of mind. Although a reference to a quality of mind is implied in at least one of Gerard's cases—pleasure taken in regularity as design—the notion of qualities of mind does not play a central role in his theory.

Alison's argument about the causes of taste experiences can be summarized as follows:

1. Emotion is always present in taste experiences.
2. Qualities of matter as such cannot evoke emotion.
3. The only alternative candidate for evoking emotion is qualities of mind.
4. Therefore, qualities of mind must always be involved in the causes of taste experiences and are the sole causes of taste experiences.

It was noted earlier that in the first edition of his book Alison presents a *convincing* argument *against* the view that only qualities of mind can evoke emotion and by implication rejects the conclusion of the argument just stated. However, by the fifth edition and perhaps earlier, he had suppressed his convincing argument in order to draw the conclusion he had presumably wanted to draw all along. My earlier arguments have undermined Alison's first premise that emotion is always present in taste experiences, and I shall next show to be false his second premise, that qualities of matter as such cannot evoke emotion. Consequently, Alison's conclusions about the causes of taste experiences are totally unsupported.

I shall now try to support my claim that Alison's view that qualities of matter as such cannot evoke emotion is false. It is true that qualities of matter are not the sorts of thing that typically evoke our emotions. A pebble on one's path, for example, does not typically evoke any emotion. However, a large rock blocking one's path may evoke anger, and a towering rock may evoke awe, and we do not have to associate either physical object with some quality of mind in order to respond emotionally to it. If we do, say, find the towering rock expressive of God's power and intelligence, this adds to the experience, but it is not identical with finding the rock sublime and awesome. Furthermore, an unbeliever may feel awe and find the towering rock sublime without finding it expressive of any quality of mind—divine or otherwise. The universal premise that Alison needs for his overall argument is just too strong. But it is not just that Alison's claim is false; even addressing this whole matter in terms of evoking emotion is misguided. Emotion is not a universal feature of taste experiences, and virtually every other taste theorist in focusing on pleasure rather than emotion as the central affective aspect of such experiences shows an awareness of this fact. Alison, in focusing on emotion, is virtually alone.

Alison is actually after more than just a necessary connection between the beauty and sublimity of objects and the feeling of simple emotion in observers of those objects. What he is really claiming is that the feeling of a simple initiating emotion is a part of what *makes* objects beautiful or sublime. Alison blurs the line between the objects of perception and the affective aspects of experience. He is not just claiming that sublime or beautiful objects always evoke emotion, he is claiming that the feeling of an emotion is necessary for something's being beautiful or sublime. For example, he writes concerning the changes that one's taste undergoes as one grows up,

> As soon as any class of objects loses its importance in our esteem [ceases to arouse emotion], as soon as their presence ceases to bring us pleasure [by ceasing to arouse emotion], or their absence to give us pain, the beauty in which our infant imagination arrayed them disappears, and begins to irradiate another class of objects, which we are willing to flatter ourselves are more deserving of such sentiments, but which have often no other value, than in their coincidence with those new emotions that begin to swell in our breasts. (pp. 96–97)

A little later, in describing the conditions for experiencing beauty or sublimity, Alison may appear to be denying the thesis that emotion helps make objects beautiful. Here he writes, concerning the effects of fatigue and the like on the emotions required for the proper experiences of objects of taste, "It is not that the objects of such pleasures are changed. . . . Whenever we return to the state of mind favourable to such emotions, our delight returns with it, and the objects of such pleasures become as favourite as before" (p. 100). It is, nevertheless, implied by Alison's view that the taste properties of objects of perception are changed by the affective aspects of experience. What, I think, Alison intends in this last quotation is that although objects do not change in their potential to arouse emotion and thereby pleasure, fatigue and the like can cause them to not function to do so, and thus they fail to be beautiful or sublime.

In any event, Alison has a deep, ulterior motive for finding a necessary connection between emotion and objects of beauty and sublimity, but he has no argument or evidence to support his claim. The motive is that he ultimately wants to make qualities of mind the foundation of beauty and sublimity. To do this, he maintains the false thesis that qualities of mind alone and not material qualities can provoke emotions. In order to make this whole move work, he also has to maintain the false thesis that emotion is a constant feature of the experience of beauty and sublimity.

I turn now to a critical examination of the core of associationism—*the principle of the possibility of the coalescence of ideas*—which functions together with *the association of ideas* to allow Gerard and Alison to develop the particular theories of taste that they do. Gerard begins using the coalescence principle at the very beginning of his book. In this first use, he speaks only of the coalescence of pleasures; it is only later that he uses the principle in connection with taste notions such as beauty and sublimity. He writes of the coalescence of pleasures early in his book during his discussion of novelty,

Any agreeable passion or emotion which a new object happens to produce, will run into the pleasant sentiment that naturally arises from its novelty, and will augment it. A new suit of cloaths gives pleasure to a child, by its being different from his former; it likewise excites his pride, and gives him an expectation of attracting the notice of his companions.[5]

As I noted earlier, Gerard appears to think that the pleasure of the pride taken in the new clothes is swallowed up by and adds to the pleasure of novelty, such that the pleasure of novelty is greater than it would be without the pleasure produced by pride. Gerard also claims at other points in his discussion of novelty that distinct pleasures coalesce, but these accounts do not add anything new to his view, and I shall not discuss them.

It seems to me that Gerard is guilty of a confusion when he thinks that different pleasures can merge, with the identity of one pleasure being absorbed into that of another pleasure and the result that the latter pleasure is increased in quantity. In the kind of case he describes, it is true that there are two sources of pleasure and that the two pleasures make the situation more pleasant than it would be if one were missing. But the two pleasures remain tied to and are identified by their sources; they do not merge to produce one large pleasure of novelty. In the described pride-novelty case, there is an additional problem: the two pleasures are of different types. Gerard calls the (novelty) pleasure that is supposedly derived from moderate mental exertion a *sensation,* and this has at least some plausibility because if the working of the body—say, the taste buds of the tongue—can produce pleasant sensations, then perhaps the workings of the mind can produce pleasant sensations. The pleasure taken in being the proud possessor of a new suit of clothes is not, however, a sensation, although if one is proud enough one might feel pleasant, tingling sensations in addition to the pleasure taken in having the new clothes. It is completely implausible that a nonsensational pleasure could "run into" a sensation of pleasure. As just noted, it is also implausible that a nonsensation pleasure could "run into" another nonsensational pleasure or that a sensation of pleasure could "run into" another sensation of pleasure.

I am not aware of any instance in which Alison claims that distinct pleasures coalesce into one pleasure. Both Gerard and Alison, however, use the coalescence principle in connection with other kinds of ideas. They both claim that two associated ideas can coalesce such that the idea of an object that has a particular taste quality can coalesce with the associated idea of an object that lacks that particular taste quality and also that as a result of this coalescence the object that lacks the taste quality can acquire it. This thesis, which is fundamental to the associationism of Gerard and Alison, is most clearly stated in a passage from Gerard quoted earlier.

It is the nature of association, to unite different ideas so closely, that they become in a manner one. In that situation, the qualities of one part are naturally

5. *An Essay on Taste,* Gerard, p. 9.

attributed to the whole, or to the other part. At least, association renders the transition of the mind from one idea to another so quick and easy, that we contemplate both with the same disposition; and are therefore similarly affected by both. Whenever, then, any object uniformly and constantly introduces into the mind the idea of another that is grand, it will, by its connection with the latter, be itself rendered grand.[6]

Gerard begins this passage is a somewhat tentative way by saying that two ideas "become in a manner one." The passage ends, however, by flatly asserting that an idea of a sublime thing by association causes another thing to become sublime, thereby implying that the two ideas involved literally coalesce.

An example Gerard gives of the association of ideas resulting in the coalescence of ideas and thereby making something sublime is that of a certain kind of sublime painting. Such paintings, which may even be miniatures, are sublime, he claims, because they are associated with (represent) sublime originals (sublime scenes). Alison has the same alleged phenomenon in mind when he speaks of the idea of a sublime military victory diffusing over the sight of the field of Agincourt and giving the scene "a sublimity which does not naturally belong to it" (p. 76).

Are Gerard and Alison right in their claim that ideas coalesce? Consider two paintings. One is a wonderfully executed, vigorously organized, luminously colored painting of a particular Alpine scene entitled *The Matterhorn*. The other is a poorly executed, amateurishly organized, muddy-colored painting of the same scene also entitled *The Matterhorn*. Assume that the first painting is sublime, and grant for the moment that it is sublime because of the functioning of the association and coalescence of ideas in the way Gerard describes. No one would be in the least tempted to say of the second painting that it is sublime, even though it always introduces into the mind the idea of a sublime object; the most that could be said of it is that it is an awful painting of a scene known to be sublime. Gerard is just wrong in his universal claim that "Whenever . . . any object uniformly and constantly introduces into the mind the idea of another that is grand, it will, by its connection with the latter, be itself rendered grand." Having noted that, in the case of the second painting, association is not sufficient to make it sublime, it can be seen that even in the case of the sublime first painting or any other sublime painting that it is not sublime because of its association with a sublime scene. The sublimity of the first painting is achieved in connection with a sublime scene, but its sublimity is not achieved simply because it is associated with a sublime scene by means of representation. The simple fact is that no matter how fast or efficiently the association of ideas brings an idea into the mind, given the occurrence of another idea or experience, the occurrent idea or experience and the ideas it calls forth do *not* become one idea. The experience of the painting and the idea of the experience of the sublime scene it is associated with by means of representation do not become

6. Gerard, *An Essay on Taste*, pp. 18–19.

one idea. When the experienced painting and the experienced sublime scene resemble one another closely (in the way that paintings and what they represent can resemble), as by hypothesis they do in the case of the first painting, it is perhaps easy to slip into the view that the two experiences (ideas) coalesce into one idea. It is not, however, difficult to see that when the experienced painting and the experienced sublime scene differ very greatly in appearance that the two experiences (ideas) do not coalesce into one idea. It may, for all I know, be a *necessary* condition of a painting's being sublime that it represent or suggest a sublime thing, but it is certainly not a *sufficient* condition of a painting's being sublime that it represent or suggest a sublime thing, as Gerard's statement implies.

The same argument applies also to Alison's contention that the historical associations of the sublime military victory give the field of Agincourt "a sublimity which does not naturally belong to it." A person viewing the field at Agincourt may certainly feel a kind of awe at being on the site, but the sublime object is not the view of the present field but the long-past military victory that is no doubt envisaged as preceded by King Henry's stirring speech, as portrayed by Shakespeare. Alison's use of the coalescence principle leads him into the mistaken view that two distinct objects of attention collapse into one.

In the same context in which Gerard makes his claims about paintings made sublime because they represent sublime scenes, he also claims that the style of words and phrases can be made sublime because they are commonly and frequently used by persons of sublime character. Gerard is mistaken here in the same way that he is mistaken in connection with the paintings discussed previously. Words and phrases may become trendy, but they do not become sublime because they are frequently and commonly used by persons of sublime character. The idea of a person's sublime character and the idea of his or her frequently used utterances do not become one idea simply because they are associated. When words and phrases are sublime, they are so because of their sounds and meanings.

At some points, Alison uses the coalescence principle in a way that raises an additional problem. For example, he speaks of the beauty of residences of persons we admire.

> The scenes themselves may be little beautiful; but the delight with which we recollect the traces of their lives, blends itself insensibly with the emotions which the scenery excites; and the admiration which these recollections afford, seems to give a kind of sanctity to the place where they dwelt, and *converts everything into beauty* which appears to have been connected with them. (pp. 75–76; italics mine)

In this passage Alison is not claiming that the idea of the residences that are of little or no beauty coalesces with an idea of something of beauty to make the residences beautiful; rather, he is claiming that the idea of the residences coalesces with ideas such as delight and admiration to make the residences beautiful. In this case, the coalescence of ideas is alleged to produce beauty out of ideas that themselves do not involve beauty! In this case, there is not only the mystery of how two distinct ideas can coalesce but also the mystery of where the beauty is supposed to come from. The answer is that it does not come from anywhere and the situation Alison describes is not one in which beauty is present. Alison is right that being present in such places as the residences of persons we greatly admire produces in us feelings of a kind of sanctity, and we frequently linger in such places and muse about the persons and their presence among the objects that we are now among. Nevertheless, the undoubted pleasure that we take in the experience of such objects does not convert them into objects of beauty. Many of these objects are just ordinary looking, and some may even be ugly. Of course, some of the objects many be beautiful, but not because of their associations.

The notion that the coalescence of ideas can produce beauty and sublimity of matter out of ideas that themselves do not involve beauty or sublimity is absolutely crucial for Alison, although not for Gerard. Remember that on Alison's view nothing in the material world is beautiful or sublime in itself and that all beauty and sublimity of matter are acquired by means of association, which ultimately leads back to qualities of mind. Since qualities of mind cannot possess material beauty or sublimity (not being material), material beauty and sublimity can, for Alison, come ultimately only from the coalescence of an idea of a material thing (which in itself he holds is neither beautiful or sublime) and a delightful, admirable, or agreeable idea of a quality of mind (which, in itself, may be neither beautiful nor sublime). Thus, on Alison's view, material beauty and sublimity can be produced by the coalescence of ideas of things that are themselves not beautiful or sublime.

I shall conclude this discussion of the coalescence principle by focusing on Gerard's and Alison's uses of it in connection with beauty of color. The two theorists are not in complete agreement about color. Gerard allows that colors "inoffensive to the eye" and colors with "splendor" can be beautiful as well as independent of associations, but Alison maintains that no color in and of itself and independent of associations can be beautiful. They do agree that colors that in and of themselves are not beautiful can *acquire* beauty by means of association and coalescence. This view is, of course, subject to the arguments used previously against the other attempts to claim that beauty can be acquired by means of the coalescence of ideas. For example, both Gerard and Alison claim that when members of a profession have a characteristic dress involving a particular color and a member of that profession is observed in that dress, as Alison writes, "we conceive that there is a propriety and beauty in such a colour" (p. 166). This kind of case, like the residence case, involves two difficulties. First, it requires the coalescence of the idea of the color and the associated idea of a profession. Second, it purports to generate beauty out of the coalescence of two ideas, neither of which involves beauty. Alison is right that we conceive a propriety in seeing a member of a profession in characteristic dress, but the most charitable thing that can be said about his claim concerning beauty is that perhaps he confuses beauty with propriety.

Perhaps the coalescence principle has received sufficient rebuttal, but Alison's claim about persons such as the blind Scottish poet Blacklock provides a fitting conclusion to this discussion of beauty of color. Alison asserts that blind persons such as Blacklock can "receive the same delight, from the ideas which they associate with colours, that they do who see" (pp. 166–67). Remember that according to Alison the beauty of color resides only in the associations of color and has nothing to do with the perceptible aspects of color. Imagine Blacklock and his contemporary Allan Ramsey, the Scottish painter, standing in front of Ramsey's portrait of Hume. Blacklock has just received a very complete and accurate description of the colors in the portrait. It can be agreed that Blacklock and Ramsey can have all the same associations that can be gotten from the colors of the painting and all the same delights that such associations give. On Alison's theory, that is all the delight that there is to be gotten from the beauty of the colors in the painting. Alison is asking us to believe that Blacklock and Ramsey receive "the same delight" from the beauty of the painting's colors! He is asking us to believe, so far as beauty of color is concerned, that Blacklock's and Ramsey's experiences are identical. It is tempting to believe that Alison is either as handicapped concerning color as Blacklock or that he is a not-so-unusual example of the philosopher who sticks to the theory no matter what.

The associationist's view that objects can acquire taste properties such as beauty and sublimity either from being associated with ideas of objects that have these taste properties or from being associated with agreeable ideas *of any sort,* even when the referents of the agreeable ideas do not have taste properties themselves, is a fantastic notion. In addition to the fact that this conclusion relies on the dubious notion of the coalescence of ideas, it ignores the fact that taste properties such as beauty and sublimity are characteristics that derive from and depend on other characteristics of the objects themselves. When we speak of the beauty or sublimity of objects, we are speaking of characteristics they have by virtue of the perceptual or conceptual features of the objects themselves. Anything these objects are associated with is irrelevant to their beauty or sublimity.

I have now critically evaluated those aspects of Alison's theory that Gerard does not share and the aspects of their theories that the two have in common. I believe that nothing of value survives this criticism and, consequently, that nothing can be salvaged from Alison's theory of taste or from those parts of Gerard's theory that are shared with Alison. I move now to a consideration of aspects of Gerard's theory that are not shared by Alison.

Gerard, unlike Alison, retains the Hutchesonian language of the internal senses, although he is very conscious of how different his account of the internal senses is from Hutcheson's. For Hutcheson, the internal senses are affective "black boxes" which, we know not how, produce pleasure when the mind is aware of certain specific characteristics. Gerard, however, gives accounts of the inner aspects and workings of the internal senses. For example, he claims that when the sense of novelty produces pleasure, it does so because conceiving of the novel object requires a moderately difficult exertion of the mind and this moderate mental exertion produces pleasure. Similarly, the difficulty of the mental exertion involved in conceiving of objects of great amplitude produces the pleasure involved in the experience of that kind of the sublime. Also, simplicity in a sublime object makes for facility of conception, which also produces pleasure. The uniformity involved in beautiful objects makes for the facility of their conception, which produces pleasure. The variety involved in beautiful objects enlivens the mind and gives it employment, which is pleasant. The pleasure derived from the sense of imitation comes from the comparison one makes between the imitation (copy) and what is represented (the original). "As comparison implies in the very act a gentle exertion of the mind, it is on that account agreeable."[7] Gerard also identifies another kind of pleasure involved in the experience of imitation that is not a pleasure produced by the sense of imitation but is simply an additional pleasure. He writes of this pleasure, "As a farther energy is requisite for discovering the original by the copy; and as this discovery gratifies curiosity, produces an agreeable consciousness of our own discernment and sagacity, and includes the pleasant feeling of success; the recognising resemblance, in consequence of comparison, augments our pleasure."[8] Gerard identifies similar *success* pleasures in the cases of the other internal senses. I mention success pleasures because shortly I will compare them to the pleasures of internal sense.

Gerard speaks of the pleasures produced by the internal senses as deriving from exertions of the mind involving the moderately difficult conceptions of objects and the easy conceptions of objects. Sometimes he just speaks of the exertion of the mind as producing pleasure. He clearly thinks that the internal senses are the cognitive faculties of the mind functioning in an ordinary employment (the conceiving of objects) and that this ordinary functioning of the cognitive faculties is what produces the pleasure basic to the experience of novelty, sublimity, beauty, and the other taste properties.

Gerard objects to Hutcheson's conception of the internal senses as ultimate and original senses because he claims to have evidence that they are derived and compounded as he has described them—derived from the cognitive faculties and compounded from the various cognitive faculties. He states in the middle of the long footnote at the beginning of Part 3, "We *find, on examination,* that uniformity and proportion are agreeable, as they enable us to conceive the object with facility; and variety, as it hinders this facility from degenerating into langour"[9] (italics mine). No doubt he thinks we *find on examination* that it is the moderate difficulty in conceiving a novel object that produces the basic pleasure involved in cases of novelty and so on for sublimity, imitation, and the like.

It seems to me, however, that what we *find on examination* in these cases is that we are pleased by uniformity and/or proportion, that we are pleased

7. Gerard, *An Essay on Taste,* p. 47.
8. Gerard, *An Essay on Taste,* p. 47–48.
9. Gerard, *An Essay on Taste,* p. 147.

by variety, that we are pleased by novelty, and so on. We also find in the case of uniformity and proportion that they enable us to conceive an object with facility, in the case of variety that it prevents boredom, and in the case of the conceiving of a novel object that it requires moderate mental exertion. What one, however, does *not* find on examination of one's consciousness is that conceiving with facility, preventing boredom, and conceiving with moderate difficulty are the causes of the pleasures we feel in these cases, although it is, of course, logically possible that these mental exertions are the causes of the pleasures. We are conscious, for example, of the fact that a particular conception was easy—it took little time and effort—but we are not conscious of the workings of the cognitive faculties that accomplish this easy conceiving and conscious, consequently, of these workings being the source of the pleasure we feel.

It seems to me that Hutcheson and Gerard are in the same boat insofar as their notions of internal sense are concerned. They are both entitled to make the kind of claims that affirm that certain perceptual qualities are pleasing because the perceptual qualities and being pleased are the kinds of things that are found in consciousness. Neither is entitled to his claim about the nature of the mental mechanism that is responsible for the pleasure because there is no evidence in consciousness (or anywhere else) to support either the contention that the pleasure is produced by an innate sense or the contention that the pleasure is produced by the workings of the cognitive faculties. By the way, Hutcheson does not claim that we are aware of the sense of beauty in consciousness; he argues (badly) to the conclusion that the sense of beauty is the source of pleasure.

Contrast what Gerard says about what I called success pleasures with what he says about the pleasures of internal sense. He writes, for example, of success pleasures that when we discover the original of an imitation we are pleased both by our success and by having the abilities that enable us to succeed. In the success cases, the awareness of our success is present in consciousness, and so is our awareness of our being pleased by the success. This kind of awareness is just what the internal sense case lacks; we are not aware of the workings of the cognitive faculties producing pleasure as we are of the consciousness of success producing pleasure. There is just no introspective evidence to show that the "internal sense" pleasure is produced by the functioning of the cognitive faculties or that it is *not* produced by a purely affective internal sense, as Hutcheson contends. Of course, there is also no evidence to show that the pleasure in question *is* produced as Hutcheson contends.

In claiming that the functioning of the cognitive faculties is productive of pleasure, Gerard is relying on a widely accepted opinion from an earlier time. Peter Kivy notes that Descartes and Spinoza, among others, held the view.[10] The fact that Gerard is following the lead of earlier philosophers explains where he got the idea, but it does not justify it. Kant was perhaps

10. Peter Kivy, *The Seventh Sense* (New York: Burt Franklin & Co., 1976), p. 182.

relying to some extent on this tradition when he maintained that the cognitive faculties in free play are productive of pleasure.

Alison, perhaps realizing the hopelessness of trying to establish a standard of taste for an associationist theory, makes no attempt to do so. Gerard, apparently failing to realize the hopelessness of such an attempt, tries to develop an account of a standard of taste, although in doing so fails to take account of his associationism. There is thus in Gerard's attempt at establishing a standard of taste a double failure. As noted at the end of the last chapter, he fails completely (a third failure) to cope with the problem of the variation of affective response and, consequently, fails to establish a standard of taste, even for a nonassociationist theory of taste. Gerard himself explicitly acknowledges the relativistic threat of affective variation, but having done so then says nothing that even tends to counter the threat.

What, if anything, is Gerard's positive contribution to the advancement of theorizing in the taste mode? Hutcheson had identified the complex property of uniformity in variety as the beauty-making property, suggested that there are analogous properties that are grandeur-making and novelty-making, and maintained that moral content can be valuable in art. Thus, Hutcheson suggests that there are at least four taste characteristics that are valuable in art and nature. Gerard identifies thirteen characteristics as valuable in objects of taste—natural or artistic. They are novelty, quantity, simplicity, uniformity, variety, proportion, utility, color less hurtful to the eye, splendor of color, harmony, imitation, incongruity, and virtue. Of these thirteen, utility is certainly suspect as a taste property. Color is certainly a domain of taste value, although one of Gerard's reasons for thinking color valuable (less hurtful to the eye) is curious. So, then there are twelve. Gerard identifies these properties within the context of his discussion of the seven senses of taste, but I believe it is the multiplication of the number of valuable characteristics that is important, rather than the multiplication of the number of senses of taste. There are many, many different characteristics—aesthetic and otherwise—that contribute to the value that art and nature have for us from the point of view of taste, and, insofar as Gerard moves in the direction of identifying a larger number of such characteristics than Hutcheson does, his theory is an advance over Hutcheson's.

4

Taste and Purpose: Immanuel Kant

The theory of taste Kant presents in his *Critique of Judgment* (1790)—known as the third *Critique*—is notoriously difficult to understand. The exposition of his theory is usually encountered as the so-called four moments from the beginning of the "Critique of Aesthetic Judgment" in the *Critique of Judgment,* and in this form it is, I believe, virtually impossible to understand. It is not just that his writing is so bad; he frequently just does not provide the information required for explaining why he draws the conclusions he does. For example, his conclusion that "beauty is an object's form of purposiveness," in the third-moment context in which he draws it, is baffling. This conclusion, by introducing the notion of purpose as an integral aspect of beauty, deviates sharply from the kind of conclusions that the other theorists of taste drew about the nature of beauty. (Hume does say that a critic ought to take account of an artist's purposes, but he does not claim that such purpose is an integral aspect of beauty.) The notion of purpose (as perfection) plays a large role in the theories of Kant's rationalist German predecessors such as Wolff and Baumgarten, but these theorists were not theorists of taste. The German rationalists were, no doubt, the historical source of Kant's conception. Because of the radically innovative nature of Kant's connection of beauty and purpose within the theory of taste tradition, Kant's conclusion has a special need for elucidation, an elucidation he does not give. Kant is just as unclear, in the context in which he draws it, about the justification for his conclusion that the faculty of taste consists of the cognitive faculties functioning in a noncognitive way. These two notions—the nature of the object of taste (beauty) and the nature of the faculty of taste—constitute the core of any theory of taste. Kant's reasons for drawing the conclusions he does about these two notions, in the context he does, are obscure.

The notions of the object of taste and the faculty of taste are *standard* notions of all theories of taste, although, of course, the various theories have different accounts of their natures. That experiences of taste are disinterested, pleasant, and universal are three other standard features of the theory of taste, at least as envisaged by Hutcheson. In any event, Kant's theory contains accounts of all five of these standard Hutchesonian features.

The first great impediment to understanding Kant's theory of taste is the order in which he presents the two main parts of the *Critique of Judgment*. In Part 1 of the third *Critique,* the "Critique of Aesthetic Judgment," Kant tries to fit the eighteenth-century conception of taste into his philosophical system, a system that includes the teleological picture of the world as the realization of God's purpose. The exposition of his teleological scheme, however, is not given until Part 2 of his book! Many, perhaps most, persons interested in Kant's theory of taste tend to ignore or dismiss its teleological context. Perhaps they ignore it because his discussion of teleology follows the discussion of taste in the *Critique of Judgment,* and people interested in aesthetics just stop reading when they come to the end of the exposition of his theory of taste; perhaps they dismiss the teleology because they do not take it seriously. In any event, Kant's theory of taste is typically read without its context. It is, of course, clear from Part 1 alone that Kant's theory of taste has a teleological aspect; the problem is that without Part 2, the fully developed teleology, the teleological aspect of his theory of taste seems unmotivated. His theory just cannot be fully understood independently of its teleological matrix.

Kant's *Critique of Pure Reason* (known as the first *Critique*) was an attempt to reform and rein in the theoretical excesses of rationalism by submitting rationalism to critical restraints. By the end of the third *Critique,* however, Kant's philosophical beliefs, with their overarching teleological, theological matrix, had come to resemble a seventeenth-century metaphysics of a Cartesian or Leibnizian sort, although it was *morally* rather than theoretically based.

Logically speaking, I believe Kant placed the two main parts of the third *Critique* in the wrong order. The teleological part should come first; the account of his theory of taste should follow because it is developed (1) by *deriving* central notions of his theory of taste from his teleology and (2) by working out accounts of what Kant takes to be the standard features of the theory of taste (gleaned from thinkers such as Hutcheson and Burke) within his own teleological system.

Kant tries to accommodate all the standard elements of the theory of taste within his grand teleological scheme in three ways: (1) He characterizes the notions of the object of taste (beauty) and the faculty of taste, two central concepts of taste, in terms of purposiveness, the central concept of teleology. (2) He claims that judgments of taste are a kind of reflective judgment, and reflective judgment is a notion that has its origins in his teleology. (3) He nests the other standard elements of taste—disinterestedness, pleasure, and universality—within his teleological scheme. In Kant's theory, the mechanism of taste is subsumed under and becomes an integrated aspect of the teleological structure of the world.

Although Kant's discusssion of taste precedes his discussion of teleology in the body of the *Critique of Judgment,* in both the unpublished first introduction and the published (second) introduction, he puts primary stress on teleology and outlines its place in his philosophical system. Also, in his 1787 letter to Reinhold, in which Kant first announces that he has found the solution to the problem of taste with the discovery of the relevant a priori principle, he writes, "So now I recognize three parts of philosophy, each of which has its a priori principles, which can be enumerated and for which one can delimit precisely the knowledge that may be based on them: theoretical philosophy, teleology, and practical philosophy. . . ."[1] Kant is clearly indicating here that his theory of taste is to be developed within his teleology. In fact, since Kant's teleology is his broadest and most inclusive scheme, his critical philosophy and his practical philosophy, as well as his theory of taste, are nested within it. Because Part 2 of the *Critique of Judgment* is primary, I shall preface my discussion of Kant's theory of taste with an account of his teleology. While I shall not discuss every detail of his teleology, I shall discuss enough of it to set the stage for his theory of taste.

In addition to the problem of the ordering of the two main parts of the book, there is a second aspect of the *Critique of Judgment* that makes it difficult to comprehend, namely, the enormous redundancy of its exposition. Kant divides his book into one hundred subsections under numerous headings. When he begins a subsection, he tends to start all over again with the statement of his theory, thereby going over ground that has already been gone over innumerable times. This procedure raises the distinct possibility that Kant will tell different stories in different places. Also, this extravagant redundancy greatly increases the distance between the discussions of the central elements of his theory and thus obscures the connections among them. Incidentally, if this redundancy could somehow be removed, the third *Critique* would be reduced from a lengthy book to a relatively short essay. At least in part as a result of Kant's method of exposition, the development of his teleology and his theory of taste is more by repetition than by argument.

In addition to the problems of the reversed order of the two main parts of the third *Critique* and the extravagant redundancy of the exposition of the overall theory, there is a third problem. I do not think that there is any one place in the third *Critique* where Kant manages to give a continuous, complete, and properly ordered account of his overall theory. His repeated starting over to state his theory at the beginning of the various sections of his text is in part, I believe, an attempt to give a continuous, complete, and properly ordered account of his theory, but he never succeeds in doing so. There is, I believe, a complete theory in the book, one that Kant has scattered the elements of throughout the length and breadth of Part 1 and Part 2. The task of giving an account of the overall theory of the third *Critique* is like the task a paleontologist faces in attempting to assemble the skeleton of a prehistorical animal whose fossilized remains have been scattered over a

---

1. Immanuel Kant, *Philosophical Correspondence, 1759–99.* Arnulf Zweig, ed. (Chicago: University of Chicago Press, 1967), p. 128.

large area. There is a "patchwork" theory of the first *Critique;* I have a "scattered-elements" theory of the third *Critique.*

Kant's use at the beginning of his book of the apparently highly organized "four moments" to set forth his account of his theory of taste gives the impression that he is following an order in which each moment logically follows from the one preceding it. This impression is strengthened when, at the beginning of the second moment, which is concerned with universality, he says that the doctrine of the second moment "can be inferred" from the doctrine of disinterestedness worked out in the first moment. He could perhaps with equal plausibility maintain that the doctrine about necessity in the fourth moment can be inferred from the doctrine of the first moment. The doctrine of the third moment that "beauty is an object's form of purposiveness," however, just comes out of the blue and does not follow from anything else in any of the other three moments. In the order it is presented in the four moments, the third moment is an undigested and undigestable lump. Of course, as noted earlier, given the perfectionist views of his rationalist predecessors, it is easy enough to see the historical source of Kant's connection of beauty and purpose.

I shall try to do two main things in this chapter: (1) I shall try to give an account of Kant's teleological theory with its encapsulated theory of taste and to give that account in a way that places the elements of the overall theory in the order in which they are logically related to one another. (2) I shall then try to evaluate his theory of taste.

Judgment in the First *Critique*

Since the framework within which the third *Critique* is worked out was formulated in the first *Critique,* I shall briefly outline the main elements of the earlier book. Both books take the notion of judgment as a point of departure, and the third *Critique* is created by extending the notion of judgment used in the first *Critique.*

The central task of the first *Critique* was to respond to David Hume's skeptical views that we cannot know objects external to our perception and that we cannot know that our future experiences will exhibit the same uniformities that our past experiences did. Kant hoped to show that Hume's skepticism was wrong.

Kant begins the first *Critique* with a discussion of judgment. By judgment, Kant means the mind's power to connect two kinds of elements in experience, specifically the subsuming of a particular under a universal. For example, the experiencing of a particular as a tree is for Kant a judgment. The linguistic counterpart of this experience is "This is a tree." The term "judgment" is used to refer both to the experiences in which particulars and universals are connected and to the sentences that describe the experiences by connecting subjects and predicates. The following discussion of judgment will be carried out in terms of sentences.

In the first *Critique,* Kant distinguishes analytic and synthetic judgments.

An analytic judgment is one in which the predicate concept is contained in the subject concept. For example, in "All bachelors are unmarried," the predicate concept *unmarried* is contained in (is entailed by) the subject concept *bachelor,* which means "unmarried male." A synthetic judgment is one in which the predicate concept is not contained in the subject concept. For example, in "This tree is a spruce," the subject concept *tree* does not contain (does not entail) the predicate concept *being a spruce.*

Kant distinguishes two other kinds of judgments—a priori and a posteriori. Before Kant, "a priori" meant something like "not derived from experience." Kant, however, gives a new and additional sense to "a priori" when he applies it to judgments. He characterizes an *a priori* judgment as one that is *universal and necessary.* For example, "All bachelors are unmarried" and "7 + 5 = 12" are universally and necessarily true. "All bachelors are married" and "7 + 5 = 13" are universally and necessarily false. An *a posteriori* judgment is one that is not universal and not necessary. For example, "This tree is a spruce" is not universally and necessarily true or false.

Kant claims uncontroversially that all analytic judgments are a priori and some synthetic judgments are a posteriori. He further claims controversially that not all synthetic judgments are a posteriori, that is, that some synthetic judgments are a priori. The central problem of the first *Critique* is to show how synthetic a priori judgments are possible.

Kant thinks everyone will agree that mathematics is known to be true and that it is a priori, so he proceeds to argue that judgments of pure arithmetic and geometry are also synthetic. He concludes, for example, that such judgments as "7 + 5 = 12" and "The shortest distance between two points is a straight line" are synthetic. Having argued that mathematical judgments are synthetic, Kant claims to show that they are a priori because they have an intrinsic connection to time and space and that time and space are a priori forms of intuition (nonconceptual forms) that the mind imposes on our experience. Time and space are forms of intuition that are a priori in the pre-Kantian sense of not being derived from experience.

Kant thinks everyone will agree that certain very general judgments about the objects of experience are known to be true and that they are synthetic, so he proceeds to argue that they are also a priori. He concludes, for example, that such judgments as "Every event has a cause" and "Every change in an individual thing has an underlying permanence" are a priori. His explanation of how it is possible for these very general synthetic judgments, which are known to be true, to be a priori is that there are twelve innate, a priori concepts in the mind and that these a priori concepts, which Kant calls "categories," impose certain general conceptual orders on experience, for example, a general causal order and experiences of permanence (substance). The categories are a priori in the pre-Kantian sense of not being derived from experience. Kant's conclusion about a general causal order is his answer to Hume's view about knowledge of future uniformities of experience. His conclusion about substance (permanence) is his answer to Hume's view about knowledge of objects external to our perception.

Thus, Kant claims to have shown by means of what he calls "transcendental arguments" how synthetic a priori judgments are possible; the mind's a priori faculty of intuition (sensibility) imposes a spatial and temporal order on the particulars of experience, and the mind's a priori categories impose general conceptual orders—causal, substantive, and others—on the temporally and spatially ordered particulars. Since these orders are imposed on experience by the mind, *every* experience *must* have these orders; that is, experience universally and necessarily has these orders, which in Kant's terminology as applied to judgments means that they are a priori. There are, of course, many a posteriori concepts—red, cat, dog, and the like—that derive from experience that also order our experience.

Since the human mind imposes the spatiotemporal and general conceptual structures on experience, their universality and necessity is of a limited kind—the universality and necessity of these structures are confined to and do not transcend human experience. Thus, the structural characteristics of experience that are assured by synthetic a priori judgments cannot be extended beyond human experience. The characteristics of experience that derive from empirical sources cannot be extended beyond human experience either.

Based on his conclusions about judgment and the nature of experience, Kant concludes that ideas of things that transcend human experience cannot be objects of knowledge. For example, the ideas of God and of noumenal objects (things in themselves that are outside of human experience) cannot be objects of knowledge. Consequently, Kant denies that the traditional arguments for the existence of God work and concludes that theoretical knowledge of God's existence cannot be had. He does say that the idea of God and other ideas of transcendent things can serve as regulative ideas that guide our thinking and research.

The Metaphysics of Purpose

Kant's Philosophical Beliefs

I turn now to the discussion of Kant's teleology. Three kinds of beliefs can be identified in Kant's philosophical system: (1) empirical beliefs that are known to be true or false on the basis of evidence from experience, (2) transcendental beliefs that are known to be true on the basis of transcendental proofs, and (3) teleological beliefs that the human mind, because of its nature, cannot avoid believing but that cannot be known to be true in a theoretical or in a transcendental way—that is, cannot be known to be true on the basis of evidence from experience or from transcendental arguments. These three kinds of beliefs sort out into two kinds of belief structures. On the one hand, there is an epistemological belief structure that involves the empirical and transcendental beliefs. I have just outlined this first-*Critique* picture in the last section. On the other hand, there is the teleological belief structure that involves beliefs *not restricted* to the phenomena of experience and the mental machinery that makes it possible. This second picture involves all the various Kantian supersensibles: God, noumenal selves, and the rest of the noumenal world external to these selves. The teleological picture contains the epistemological picture as a substructure. The central task of the *Critique of Judgment* is to justify believing in an unexperienced teleological world that surrounds and supports the epistemological world from which we longingly peer out. Kant seeks to accomplish this justification with a two-step procedure: He attempts, first, to discover something about the machinery with which we know phenomena that will connect us in our epistemologically restricted world to the hidden teleological world and then, second, to find some justification for believing in this connection and the noumenal world at the end of the connecting rainbow.

Seeking System

In both of the introductions that Kant wrote to the third *Critique,* after first outlining the results of the first *Critique* and second *Critique,* Kant begins to talk about judgment. For Kant, judgment is the mind's ability to relate particulars and universals. There are, he claims, two kinds of judgment. When the mind already possesses a universal, it can subsume particulars furnished by intuition under that universal (concept) and thereby produce the phenomena of experience, which is, of course, a *unified* experience. When judgment works in this way, Kant calls it *determinate* judgment. Such judgments involve a priori universals (the categories) and a posteriori universals. In cases of determinate judgment, a priori and a posteriori universals work together with intuitions to produce *unified* experience. Except for the new terminology, the claim about determinate judgment is essentially the doctrine of the first *Critique.* Kant calls the second kind of judgment *reflective* judgment. When intuition furnishes the mind with a particular for which it does not possess a universal, the mind must seek an a posteriori universal under which to subsume it. This seeking is what Kant means by reflection, and it is a seeking for unity. Reflective judgment, like determinate judgment and because it is a kind of judgment, seeks *unity.* It seeks unity within the empirical domain.

Kant asserts that there is a transcendental *principle* of reflective judgment. When he uses the expression "transcendental principle" here, he is not referring to a principle of the fundamental truth kind; that is, he is not talking about a propositional entity. He is using the word "principle" in the sense of "ultimate source or origin," not "fundamental truth." There are principles or maxims of the fundamental truth (propositional) kind such as "Nature takes the shortest way" and the like that are involved with the transcendental principle of judgment, but the two different kinds of principles should not be conflated. The transcendental principle of reflection of which Kant speaks is the cognitive faculties' drive to seek a posteriori unity—the unity or systematicity of empirical experience and empirical laws.

Reflection (the seeking of a posteriori unity) may succeed or fail. An example of its success would be Newton's subsumption of the motion of terrestrial falling bodies and the motion of the planets under the new theory of gravitation. (Kant treats a general thing such as a theory as a universal.) Another example of successful reflection would be the subsumption of a variety of species of animals under a particular genus. If Newton had not been able to think of the new synthesizing theory, then his reflective judgment would have failed. Newton's success revealed the systematic relation among some of nature's physical laws that up until then had not been known. Likewise, the subsumption of a number of species of animals under a genus reveals hitherto unknown systematicity in the structure of organic nature. Systematicity can thus be discovered both in the physical laws of nature and in the structure of organic objects of nature. When reflective judgment succeeds in finding an a posteriori universal for a particular, as in the case of Newton, Kant claims that one feels the pleasure that one feels when an aim is realized. Since such pleasure is based, Kant claims, on an a priori foundation—namely, the cognitive powers' drive for a posteriori unity—it can be considered universal and valid for everyone; that is, such pleasure is universal because it derives from the realization of a drive that everyone has as a result of the drive's origin in the cognitive powers themselves. The success of reflective judgment's drive for systematicity is always in doubt, and the success is pleasant. By contrast, when the categories of the understanding (the a priori concepts) are applied to particulars, no pleasure is produced because this application comes about automatically and without any sense of success. Then again, it appears that Kant believes that when any a posteriori concept is applied to an intuition, pleasure results. He writes in the published introduction, first, of the pleasure resulting from the discovery of an empirical concept and then of the residual pleasure that occurs in the subsequent routine application of such concepts that

> this pleasure was no doubt there at one time [the time of the discovery of the concept], and it is only because even the commonest experience would be impossible without it [pleasure] that we have gradually come to mix it [pleasure] in with mere cognition and no longer take any special notice of it [pleasure].[2]

Kant notes that the empirical laws and the structure of nature might have been so complicated and unconnected that the human mind (the subject of experience) would not have been able to deal with them. In fact, however, the laws and structure of nature exhibit a systematicity that enables our minds to grasp them. The subject of experience (the mind) and the systematicity of nature thus fit harmoniously together with the mind grasping the system. There is, then, a mental or subjective fit (fit of the subject) with nature.

At any given time, we will have discovered some degree of systematicity

---

2. Immanuel Kant, *Critique of Judgment*. Werner S. Pluhar, trans. (Indianapolis: Hackett Publishing Co., 1987), p. 27. All subsequent internal page cites in this chapter to Kant are to this edition.

in nature. Before Newton, Galileo's discovery of the law of falling bodies and Kepler's discovery about the orbits of the planets had introduced system into *two* domains. Newton's theory of gravitation brought these two systems into *one* domain and, thus, increased the degree of systematicity of physics. At any given time, it is possible that all the systematicity of nature will have been discovered, and continued research will be frustrated. Kant claims, as noted, that there is an a priori principle of judgment (analogous to the a priori structures of the understanding) that drives us to seek systematicity in nature. Unlike the a priori categories of the understanding that guarantee that our experience will *necessarily* have certain systematic features—causality and substantiality, for example—the a priori principle of judgment cannot guarantee that nature will continue to exhibit additional *contingent* systematicity. Such judgment is merely reflective and may succeed or fail. Determinate judgments, insofar as they involve the *categories* of the understanding, can never fail. Determinate judgments with empirical content may, of course, be false.

After discussing the relation of *subjects*—that is, the things that know— to nature, Kant turns his attention to the *objects* of nature, that is, things in nature that are known. He notes that these objects are of two kinds: aggregates and systems. Aggregates—for example, earth, stones, minerals—like everything else are embedded in the a priori laws of the understanding and in the contingent systematicity of nature's laws and structure, but aggregates themselves *exhibit* no systematic form. In contrast, systems—for example, animals, plants, flowers, crystal formations—*exhibit* a systematic form in which their elements fit together, in addition to being embedded in the a priori laws of the understanding and nature's contingent laws and structure. Animals, plants, and the like are thus systems within a system of nature.

Thus far, virtually everything that I have said about Kant's view of reflective judgment—that is, the seeking of systematicity—has not involved teleology. I have developed the account of Kant's view in this way because the seeking of systematicity need not involve any commitment to teleology. For example, an antiteleological philosopher such as Hume could agree that human beings seek systematicity in nature for pragmatic reasons quite independently of any teleological concern. Kant, however, from the very beginning, casts his account of reflective judgment's quest for systematicity in teleological terms, so that for him systematicity is a teleological notion. The points I want to bring out forcefully here are that systematicity and teleology are not necessarily related and that an argument is required to show that systematicity is a teleological notion. One can seek systematicity without seeking purpose.

Kant does not give an argument at this point; he says, in effect, that we just cannot help regarding systematicity teleologically. For example, he writes of systems, "that their shape or inner structure is of such a character that we must, in our power of judgment, base their possibility on an idea [meaning by 'idea' an agent's intentional idea]. . . . Insofar as nature's products are aggregates, nature proceeds *mechanically, as mere nature;* but insofar as its products are systems . . . nature proceeds *technically*, i. e., it proceeds also as *art*" (pp. 405–6). Within his cannot-help-but-believe teleological systematicity, Kant distinguishes two kinds of system or fit: (1) what he calls a "subjective" fit between the *subject* of experience and the systematicity of the laws and structure of nature and (2) a fit among the elements of those objects that are systems. But even if we cannot help but believe that all the elements of systematicity are teleological, it has not been shown that they are teleological. (Kant, of course, never claims that they can be shown *theoretically* to be teleological.)

Seeking Purpose

As one would expect, given the nature of his critical philosophy, Kant's use of teleological language in theoretical contexts is of a hypothetical and heuristic kind that speaks of the systematic aspects of nature *as if* they were purposive. At least, this is his official line, but he is not always so careful. In the first introduction, for example, in speaking of the conception of the mind's ability to know nature, he writes, "In other words, this concept would have to be that of a purposiveness of nature for the sake of our ability to cognize nature" (p. 392). Strictly speaking, when Kant writes without hypothetical qualification of the aspects of nature that enable subjects to know nature as a whole, he should speak only of the systematicity of nature rather than of the purposiveness of nature, since, as noted in the last section, systematicity and purpose are not necessarily related; that is, when he speaks without qualification of the fit between knowing subjects and nature, he should speak of subjective systematicity rather than subjective purposiveness. Of course, Kant repeatedly states that teleological conceptions do not yield knowledge and that they are regulative only. Nevertheless, he seems to feel free on occasion to equate the systematicity of nature with a purposiveness of nature without the qualification that such purposiveness is merely heuristic. When speaking of objects of nature such as plants and animals, Kant is also usually careful to say that these natural systems are to be conceived of as purposive only in a hypothetical and heuristic sense. Nevertheless, he does sometimes speak about natural systems in a very curious way. For example, he writes, "For though experience can show us purposes [i.e., systems], nothing in it can prove that these purposes are also intentions" (p. 423). And a few pages later, in speaking of systems, he writes that "we leave undetermined whether their purposiveness is intentional or unintentional" (p. 426). Astonishingly, Kant here, as elsewhere, is claiming to distinguish between intentional purposes and *unintentional* purposes! Kant himself, at the beginning of the third moment, appears to characterize purpose in terms of intention. His curious notion of unintentional purpose will allow him to speak of purposes without having to be committed to the existence of a being whose intention lies behind those purposes without saying that such talk is merely heuristic! Thus, on occasion, Kant speaks of both subjective systematicity and systems as purposive without the qualification that such purposiveness is merely heuristic, and he also thinks he can speak meaningfully of unintentional purposes.

When Kant speaks of either systematicity of objects (systems) or subjective systematicity as unintentional purposes, he is, in effect, introducing a technical term that is at odds with the way in which we usually understand the notion of a purpose. This way of talking allows the use of a teleological-sounding expression, "unintentional purpose," as a synonym for the not necessarily teleological notion of the systematicity of nature and thereby covertly supports the belief that certain aspects of nature are, in fact, teleological. It is a subtle way of edging into a belief about the teleological world that supposedly surrounds and supports our epistemological world.

As noted, however, Kant, for the most part, is careful to keep his teleological remarks hypothetical and heuristic. In this *as if* vein, he conceives of reflective judgment's quest for systematicity as enabling us to form the *idea* of nature as the art or technic of a supersensible deity in order to guide our thinking and research. But it is not just that the quest for systematicity enables or allows us to do this; he thinks that given the nature of our cognitive faculties that "we are absolutely unable to form a concept of [how] such a world is possible except by thinking of it as brought about by a supreme cause that *acts intentionally*" (p. 281). Viewed in this way, the systematicity of nature would be conceived of hypothetically, but inevitably, as the *intentional* creation of God's understanding.

Given this grand scheme, how does Kant picture it in detail? First, remember that on Kant's epistemological—that is, first-*Critique* view—the categories of the human understanding impose a necessary structure on human experience, for example, the necessity of a causal and substantive structure. Such a generalized causal structure, Kant maintains, leaves undetermined the content of the specific causal laws of nature. The actual laws of nature are contingent and must be discovered by empirical inquiry. When one moves to Kant's grand teleological scheme, however, one can envisage that what human beings experience as the *contingent* laws and structure of nature are really *necessary;* that is, in the teleological picture, the laws and structure of nature and their systematicity are seen as the necessary result of the deity's creative understanding. In the teleological scheme, God's understanding is pictured as operating in a way somewhat analogous to the way in which the human understanding operates when it produces the causally necessary structure of experience. Human understanding is seen as imposing a necessary causal structure, and the divine understanding is seen as imposing a *specific* necessary structure and a *specific* set of necessary causal laws. In this hypothetical, teleological picture, all of nature's contingency is seen as converted into creation's necessity.

Finally, in his hypothetical, teleological picture, Kant sees the purposiveness of the human mind's fit in its cognizing of nature as a part of the overall purposiveness of nature. He writes that once nature has been judged teleologically, and the natural purposes that we find in organized beings have entitled us to the idea of a vast system of purposes of nature, then even beauty in nature, i.e., nature's harmony with the free play of our cognitive powers as we apprehend and judge its appearance, can similarly be considered an objective purposiveness, namely, of the whole of nature [regarded] as a system that includes man as a member. (p. 260)

Kant speaks here of purposiveness as it is involved in the experience of beauty, but he clearly also has in mind purposiveness as it is involved in reflective judgment's successful discovery of systematicity in nature. In this passage, then, Kant conceives of this kind of purposiveness (both the fit of the cognitive faculties in their free play in the experience of beauty and the mind's fit with nature) as a part of overall purposiveness. That is, on the one hand, he conceives of the fit between the cognitive faculties of a subject in their free play to be a fit between two different aspects of the mind of an organism. On the other hand, he similarly conceives of the fit between (1) each subject's cognitive faculties and (2) the systematicity of nature to be a fit between different aspects of nature, so that all of nature, including subjects, becomes one object. He thus pictures all of nature as a kind of organism—the Supersensible's Super Organism.

Kant repeats incessantly two theses throughout the "Critique of Teleological Judgment." The first thesis is that we cannot help believing that first organisms and then all of nature are the intentional creations of God. The second thesis is that we cannot, however, justify this belief theoretically. For example, at one point he asks whether all of his talk about teleology proves that God exists, and his answer is an unequivocal

No; all it proves is that, given the character of our cognitive powers, i.e., in connecting experience with the supreme principles of reason, we are absolutely unable to form a concept of [how] such a world is possible except by thinking of it as brought about by a supreme cause that *acts intentionally.* (p. 281)

Near the end of the "Critique of Teleological Judgment," as a kind of summation, Kant devotes a long subsection to explaining his rejection of the Design Argument, which he calls "Physicotheology." This amounts to saying what has already been said so frequently, that the existence of God, the designer, cannot be inferred from the order exhibited by nature. This leaves us with the unavoidable belief in God, the designer, but without a theoretical justification for that belief. In effect, the doctrine of the first *Critique* generates but cannot justify this belief as knowledge.

Purposiveness Gained

The doctrine of *Critique of Practical Reason* (known as the second *Critique*) comes to the rescue. I shall give only a sketchy account of this rescue, as I am primarily interested in Kant's conclusions and their implications for his theory of taste.

At the end of the "Critique of Teleological Judgment," in a discussion of belief, Kant distinguishes three kinds of cognizable things:

1. matters of opinion
2. matters of fact
3. matters of faith (p. 360)

Matters of *opinion* are about things that are not known to exist but that are possible within the empirical domain. Kant gives as an example the question of whether there is life on other planets.

Matters of *fact* are about things whose objective reality can be proved. Any law of science would be an example of a matter of fact. Kant claims that the objective reality of one and only one rational idea can also be proven— the idea of human freedom. Hence, it is a matter of *fact* that freedom exists. He claims that freedom "proves . . . that it has objective reality, by the effects it can produce in [nature]" (p. 368).

Matters of *faith* are about things that transcend theoretical reason but "that we have to think a priori . . . in reference to our practical use of reason in conformity with duty" (p. 362). Kant claims that there are three and only three objects of faith. First, there is the highest good that pure practical reason commands us to achieve using our freedom. Second and third, there are the existence of God and the immortality of the soul, which are, Kant argues, necessary conditions for the achievement of the highest good (p. 362).

The alleged *fact* of freedom plus the alleged *commands* of practical reason allegedly lead to *faith* in the highest good, the existence of God, and the immortality of the soul. Thus, Kant claims to justify belief in the three ideas of reason—freedom theoretically and God and immortality practically. Through the fact of freedom, Kant asserts,

> it [is] possible to connect the other two ideas with nature, and to connect all three with one another to form a religion. Therefore, we have in us a principle that can determine the idea of the supersensible within us, and through this also the idea of the supersensible outside us, so as to give rise to cognition [of them], even though one that is possible only from a practical point of view. (p. 368)

Thus does Kant claim to achieve a justified belief in the grand teleological scheme that completes the philosophical system of the three *Critiques*.

Kant's Teleological Theory of Taste

The Transition to the Theory of Taste

Now that an account of Kant's teleology and his justification for believing in it are in place, the transition to the theory of taste can begin. I shall first try to show that the two core notions of his theory of taste—his conceptions of the object of taste and the faculty of taste, which are so obscure in the context of the four moments—are derived from his teleology. His conception of the object of taste (beauty) is derived wholly from his teleology, and his conception of the faculty of taste is derived, with some assistance, from the same source. These derivations make Kant's claim that beauty is an aspect of purposiveness less baffling. These derivations also make his claim that the faculty of taste is some cognitive faculties in reflection at least understandable.

What, in Kant's view, does the universe as a vast system of purposes mean for the theory of taste? In the very first paragraph of Part 2, the "Critique of Teleological Judgment," Kant writes, in the hypothetical way appropriate at that point in his text, about what at the end of Part 2 he is assured of, namely, the purposivenes of nature. This passage, read assertively with purposiveness assured, serves as a conclusion for Part 2 and provides the basis for a transition to the theory of taste in Part 1, the "Critique of Aesthetic Judgment."

> Transcendental principles do provide us with a good basis for assuming that nature in its particular laws is *subjectively* purposive for the ability of human judgment to take [it] in, making it possible to connect the particular experiences to [form] a system of nature; and we can then expect that the many natural products in such a system might include some that, as if adapted quite expressly to our judgment, contain certain specific forms: forms that are commensurate with our judgment because, as it were, their diversity and unity allow them to serve to invigorate and entertain our mental powers (which are in play when we engage in judging) and hence are called *beautiful* forms. (p. 235)

Kant begins this passage by talking about transcendental principles, meaning, of course, to focus on judgment's drive for empirical systematicity. Reading the passage as if it were the conclusion of the "Critique of Teleological Judgment," the seeking of assumed systematicity that could fail at any point becomes the seeking of purposiveness that is assured. Kant speaks first of subjective purposiveness—the purposive systematicity of nature that enables us to comprehend nature as a whole. This kind of purposiveness involves the relation between knowing *subjects* and the world, hence, his name for it, "subjective purposiveness." The system of nature involves not only the laws of science and the structure of organic nature but also all the individual *objects* in nature, what in the passage Kant refers to as "the many natural products." All the natural products or objects of nature fall under the laws and structure of science and, hence, are commensurate with human judgment; that is, all the objects of nature are knowable and as part of a system of nature fall under subjective purposiveness, the fit between the cognitive faculties and the objects of nature. In this passage, Kant divides the natural products of the system of nature into two groups: objects that lack and objects that have a specific form (diversity and unity), which is expressly adapted to our judgment so as to invigorate and entertain our mental powers. He claims that the objects with this specific form are the objects that have the beautiful forms. It is the objects with this specific form that exhibit the purposiveness in which the parts of an object fit together in a special way. It is clear that in this passage Kant is concerned only with *natural* beauty, and I shall be concerned in what follows only with his view of natural beauty until I indicate otherwise.

The Object of Taste

In the particular kind of case Kant is talking about in the just quoted passage, the beautiful forms are seen as having a *special* fit within subjective purposiveness (the fit between knowing subjects and the objects of the cognitive faculties). The question remains, how are the two groups of objects—those that have the special fit and the specific form (the beautiful form) and those that lack it (the nonbeautiful form)—to be characterized in the Kantian theory of taste? As noted in my account of his teleology, Kant distinguishes between two kinds of objects in nature—systems and aggregates. I think it is systems and aggregates that he has in mind when he speaks of the objects that have the specific form that invigorates and entertains the mental powers and is the beautiful form and of the objects that lack the specific form, so that when Kant concludes in the third moment that "beauty is an object's form of purposiveness," he must be claiming that it is the form of systems that is the (natural) beautiful form. All of the systems that Kant mentions, except crystal formations, are organisms. So, it is the forms of organisms plus forms that closely resemble the forms of organisms, such as those of crystal formations, that Kant has in mind when he speaks of beautiful form. But what is the argument that supports the conclusion that natural beauty is the form of systems of this kind?

I do not believe that Kant gives anything like a straightforward argument to justify his conclusion. There are, however, several passages in the "Critique of Teleological Judgment" where he makes remarks that go some way in suggesting why *he thought* that the forms of systems are the beautiful natural forms.

At one point in talking about the grand teleological picture, Kant speaks of "the unfathomably great art that lies hidden behind nature's forms" (p. 334). It is unclear here whether Kant, in speaking of "great art," is talking about all of the forms found in nature or just about the forms he calls "systems." In many places he speaks of the idea of all of nature as a technic. Nevertheless, even though Kant thinks that we cannot avoid believing that the whole system of nature is God's art, and in the end he thinks this belief is justified, he admits that there are aspects of nature that have the appearance of being devoid of system—what he calls "aggregates." So, "aggregates" or "lumps" appear to be scattered profusely through God's art, conceived of as the whole of nature, and this would seem to disqualify the *whole* of nature as God's *great* art. Fortunately, very near the end of the "Critique of Teleological Judgment," Kant is more specific about the great art he is thinking about. Here he writes of his belief that the supreme being "manifests itself with such unfathomable artistry in the purposes of nature" (p. 372). Here, in speaking of "the purposes of nature," he is clearly thinking about systems as God's unfathomably *great* or fine art, as distinguished from the whole of nature with its many lumps. So, *within* the whole of nature (the system of God's lumpy art), there are systems that Kant thought of as God's fine art. Now Kant thinks that the goal of fine art is the realization of beauty, for he writes that "what is essential in all fine art is the form that is purposive for our observation and judging" (p. 195); that is, he thinks that the form of purposiveness—beauty—is the goal of fine art. Kant must have thought that surely if any being's fine art would be beautiful, God's fine art (systems) would be. Thus, he must have thought that he had good reason for believing that systems are beautiful, or rather that the *forms* of systems are beautiful, since for reasons not yet mentioned he thought that only form could be beautiful. There is thus an argument of sorts for Kant's belief that "beauty is an object's form of purposiveness." I am not claiming that this is a good argument; I do not believe that a good argument can be given for Kant's conclusion because I believe his conclusion is false. I am not trying to show that his conclusion is justified; I am just trying to show how Kant's conclusion is derived within his philosophical, teleological system.

There is an objection to Kant's conclusion that "beauty is an object's form of purposiveness" to which Kant does not give an answer but to which he could have given an answer. This is the problem of how to account for the ugly individuals within a species of organisms; on Kant's view, every member of a species of organisms is purposive because it is an organism, but some members of almost every species are undeniably ugly. I believe that Kant could counter this objection by arguing that the ugly members of a species constitute a falling away from the purposive form of the species; that is, they are in some degree deformed and do not truly exemplify what God intended. (This answer, of course, raises the theological problem of natural evil in a special form, and I have no idea how it could be resolved.)

Thus far in the discussion of the passage quoted at the beginning of my discussion of Kant's theory of taste, the notion of subjective purposiveness has been passed over very quickly in order to get on with the discussion of the object of beauty. But there remains a puzzle about subjective purposiveness: Why does Kant believe that the forms that are commensurate with the mental powers in such a way as to invigorate and entertain them are the beautiful forms?

In the quoted passage from the beginning of the "Critique of Teleological Judgment," Kant talks about subjective purposiveness, but he actually focuses on it narrowly, that is, not on the *general* notion of the fit between knowing subjects and the objects of knowledge, but on the more fine-grained notion of the *special* fit between the cognitive faculties and a certain *subset* of the objects of nature. So there is a *general* subjective purposiveness that obtains for all of nature and a *special* subjective purposiveness that obtains for a certain subset of the objects of nature. (This passage, by the way, is the only place of which I am aware that Kant mentions uniformity and variety as properties of form that play a role in the experience of beauty, but

I am not interested in this point at the moment.) What is the justification for Kant's conclusion that beauty is the form of the objects of nature that fit with the cognitive faculties in the special way? What is it about the forms of these objects that makes them and only them beautiful? As far as I can tell, Kant does not say here *or anywhere else* what justifies the inference or even why he believes that the inference is plausible. Why did Kant think he could claim that the forms that are commensurate with judgment in a special way so as to invigorate and entertain our mental powers are the beautiful ones?

So even if Kant's belief that the forms of systems and only those natural forms are beautiful were justified, there is still the problem of the justification of the claim that the forms that are commensurate with judgment in a special way are the beautiful forms. Even if Kant does not give any argument to support this claim, there are considerations in his teleological scheme that may have led him to his conclusion that the especially commensurate forms are the beautiful forms. Consider as a first premise the view that the forms of systems are identical with the beautiful natural forms; Kant certainly thought he was entitled to this premise—it is the conclusion of the third moment (when only natural beauty is in question). Then, if, as a second premise, Kant believed that the forms of systems and only the forms of systems (in cases of natural beauty) are commensurate with judgment in a special way so as to invigorate and entertain our mental powers, one can conclude that the forms commensurate with judgment in this way are identical with the beautiful natural forms. That is, Kant may have had in mind the following argument, which I shall state without bothering to put in the qualification about *natural* beauty:

1. The forms of systems are identical with the beautiful forms.
2. The forms of systems are identical with the forms that are commensurate with judgment in such a way as to invigorate and entertain our mental powers.
3. Therefore, the forms that are commensurate with judgment in such a way as to invigorate and entertain our mental powers are identical with the beautiful forms.

What in Kant's teleological system could have led him to believe the second premise?

Consider part of the long passage I quoted earlier: "we can . . . expect that the many natural products in [the system of nature] . . . might include some that, as if adapted quite expressly to our judgment, contain certain specific forms: forms that are commensurate with our judgment." Kant begins here by referring to "the many natural products" in the system of nature. These products divide, we know, into two exhaustive kinds: aggregates and systems. He goes on in this passage to refer to "certain specific forms" that are commensurate with judgment in such a way as to invigorate and entertain the cognitive faculties. Of course, all forms are commensurate with judgment in some way, since this commensurability is the basis for the knowledge we have of objects. Kant must have thought that the form of systems is commensurate with judgment in the special way that invigorates and entertains because the forms of systems are the only alternative to the forms of aggregates. And, he must have thought aggregates would be just too unstructured to be commensurate with judgment in the *special* way that invigorates and entertains the cognitive faculties. (Of course, the forms of aggregates are sufficiently commensurate with judgment in a general way for us to have knowledge of them.)

So, Kant may have had something like this reasoning in mind to support the second premise of the formulated argument, for this premise would allow him to conclude, as he does, that the especially commensurate forms are the beautiful forms.

Kant's view, derived from his teleology, is then (1) that the beautiful natural forms are the forms of systems and (2) that these forms are "adapted quite expressly to our judgment" (*special* subjective *purposiveness*). This derivation indicates, I think, why Kant thinks he can claim in the third moment that "beauty is an object's form of purposiveness," a claim that, if approached only through the four moments of the theory of taste and in the order in which Kant presents them, is completely baffling. This derivation shows how Kant's teleology underlies and supports one of the central notions of his theory of taste—his conception of the *object of taste* as the form of purposiveness that has a special subjectively purposive relation to our cognitive faculties.

Kant's conception of beauty as the form of purposiveness has two poles, one of which is anchored in the world of objects and one of which is anchored in the world of subjects. *Systems* exhibit the form of purposiveness in experiential objects of the world. The human subject's mind itself exhibits a higher order form of purposiveness in its *special fit* interaction with the form of systems. It is the form of purposiveness exhibited by natural systems in the world of experience that I shall have in mind when I speak of the object of (natural) beauty.

There is an important consideration that is directly connected to the notion of the object of taste—the question of principles of taste. For example, in Hutcheson's theory, it is alleged that uniformity in variety is the object of taste, and it is implied that "objects that possess uniformity in variety are always beautiful" is *the* principle of taste.

Kant appears in a number of places to deny the possibility of any kind of principle or principles of taste. He clearly denies principles such as Hutcheson's that identify beauty with a property such as uniformity in variety. For example, in the first sentence of a section entitled "An Objective Principle of Taste Is Impossible," Kant writes, "By a principle of taste would be meant a principle under which, as condition, we could subsume the concept of an object and then infer that the object is beautiful. That, however, is absolutely impossible" (p. 149). Although he speaks in this quotation without qualification of a principle of taste, his section heading specifies that he is talking about an *objective* principle of taste. So, he explicitly means to deny that there could be an *objective* principle of taste, namely, a principle in which the predicate beautiful expresses a concept and refers to a property such as uniformity in variety.

In the passage quoted, Kant appears also to deny that it is possible to infer that an object is beautiful. Does he mean that this cannot be inferred from *any* principle or only that it cannot be inferred from an *objective* principle? I think many people take Kant to be denying the possibility of *any* principle of taste and of *any* inference to the conclusion that an object is beautiful.

Kant's denial of the possibility of an objective principle of taste, however, leaves open the possibility for him of a *subjective* principle of taste and thus for the possibility of inferences to a conclusion that an object is beautiful. Kant's assertion in the third moment—"*Beauty* is an object's form of *purposiveness* insofar as it is perceived in the object *without the presentation of a purpose*"—certainly has all the earmarks of a principle that identifies beauty with (for short) an object's form of purposiveness. For Kant, the form of purposiveness does not express a concept or refer to an empirical property because it involves only intuition and not the understanding (the faculty of concepts). Thus, the form-of-purposiveness principle is not an objective one, that is, not a principle of the kind that Kant explicitly denies. Given Kant's subjective principle, the following inference is constructible:

1. Beauty is an object's form of purposiveness.
2. This object (intuition) exhibits the form of purposiveness.
3. Therefore, this object (intuition) exhibits beauty.

Thus, Kant's theory of taste does have a (subjective) principle of taste and does allow for inferences to the beauty of objects (intuitions). Neither of the two premises of this argument is a determinate judgment, and its conclusion is not a determinate judgment either. That is, none of the three expresses a concept; the premises and the conclusion refer only to objects of sensibility (the forms of space and time).

The Faculty of Taste

Once it is seen how Kant's conception of the object of taste (beauty) derives from his teleology, the question quite naturally arises, Do other aspects of his theory of taste stand in a similar relation to his teleology? It can be shown, I think, that his conception of the nature of the *faculty* of taste can also be derived, with a little assistance, from his teleology. His notion of the object of taste's special relation to the cognitive faculties is a clue to what his account of the faculty of taste will be.

It is Kant's notion of judgment, especially reflective judgment, the centerpiece of his teleology, from which his conception of the nature of the faculty of taste primarily derives. I shall now try to show how Kant's view of the principle of judgment provides the foundation for his conception of the faculty of taste.

Kant takes several propositions inherited from earlier theorists of taste for granted, and they, together with the notion of judgment, determine the way in which he conceives of the faculty of taste. The propositions are:

1. There are judgments of taste (beauty).
2. The notion of beauty is *not* a concept (a universal).
3. Experiences of beauty are pleasant.

The view that the notion of beauty is not a concept is, of course, a purely Kantian formulation, but it has its antecedents in Hutcheson's view that "beauty" refers to a feeling (pleasure) in us and Hume's view that "beauty is no quality in things themselves." The first two propositions listed function as premises in the argument that yields Kant's conception of the faculty of taste. The third proposition, that experiences of beauty are pleasant, does not function as a premise in the argument but is rather a proposition that Kant takes for granted and that his conception of the faculty of taste must account for.

There are in Kant's philosophical system two, and only two, kinds of judgment: determinate and reflective. If there are judgments of taste and the notion of beauty is not a concept, then judgments of taste cannot be determinate judgments because determinate judgments require that a concept or universal be applied to an intuition. It follows that judgments of taste are reflective judgments, that is, judgments that are a search for a concept for an intuition. Since judgments of taste are reflective judgments and reflective judgments are a particular way in which the cognitive faculties function, the faculty of taste (the mental entity that underlies experiences of taste) has to be the cognitive faculties searching for a concept under which to subsume an intuition. But since the notion of beauty is not a concept, the faculty of taste's search can never succeed in the way that reflective judgments can sometimes succeed, and thus beauty cannot be linked to concepts in the way that concepts are linked in a theory and to other theories in the system of nature. There are then two kinds of reflective judgments: (1) the kind such as Newton's search for a unifying theory, a search that may succeed and generate pleasure or fail and not generate pleasure; and (2) judgments of taste that must *always* fail to find a concept, since the notion of beauty is not a concept. For Kant, then, the faculty of taste is the cognitive faculties in *what would appear to be* a necessarily unsuccessful search for the concept of beauty. Thus, Kant's notion of judgment plus certain theory-of-taste propositions he takes for granted generate his own particular conception of the faculty of taste as the cognitive faculties in a futile search. I take it that Kant's view must be that we have a sense that in cases of the experience of beauty no concept can be found and that because of this sense (realization) we can contemplate the content of an intuition.

It remains to be explained how, on Kant's theory, the pleasure of the experience of beauty can be generated out of a search that cannot possibly succeed. This explanation will also fill in the details of the way in which the Kantian faculty of taste functions.

Kant takes it for granted that there are judgments of taste and that experiences of beauty are pleasant. These particular reflective judgments cannot produce their pleasure in the way that Newton's success in finding a universal did, because in these cases there is no universal to be found. But since it is taken for granted that judgments of taste are pleasant, a way must be found to show how the cognitive faculties (which are known to be the faculty of taste) can produce pleasure in a way that does not involve the *success* of finding a universal for an intuition. Since the pleasure of a judgment of taste must be produced without the success of finding a new universal, the pleasure must be derived from reflection as it deals merely with the contemplation of an intuition all by itself and without relation to any determinate universal. The pleasure of taste then must be derived from the cognitive faculties in reflection, but since the usual kind of success of reflective judgment is absent, the only possible source of the pleasure of taste would have to be the cognitive faculties functioning in some way independently of the synthesizing of an intuition and a universal. So, the source of the pleasure has to involve what is uniquely involved in experiences of beauty, and what is unique in these cases is the cognitive faculties dealing only with the contemplation of an intuition with a special form in a way that does not involve the synthesis of intuition and determinate universal. What is unique, since it is all that is left after the requirement that the notion of beauty is not a determinate concept has been taken account of, is the purposively attuned cognitive faculties themselves functioning with an intuition with a special form independently of the intuition's synthesizing with a determinate universal. It is then a special-form intuition in its interaction with the cognitive faculties that has to be the source of the pleasure of taste because that is all that is left. Kant calls this remainder process the "harmonious free play" of the cognitive faculties. It is called "free play" because the engagement or connection the cognitive faculties ordinarily make between intuition and universal is lacking. It is called "harmonious" because the cognitive faculties are purposively attuned to one another in *all* their interactions and, hence, harmonious in their free play interactions. Additionally, in the case of beautiful forms, there is the *special* fit that invigorates and entertains the cognitive faculties. I take it that Kant must think that it is the special fit between intuitions of the forms of systems and the cognitive faculties that is invigorating and entertaining, that is, pleasant. It is not, however, that one can "clearly see" in Kant's theory how the pleasure arises; it is rather that this process must be the source of the pleasure because it is all that is left to be the source.

Notice that, on Kant's view, the faculty of taste (the cognitive faculties) is a universal and necessary feature of human beings and that in experiences of beauty the faculty of taste functions independently of contingency (empirical universals). Thus, on his view, judgments of taste and their pleasures have a universal and necessary basis. It is what a judgment of taste *lacks* (as compared to a empirical judgment)—namely, an empirical universal—that assures that it is universal and necessary.

At this point, an aspect of Kant's conception of the object of taste that was left unaccounted for earlier can now be addressed. Kant concludes that "beauty is an object's form of purposiveness," and my earlier discussion focused solely on the purposiveness aspect of his claim. But why the *form* of purposiveness?

It has just been shown that on Kant's view, in order to take account of his view that the notion of beauty is not a concept, beauty must be confined to what can be found in an intuition independently of a synthesis with a universal. Only spatial or temporal form can be found in such an intuition. Of course, not every experience of spatial or temporal form is beautiful, and Kant tries to take account of this fact by claiming, as has been shown, that only a certain subset of spatial or temporal forms is beautiful, namely, the spatial or temporal forms that exhibit purposiveness (systems). Note that while the mind's forms of intuition are, according to Kant, the source of the spatial and temporal structure of the objects of experience, the specific spatial or temporal form that a form of purposiveness has derives, in Kant's system, from a source external to the human mind, namely, from God. In experiences of beauty, the tracings of God's purposiveness show through in the intricate unity and variety of the forms of organisms.

To sum up, the object of taste (beauty) is an object's form of purposiveness (systems), and the faculty of taste is the cognitive faculties functioning merely with an intuition of a form of purposiveness (harmonious free play). When such functioning occurs, the pleasure of taste is produced.

Thus far, the nature of the object of taste (beauty) has been derived from and integrated with Kant's teleology, and the nature of the faculty of taste has also been derived, with some outside help, from his teleology. What remains to be shown is how, according to Kant, judgments of taste are disinterested, universal, and necessary. When that is done, an account of Kant's view of beautiful art can be developed and integrated with his account of natural beauty.

Disinterestedness

The first of the four moments in which Kant gives his exposition of his theory of taste is concerned with the disinterestedness of judgments of taste. He does not attempt to prove that judgments of taste are disinterested. He takes it for granted that such judgments are disinterested and attempts to show how the fact of their disinterestedness can be realized within his theory of taste. Thus, there is a fourth proposition that Kant takes for granted.

4. Judgments of taste are disinterested.

This proposition, like the proposition that experiences of beauty are pleasant, does not function as a premise in a Kantian argument; it is the statement of a fact to be taken account of.

That judgments of taste are disinterested was a staple of the theory of taste long before Kant. For Hutcheson, for example, this meant that the perception of the characteristic of uniformity in variety in an object triggers pleasure in a subject independently of any relation of self-interest the object has for the subject. For example, the uniformity in variety of a painting triggers pleasure in a subject regardless of whether the subject owns the painting, the painting is a portrait of the subject, the food depicted in the painting pleases the subject, and so on. When a subject has a disinterested pleasure in a painting, he might also at the same time take pleasure in owning the painting (possession interest), viewing his own likeness (vanity interest), and so on, but any of these would be a different and additional pleasure (of self-interest). The occurrence of a disinterested pleasure in viewing a painting can also, for Hutcheson, *generate* the occurrence of an *interested* pleasure in anticipation of a future disinterested viewing of the painting.

Kant begins Section 1 of the first moment assuming that the notion of beauty is not a concept and that experiences of beauty are pleasant. From these premises he concludes that judgments of taste are aesthetic and subjective, that is, not cognitive and not objective. In a cognitive judgment, an intuition is synthesized with a universal. In contrast, a judgment of taste "does not contribute anything to cognition, but merely compares the given presentation in the subject with the entire presentational power" (p. 44). It is unclear which of two things Kant is claiming here. He may be claiming that when a judgment of taste occurs, it is the kind of experience in which a synthesis is possible but in which no actual synthesis takes place; it is thus an experience that contains as its content only an intuition and a feeling of pleasure that is generated, or he may be claiming that it is the kind of experience in which a synthesis does take place, but that the subject attends only to the intuition and a feeling of pleasure in the experience, ignoring the aspect of the experience that derives from the universal in the synthesis. In the second case, the experience of the object of taste is achieved by abstracting it from its synthesized matrix. In the first case, no abstraction is required. In either case, the content of the intuition itself is the object of taste.

In Section 2 of the first moment, Kant gives an account of how a *Kantian* judgment of taste is disinterested. Before getting into Kant's account, consider *generally* what is meant in saying that a pleasure is or is not interested. A pleasure is not *interested* when the pleasure a subject takes in an object is taken solely in the object itself, independently of its relation to any other object of experience. A pleasure is *interested* when the pleasure a subject takes in an object is taken because of the object's relation to some other object in which the subject has a (self) interest.

When the notions of disinterested and interested pleasure are incorporated into the third *Critique,* they are given a novel twist. Kant writes of interested pleasure, "Interest is what we call the liking we connect with the presentation of an object's existence" (p. 45). He writes of disinterestedness, "In order to play the judge in matters of taste, we must not be in the least biased in favor of the thing's existence but must be wholly indifferent about it" (p. 46). Kant's insertion of the notion of *existence* into his characterizations of interest and disinterest is novel and initially puzzling. None of the

earlier theorists of taste even raised the question of the relevance of the
existence of the object of taste, so the question of whether interest or disinterest relates to the existence of an object of taste did not arise. Kant's introduction of the notion of existence, however, helps clear up a possible ambi-
guity about just what the object of taste is. Strictly speaking, for Hutcheson
it is not, for example, a painting itself that is the object of taste but a painting's uniformity in variety. Put otherwise, the object of taste is a particular
aspect of the painting—its uniformity in variety. So, for Hutcheson, too, the
disinterested pleasure taken in an aspect of a painting is distinct from an
interest in the existence of the painting. The reason why Kant makes the
distinction about existence that he does is that the epistemological twist he
gives to the theory of taste calls special attention to the clear distinction
between a subject's pleasure in an object of taste and a subject's pleasure in
the existence of an object. For Kant, an object of taste is an intuition in
which the form of purposiveness is manifested, either unsynthesized with a
universal or abstracted from its synthesized matrix. But an intuition is not
the kind of thing that has full-blooded existence. Only *objects*—the result of
a synthesis of an intuition with the categories and some empirical univer-
sal(s)—can be said to exist, that is, to have a continued, self-identical persistence through space and/or time. One cannot take pleasure in the existence
of a Kantian object of taste because it is not the kind of thing that has
existence, and, consequently, it is not possible for a Kantian object of taste
to relate to an existing object of self-interest.

Many have found it puzzling when Kant says that "judgments of taste,
of themselves, do not even give rise to any interest" (p. 46). They have
thought he was saying that taking a disinterested pleasure in, say, a painting
cannot generate an interested pleasure in the anticipating of a future viewing
of the painting. But on Kant's view, a painting (an object) is not an object of
taste; an object of taste is an intuition of a certain sort and not the kind of
thing it makes sense to think of as having a self-identical persistence through
space and/or time and, hence, not the sort of thing that exists. For Kant, I
take it that viewing, say, a painting and taking a disinterested pleasure in an
object of taste (an intuition of a certain sort), plus *the assumption that the
intuition is an aspect of an object that has a self-identical persistence through
space and/or time* (the painting), can generate an interested pleasure in the
anticipation of a future viewing of the painting.

It is now clear how Kant's accounts of disinterested and interested pleasure are special cases of the way these notions are ordinarily understood by
earlier philosophers such as Hutcheson.

This ordinary understanding of disinterested pleasure is that a pleasure
is disinterested when the pleasure a subject takes in an object is taken solely
in the object itself independently of its relation to any other object. For Kant
also, a pleasure taken in an object of taste (an intuition) has to be disinterested because pleasure taken in an intuition is pleasure taken in an object
that does not qualify for existence and, hence, cannot stand in relation to an
existing object of self-interest.

The ordinary understanding of interested pleasure is that a pleasure is interested when the pleasure a subject takes in an object is taken because of the object's relation to something else in which the subject has a (self-) interest. For Kant, a pleasure taken in an object of taste (an intuition) cannot be interested because an interested pleasure depends on its object to be an *existing* object standing in relation to another *existing* object of self-interest, and an intuition is not the sort of thing that qualifies for existence.

Universality and Necessity

Hutcheson tried to show that judgments of taste are universal by showing that everyone has a *sense* of beauty, that is, a faculty of taste on which such judgments are based. He tried to show by means of a thought experiment that the faculty of taste is universal by showing that in very simple cases (e.g., a square compared to a triangle) that everyone will prefer greater uniformity to lesser uniformity. Any disagreements over beauty could, Hutcheson thought, be explained as a result of the confusion introduced by complexity in nonsimple cases.

Kant thinks that his approach in the second moment to showing that judgments of taste are universal has to be of a very different sort from Hutcheson's and cannot involve an empirical appeal to what people prefer. In fact, Kant admits that there are disagreements of taste and takes his task to be to show how judgments of taste are validated and, hence, that validated judgments ought to be universally agreed with.

In the title of the first section of the second moment, Kant asserts that "The Beautiful Is What Is Presented without Concepts as the Object of a *Universal* Liking" (p. 53). In this first section he argues that the universality of judgments of beauty can be deduced from their disinterestedness. Since the pleasure taken in an object of beauty is disinterested, it is not based on any private interest. Kant concludes that it must, therefore, be based on something that is nonprivate and universal in all humans. A universal basis means that judgments of beauty can justifiably claim to be subjectively universal—subjectively because, although not based on concepts, they are based on mental features that all *subjects* have in common.

In the third section of the second moment, Kant again pursues the topic of universality. He seems at first to use an "ordinary language" point of view that when we say that something is beautiful we are just making a universal claim—"in a judgment of taste about beauty we always require others to agree" (p. 57). But at the end of the section, he returns to his "disinterestedness entails universality" argument, arguing that if one is *conscious* that a pleasure is not based on any interest, then one "counts on everyone's assent" (p. 60).

In the middle of this third section, Kant asserts that all judgments of beauty are *singular* judgments because the notion of beauty is not a concept; that is, the predicate "beautiful" does not express a concept, so no generality can be attained. His example of such a singular judgment is "This rose is beautiful." Kant then makes an astonishing and, I think, contradictory claim. He writes,

> I may look at a rose and make a judgment of taste declaring it to be beautiful. But if I compare many singular roses and so arrive at the judgment, Roses in general are beautiful, then my judgment is no longer merely aesthetic, but is a logical judgment based on an aesthetic one. (p. 59)

But "Roses in general are beautiful" cannot be a logical judgment. If the notion of beauty is not a concept and logical judgments require predicates that express concepts, then any judgment with "beautiful" as its predicate cannot be a logical judgment! I do not think this slip has any general consequences.

Kant has concluded thus far in the first two moments that judgments of beauty are disinterestedly pleasant and universal. In the final section of the second moment, he tries to answer the question: "What is the nature of the mental basis for this kind of universal pleasure?" Since the judgments are universal, their basis must be something that all humans have in common. The statement of Kant's argument concerning this basis—the central notion of which is something he calls "universal communicability"—is very obscure. Paul Guyer claims that "universal communicability" is just another way of speaking of "universal validity," and I will read it this way too.[3] In the exceedingly obscure first part of this argument, Kant appears to conclude that the pleasure of experiences of beauty must come as a consequence of the functioning of the universal basis. He then writes,

> Hence it must be the universal communicability [validity] of the mental state, in the given presentation, which underlies the judgment of taste as its subjective condition, and the pleasure in the object must be its consequence. Nothing, however, can be communicated [validated] universally except cognition, as well as presentation insofar as it pertains to cognition; for presentation is objective only insofar as it pertains to cognition, and only through this does it have a universal reference point with which everyone's presentational power is compelled to harmonize. (p. 61)

I take Kant to be arguing that the cognitive faculties are the only mental faculties that all humans have in common that could function as a basis (a faculty of taste) for universally valid experiences of beauty. He then argues that since beauty is not a concept, to produce the pleasure of taste, the cognitive faculties of the imagination and the understanding must function in a free play (independently of the application of a universal) and in the harmony that characterizes all of their interactions. He then claims that it is the sensation of this pleasure that tells us that the harmonious free play of the cognitive faculties is occurring.

The fourth moment, which is concerned with the *necessity* of judgments of taste, is parallel of the second moment. Kant begins by asserting that "we

---

3. Paul Guyer, *Kant and the Claims of Taste* (Cambridge, Mass.: Harvard University Press, 1979), pp. 282–83.

think of the *beautiful* as having a *necessary* reference to liking" (p. 85). And he goes on to explain that the necessity in a judgment of taste is "a necessity of the assent of *everyone* to a judgment that is regarded as an example of a universal rule that we are unable to state" (p. 85). This necessity, like universality, involves a demanded *assent*. Kant's argument for explaining the necessity of judgments of taste is parallel to that used for explaining their universality, except that here for the first time he calls the mental faculty all must have a "common sense" before going on to identify it as the imagination and understanding in harmonious free play.

It is worth noting that the universality and necessity of synthetic a priori determinant judgments such as "Every event has a cause" means that the judgment is universally and necessarily true. The universality and necessity of reflective judgments of taste cannot be a universality and necessity of truth; they have a universality and necessity of *assent*. The universality and necessity of truth and the universality and necessity of assent are supposed to derive from the same faculties functioning in different ways. It is the sameness of faculties that is supposed to ensure universality and necessity in both cases, and it is the functioning in different ways that determines truth in the one case and requires assent in the other.

Beauty of Art: Human and Divine

Kant follows the four moments with a forty-three page discussion of his theory of the sublime, which I shall ignore.

He follows his account of the sublime with sixty-six pages (twenty-five sections) under the title "Deduction of Pure Aesthetic Judgments," only the first half of which, however, is devoted to a discussion of judgments of taste. The title of this sixty-six page discussion raises the hope of additional argument to support Kant's view of the nature of the faculty of taste, but none of its sections contains any new argument; disappointingly, Kant simply repeats what he has said earlier in the four moments and elsewhere.

At the midpoint of the twenty-five sections entitled "Deduction of Pure Aesthetic Judgments," Kant unexpectedly (given the title) begins a discussion of fine art. The main purpose of this whole discussion is, I think, to show how the notions of beautiful art and beautiful natural objects are both *aesthetically pure* and can both be subsumed under his formalist theory of beauty.

Kant first contrasts agreeable art, which derives its pleasure from sensation, with fine or aesthetic art, which derives its pleasure from form, the latter, of course, being the kind of art capable of beauty. He then launches into a lengthy discourse on artistic genius as the ability to create beautiful art despite the fact that the notion of beauty is not a concept. He compares scientific creations with creations of artistic beauty; the former can be explained and taught because they are a matter of concepts, but the latter cannot be explained and taught because the notion of beauty is not a concept.

None of Kant's remarks about agreeable art, aesthetic art, or artistic and scientific creation is very surprising; they are straight out of the established Kantian line. What comes next, however, is surprising. In order to accomplish the synthesis of natural and artistic beauty as the form of purposiveness, Kant at this point introduces the entirely new notion of *aesthetic ideas,* which on its face does not appear to be a formalist notion at all. Aesthetic ideas, he claims, are the products of genius, that is, artistic talent. He defines this new notion as follows:

> by an aesthetic idea I mean a presentation of the imagination which prompts much thought, but to which no determinate thought whatsoever, i. e., no [determinate] *concept,* can be adequate, so that no language can express it completely and allow us to grasp it. It is easy to see that an aesthetic idea is the counterpart of a *rational idea,* which is, conversely, a concept to which no *intuition* (presentation of the imagination) can be adequate. (p. 182)

Kant's choice of terminology is misleading here; what he calls "an aesthetic *idea*" is not a kind of concept or idea but is a kind of *intuition*. Aesthetic ideas (intutions), he says, "strive toward something that lies beyond the bounds of experience" (p. 182). After characterizing "aesthetic ideas" and commenting on the notion at length, Kant, at the beginning of a section on fine art, draws a conclusion that is clealy designed to unite his views of natural beauty and artistic beauty. No elucidation follows the paragraph; it is followed by a tedious account of the division of the arts. The paragraph reads,

> We may in general call beauty (whether natural or artistic) the *expression* of aesthetic ideas; the difference is that in the case of beautiful art the aesthetic idea must be prompted by a concept of the object, whereas in the case of beautiful nature, mere reflection on a given intuition, without a concept of what the object is [meant] to be, is sufficient for arousing and communicating the idea of which that object is regarded as the *expression*. (p. 189)

In this passage, Kant uses "idea" in two senses. He speaks of the expression of aesthetic *ideas,* by which he means the occurrence of a particular kind of *intuition*. But at the end of the passage, he speaks of the *idea* that this particular kind of intuition expresses. This last use of "idea" appears to refer to a mental content, which is expressed and "lies behind" an intuition, which is the idea's expression.

Kant is clearly claiming that *both* natural beauty and artistic beauty are the expression of aesthetic ideas (intuitions); that is, he is presenting a *single* theory in which he identifies beauty (the form of purposiveness) with the expression of aesthetic ideas (intuitions). This single theory must show how the expression of aesthetic ideas (intuitions) is a form of purposiveness in both kinds of cases.

Kant makes no attempt to explain how this can be; he just rambles on about the division of the arts. A Kantian explanation, however, can be given. Consider the example and explanation of an aesthetic idea (intuition) that Kant gave in his discussion of artistic beauty, namely, Jupiter's eagle—a representation of an eagle with lightning in its claws. The intuition that derives from the representation of Jupiter's eagle obviously has elements that synthesize with concepts, namely, the concepts of *eagle, claws,* and *lightning.* An aesthetic idea (intuition) as Kant defines it is, however, a very special kind of intuition. The intuition *as a whole* strives for something beyond the bounds of experience, and it is not an intuition to which any concept is adequate. An aesthetic idea in art (e.g., Jupiter's eagle) is an intuition that contains some elements that synthesize with determinate concepts (e.g., *eagle* and *claws*), but the aesthetic idea (intuition) itself as a whole is not exhausted by the elements that synthesize with these mundane concepts. An aesthetic idea in art then turns out to be an intuitional *structure* that may contain some elements that synthesize with determinate concepts but must have other elements that do not. Thus, Kant's view that beauty is not a concept and his formalistic account of natural beauty can be reconciled with his account of artistic beauty as the expression of aesthetic *ideas* (intuitions) because for Kant the notion of idea in an aesthetic idea (intuition) is a very special, technical kind of notion. The expression of aesthetic ideas (intuitions) in the case of art turns out to be the expression of intuitional structures that may contain elements that synthesize with determinate concepts but must also have elements that do not. These intuitional structures (aesthetic ideas) as a whole do not synthesize with any determinate concept. Thus, in the case of the beauty of art, the beauty is formal—the form of a set of intuitional elements. There will be two kinds of cases here. The first kind of case is one in which the art object is nonrepresentational, for example, an arabesque. In this kind of case, whatever the aesthetic idea (intuition) is that is expressed, its expression will involve only spatial or temporal forms. The second kind of case is one in which the art object is representational, for example, a painting of Jupiter's eagle. In this case, the idea (in Kant's second sense of "idea") expressed is the mighty king of heaven, and its expression is the intuition that derives from the painting of Jupiter's eagle. In this case and others like it, the intuitional structure, to which as a whole no determinate concept is adequate, is clearly not merely spatial (or temporal), so Kant's view implies a higher-order intuitional form than that of merely a spatiotemporal kind. In addition to spatial and/or temporal form, such a form would have to include representational elements that synthesize with mundane concepts but which suggest more, a more for which there is no concept.

In the case of artistic beauty, the *purposiveness* of the form of purposiveness turns out to be a human artist's purposive striving to express something beyond the bounds of experience, which, of course, is unspecifiable. Artistic beauty is a form of human purposiveness; it is teleology writ small.

Natural beauty—the purposes of nature—is teleology writ large. The *purposiveness* of the form of purposiveness in the case of natural beauty is God's purposiveness striving to intimate to human beings something beyond the bounds of their experience. The *form* of the form of purposiveness in the case of natural beauty is the form of systems. In the case of natural beauty, the ideas behind the aesthetic ideas (intuitions) expressed are God's ideas. In the end, the creation of human art resembles and mimics the divine creation of systems.

Before proceeding to the evaluation of Kant's theory, there is one final puzzle of the third moment that I shall address. The first five sections of the third moment are concerned with the notion of beauty as the *form* of purposiveness. The sixth section, "A Judgment of Taste Is Wholly Independent of the Concept of Perfection," which is an oblique attack on Baumgarten's and others' conception of beauty, continues this emphasis on beauty as form and the independence of beauty from concepts. Kant begins the seventh section of the third moment, however, with the startling assertion, "There are two kinds of beauty, free beauty . . . and merely accessory beauty. . . . Free beauty does not presuppose a concept of what the object is [meant] to be. Accessory beauty does presuppose such a concept, as well as the object's perfection in terms of that concept" (p. 76). Kant goes on to say that free beauty involves *pure* judgments of taste and that accessory beauty involves impure and applied judgments of taste. The puzzle is that, given what he says elsewhere, what he is calling "accessory beauty" here cannot be a kind of beauty. Given what he says elsewhere, beauty is what he is calling "free beauty" here. I do not know how to explain consistently what appears to be the contradiction involved in the expression "accessory beauty."

Evaluation of Kant's Theory of Taste

Lewis White Beck, in an introduction to selections from the third *Critique,* writes, "In the course of answering the deepest systematic architectonic question about the relation of morality to nature, Kant . . . wrote one of the greatest treatises on aesthetics."[4] Kant is indisputably a great philosopher, and, like Beck, many conclude that his theory of taste is a great philosophical achievement. I think this conclusion is wrong. Kant's theory of taste is so riddled with difficulties that it does not even compare very favorably with Hutcheson's relatively unsophisticated theory, and it cannot hold a candle to the highly sophisticated theory of Hume's "Of the Standard of Taste."

I shall first focus on the difficulties involved in Kant's conception of beauty. I shall then examine his arguments in support of his conception of the faculty of taste. Finally, I shall consider his teleology.

Beauty

There are at least three grave problems with Kant's conception of beauty: its general implausibility, its inadequacy for covering certain aspects of the nature of beauty, and its treatment of color.

The greatest problem for Kant's account is that his very conception of

4. Lewis White Beck, ed., *Kant Selections* (New York: Macmillan, 1988), p. 332.

beauty is entirely implausible and flies in the face of common and philosophical sense. In constructing his account of the nature of beauty, Kant seems to me to have lost sight of or to have never had in view what the task of theorizing about beauty is fundamentally about.

Kant concludes in the third moment that "beauty is an object's form of purposiveness." The form of purposiveness that Kant is talking about here is clearly the form of an object that we experience, since he explicitly specifies that he is talking about "an object's form of purposiveness." Kant's conclusion has no plausibility at all. In contrast, the views of most of the earlier philosophers of taste on this specific point—views that were known to Kant—have considerable plausibility. For example, Hutcheson's identification of beauty with uniformity in variety, while inadequate, is at least plausible because uniformity in variety is clearly a beauty-making characteristic. Philosophers and everyone else from the time of Plato and Aristotle have considered that uniformity and variety are beauty-making characteristics. Edmund Burke's citation of such qualities as smoothness and gently curving lines as beauty-making characteristics is also plausible because such qualities are present with great frequency in beautiful objects. The kind of perceptible characteristics Hutcheson and Burke specify are obviously involved with beautiful objects, and their theories thereby have at least an initial plausibility. Hutcheson, Burke, and most of the other philosophers of taste exhibit good sense in theorizing with an eye on examples from the set of objects that human beings have found beautiful. Kant's approach and claim about beauty are bewilderingly different from this sensible approach and the plausible conclusions of these earlier theorists of taste.

Some thinkers apparently take Kant's claim about beautiful objects to be a profound one. It seems to me, however, that Kant is just badly wrong. Ironically, Burke's argument against utility as a kind of beauty—an argument Kant must have been aware of since he refers to Burke's book—makes the falsity of Kant's conclusion manifest. (I am not, by the way, claiming that Kant thought that utility is a kind of beauty.) Some taste theorists had argued that utility is a kind of beauty. Burke quite correctly noted that a pig's snout is of the greatest utility for rooting in the ground but that we do not find it beautiful.[5] I concluded earlier that, according to Kant, systems (organisms) are God's fine art and that their forms are God's artistic and purposive forms. In the Kantian teleological scheme, therefore, the form of a pig's highly useful snout, as well as the forms of virtually all of its other anatomical features— useful or not—would be forms of God's purpose. This would also be true of the forms of the aspects of all organisms. In Kant's scheme, the forms of all these things would be forms of purposiveness. Of course, according to Kant, in a judgment of taste, we do not cognize the *actual* purpose of the beautiful form but only the *form* of purposiveness independently of actual purpose. Thus, according to Kant's account of judgments of taste, we ought to find a

5. Edmund Burke, *A Philosophical Enquiry into the Origin of Our Ideas of the Sublime and Beautiful.* J. T. Boulton, ed. (Notre Dame, Ind.: University of Notre Dame Press, 1958), p. 105.

pig's snout beautiful when we perceive its form of purposiveness independently of its purpose. Unfortunately for Kant's theory, we do not find the form of a pig's snout and many other "forms of purposiveness" beautiful. The truth is that while the forms of many things that, according to Kant, are forms of purposiveness are beautiful, the forms of purposiveness of many are not. To try to illustrate his thesis, in several places Kant gives lists of things that he presumably thinks everyone will agree have beautiful forms. In one place he mentions "Flowers, free designs, lines aimlessly intertwining and called foliage" (p. 49). Later, after mentioning flowers again, he writes, "Many birds (the parrot, the humming-bird, the bird of paradise) and a lot of crustaceans in the sea are [free] beauties" (p. 76). And so they are, but Kant's lists of things with forms of purposiveness are too selective. His list of birds, for example, could include starlings, vultures, and the like, whose forms of purposiveness are just as much forms of purposiveness as that of the parrot. He could also include on his list the pig, the moose, the rhino, and the like. If Kant had constructed a list of things with forms of purposiveness of any length at all, he would have realized that the form of purposiveness just cannot be equated with beauty. When Kant speaks of "*many* birds" and "*lots* of crustaceans," his language suggests that some birds and some crustaceans are not beautiful, but his commitment to beauty as the form of purposiveness apparently did not allow him to be sensitive to the implication of his own language. I am not, I want to make clear again, claiming that Kant's view is that utility or the form of utility is beautiful. I am claiming that Burke's particular counterexample to utility as a *kind* of beauty is also a counterexample to the form of purposiveness considered independently of actual purpose being *identical with* beauty.

What caused Kant to deviate from the plausible tracks established by the earlier theorists of taste and to put forth the highly implausible claim that he did? Instead of trying to draw clues from objects generally regarded as beautiful, as did such empiricist-inclined philosophers as Hutcheson and Burke, Kant tried to draw his theory of beauty out of his general philosophical system much in the manner of seventeenth-century philosophers such as Leibniz. Kant's theological teleology cannot, however, transmute the Burkean pig snout and all the other unattractive forms of organisms like it into beautiful forms. The form of purposiveness, which is not even a beauty-making characteristic, certainly cannot be identified with beauty. Even if a pig's snout is one of God's great works of fine art, its form is not a silk purse.

It is also clear that artistic beauty cannot be equated with form of purposiveness. A work of art that exhibits a form of purposiveness resulting from a human artist's efforts is no more guaranteed to be beautiful than is the form of purposiveness of an organism. The domain of art is replete with the artistic equivalents of pig snouts.

Kant was influenced by the British empiricists, but he was also still under the sway of the rationalist philosophers. His account of beauty in the third *Critique* is an attempt at a synthesis of empiricist and rationalist views, just as his first-*Critique* views were supposed to be for the domain of the metaphysics of epistemology. Whatever Kant's achievement is in the case of the first *Critique,* his attempted synthesis in the domain of taste retains too much seventeenth-century rationalism.

The first serious difficulty of Kant's implausible conception of beauty is that it is too broad; it captures many nonbeautiful things.

The second grave problem of Kant's account of beauty is that it does not allow for an explanation of how beauty admits of degrees. Two difficulties arise involving degrees. The first of these problems arises because we often find one object to be more beautiful that another. Hutcheson's theory has no difficulty in *trying* to explain this; it will try to show that the more beautiful object is more uniform or more varied than the less beautiful object. Kant's theory cannot explain variation in beauty because it is not clear how the form of purposiveness can admit of degrees. The beautiful form of a cedar waxwing is just as much a form of purposiveness as the beautiful form of the bird of paradise, but the latter is presumably a more beautiful bird. Of course, the alleged harmony in the interaction of the cognitive faculties is the sort of thing that could vary by degrees. Since, however, the form of purposiveness that supposedly sets this interaction in motion cannot vary by degrees, it is difficult to see what would cause a variation in harmony. (The case under discussion is different from the starling-vulture problem; a case such as that of the starling is a problem because its form is a form of purposiveness but is *not* beautiful.)

The second problem involving degrees is one that neither Hutcheson nor Kant comes to grips with; neither gives any explanation of the fact that we treat beauty as a threshold phenomenon. That is, while we think that beauty admits of degrees, such that many beautiful objects can be placed in an order of greater than and less than, we also think that there is a threshold below which objects are not beautiful. (The threshold need not be a sharp or narrow one.) For example, there are many beautiful people, but most people are ordinary-looking. Hutcheson treats *any* degree of uniformity as a case of beauty, with the result that for him virtually everything is beautiful. There is nothing about his theory, however, that compels him to do this. He could have said that uniformity is a beauty-making characteristic an object can have without being beautiful and that only objects with a relatively high degree of uniformity pass over the threshold and are beautiful. I do not see how Kant could take account of beauty as a threshold phenomenon, since the form of purposiveness does not admit of degrees and, hence, cannot be made to fit with the notion of a threshold. I shall pursue the notion of beauty-making characteristics and beauty as a threshold phenomenon in the chapter on Hume's theory of taste.

The third grave problem with Kant's conception of beauty is the exclusion of color from its domain. Both Hutcheson and Kant embrace a formalist account of beauty, and both reject the experience of color as such as an aspect of the experience of beauty. Both theorists do this because of certain features of their conceptions of the faculties of the mind. Hutcheson held that the pleasure derived from color (a simple idea) derives from the *external* sense of vision, but that the pleasure derived from a beautiful object (a complex idea) derives from the *internal* sense of beauty; consequently, he concluded that color as such cannot be an aspect of beauty.

Kant arrives at his anticolor conclusion in a different way. He takes for granted that there are experiences of beauty and argues they derive from cognitive faculties that everyone has in common. He held that the cognitive faculties are responsible for the formal properties (the spatiotemporal properties) of experience in such a way that makes these properties the same in all persons. Thus, he thinks that form and the pleasure derived from it can be counted on to be the same in everyone's experience. Color, by contrast, belongs to the content (not the form) of experience, so that pleasure derived from color derives from an aspect of experience that cannot be counted on to be the same in all persons. Since, according to Kant, beauty is universal, color cannot be an aspect of beauty. The experience of color does not depend on an a priori feature of the human mind. Kant writes, "To one person the color violet is gentle and lovely, to another lifeless and faded. . . . It would be foolish if we disputed about such differences with the intention of censuring another's judgment as incorrect if it differs from ours, as if the two were opposed logically" (p. 55).

Kant appears to make an exception in the case of simple colors. He writes that "insofar as as they are pure [they] are considered beautiful" (p. 71). It turns out, however, that he is not talking about colors as we perceive them with the senses but about colors whose form (uniform vibrations) we perceive by reflection. Since it is colors as perceived by the senses that are at issue here, I shall say no more about Kant's curious notion of perceiving the form of color by reflection.

I believe that if a theory claiming to account for visual beauty excludes color from the domain of beauty, this alone is sufficient for concluding that the theory is not just wrong but badly wrong.

Color is by no means the whole story concerning beauty, but it is and always has been regarded as a very important aspect of beauty. Many of the paradigm cases of beauty are cases that depend wholly or largely on color. One example will suffice. The beauty of sunsets in their earlier moments derives almost wholly from the expanses of vivid reds and oranges and other such colors and in their later moments from the expanses of mauves and such delicate colors. Horizon features may add contrast and hence form, but color itself does the main work. Only a philosopher could maintain that there is no beauty of color.

Kant sacrifices color because he believes that beauty is universal and is so because of its a priori foundations *and* that color is based on an a posteriori foundation and thus cannot be universal. Given the *whole* Kantian system, however, there is just as much reason to believe color has an a priori foundation as there is to believe that the form of purposiveness does.

For Kant, form as such is a priori because it is derived from the structure of the human mind. The specific forms that are the forms of purposiveness, however, have a source outside the human mind and are, therefore, an aspect of contingent systematicity. It is not form as such that guarantees that beauty is universal because form as such is not beautiful. A way had to be found to assure that the specific form of purposiveness, which from the human point of view is contingent, is really necessary and universal. Kant, of course, believes that the contingent systematicity of nature is really a necessary purposiveness, and this means that he believes that the apparent contingency of the forms of purposiveness has a nonhuman a priori base, God's understanding. But if one can believe that the forms of systems that appear as contingent aspects of experience have a nonhuman a priori foundation, cannot certain contingent-appearing colors have the same kind of foundation? Such an accommodation of color within the Kantian scheme would not, of course, relieve the implausibility of tying beauty to purpose.

Kant's conception of beauty as he actually worked it out, however, did claim to exclude color from the domain of beauty. Thus, while the first serious difficulty of Kant's conception is that it is too broad because it captures nonbeautiful things, the third serious difficulty is that it is too narrow in excluding beauty of color.

The fault of narrowness in excluding beauty of color and every other nonformal aspect of beauty in Hutcheson's and Kant's conceptions of beauty derives in both cases from the excessive demand that beauty be universal—from the fear of relativism. Both theorists try to ensure universality for beauty by betting on a sure thing; that is, there is complete agreement that uniformity and variety (which are clearly embedded in Kant's notion of form of purposiveness) are beauty-making characteristics, and Hutcheson and Kant seize on this fact and try to make these formal properties do the whole job. It is not clear, however, that the domain of beauty can be completely safeguarded from relativism.

The Faculty of Taste

There are two arguments that attempt to support Kant's conclusion that the faculty of taste is the cognitive faculties in harmonious free play: (1) the argument I reconstructed in "Kant's Teleological Theory of Taste" in the chapter under the heading "The Faculty of Taste" and (2) the argument Kant gives in the second moment and repeats elsewhere. The first argument moves from the following three premises:

1. There are only two kinds of judgment: determinate and reflective
2. There are judgments of taste
3. Beauty is not a determinate concept

to the intermediate conclusion

4. Judgments of taste are reflective judgments

and then on to the conclusion

  5. Experiences of taste are based on the cognitive faculties in harmoni-
     ous free play.

The second argument moves from the premises:

  1. Judgments of taste are universally valid
  2. Nothing but cognition is universally validated, and, hence, cognition
     is the only possible basis for judgments of taste

to the conclusion

  3. Experiences of taste are based on the cognitive faculties in harmoni-
     ous free play.

In order for this last argument (the one from the second moment) to be
conclusive, Kant would have to show that the cognitive faculties are the *only*
mental faculties humans have in common that could be the basis for experiences of beauty. I take it that he is trying to show this exclusivity when he
asserts, "Nothing, however, can be communicated [validated] universally except cognition." Suppose this is true; there is still a problem: if the cognitive
faculties were the only universal mental faculty of whose existence we were
certain (is validated), it would not show that it is the actual source of the
disinterested, universal pleasure of taste; it would only show that it *could be*
the source. In order for Kant's argument to be conclusive, he would have to
show that competing explanations of the source of the pleasure are ruled
out. But he makes no attempt to show this. For example, he makes no
attempt to disprove the Hutchesonian claim that all humans have a noncognitive *sense* of beauty that produces the disinterested pleasure of the experience of beauty. Kant claims that the sensation of the pleasure of taste tells
us that harmonious, free play of the cognitive faculties is going on, but this
assumes that the cognitive faculties are the source of the pleasure. The disinterested, universal pleasure could derive from a sense of beauty. There is no
transcendental argument that there is a sense of beauty, but the transcendental argument that shows how the cognitive faculties provide a basis for
knowledge shows only that the cognitive faculties *could be* the faculty of
taste. His argument that the faculty of taste is the imagination and understanding in harmonious free play is, then, inconclusive.

Notice that Kant's argument is quite different from Gerard's claim that
we find *upon examination* that the cognitive faculties are the faculty of taste.
Kant does not claim that we *experience* the cognitive faculties functioning as
the faculty of taste; he claims that his argument allows us to infer that the
faculty of taste is the cognitive faculties in harmonious free play. As just
noted, however, this inference is inconclusive.

Perhaps the first argument from my "The Faculty of Taste" in this chapter can save Kant's conclusion about the nature of the faculty of taste. This
argument depends on the intermediate conclusion that judgments of taste
are reflective judgments, but this seems very dubious to me. Why should we
think that the kind of experiences denoted by a proposition such as "This

rose is beautiful" is a kind of experience in which a person is *searching* for an empirical universal (and searching futilely to boot)? It does not seems to me that the experience of a beautiful rose, sunset, or the like is anything at all like the kind of experience that Newton underwent when he was producing the theory of gravitation. An experience of a beautiful thing is typically one of quiet contemplation. Kant himself in various places characterizes experiences of beauty as contemplative, and contemplation is a very different kind of experience from the experience of searching for a universal for an intuition or any other kind of searching. Contemplation is a nonsearching, quiescent state or activity of mind.

Kant, however, may have confused contemplation and such searching by moving back and forth between the sense of "reflection" that means contemplation and his technical meaning of "reflection" as searching for a universal. For example, he writes in the first moment that "we judge it [a beautiful object] in our mere contemplation of it (intuition or reflection)" (p. 45). In this passage, Kant's use of the expression "mere contemplation" suggests that he has a quiescent state or activity in mind, and he is thus saying that reflection is a kind of contemplation, but this kind of quiescent reflection is very different from his notion of reflective judgment as a search. Then again, because he connects contemplation with reflection, he may think he is making a connection between contemplation and reflective judgment. In any event, it is clear that it does not make sense to maintain that experiences of taste at their base are a kind of search, although some experiences of taste may involve search-like activities, for example, the reading of a murder mystery. Thus, Kant's intermediate conclusion that judgments of taste are reflective judgments must be false. This means that at least one of his premises or his inference is at fault, but I shall not trouble myself with the question of where the fault lies. So, in the end, the first argument does not fare any better than the second in supporting the claim that the faculty of taste is the cognitive faculties in harmonious free play.

Teleology

That the world is a teleological system seemed like a natural and perhaps inevitable conclusion to draw to most eighteenth-century thinkers. Hutcheson, for example, concludes *at the end* of his treatise on beauty that the sense of beauty is implanted by God, and he regards it as an exhibition of God's benevolence that he filled the world with so many beautiful things for the sense of beauty to respond to. The essential features of Hutcheson's theory of taste, however, are argued for and conceived of quite independently of either theological or teleological considerations. In the case of Kant, however, his theory of taste is inextricably intertwined with teleology: His major taste notions are conceived of in teleological terms.

The theory of evolution has long since undermined teleology in the biological domain, and the general systematicity of nature does not provide the compelling impetus toward teleology today that it apparently did in the

eighteenth century. Of course, the theory of evolution and present-day attitudes do not disprove teleology, but few philosophers today have great confidence in it. It is hard to imagine aestheticians today trying to formulate the
notions they use to talk about beauty in teleological terms.

I think some would like to write off Kant's teleology as an eighteenth-
century irrelevance, denying it any importance for his theory of taste. It is,
however, hard to see what would be left of Kant's theory if the subtraction
of teleology could somehow be accomplished. He defines beauty in terms of
purposiveness without purpose, and he characterizes the faculty of taste as
the cognitive faculties when they are invigorated and entertained by the special purposive fit between themselves and a certain subset of the objects of
nature. The subtraction of the teleological elements from Kant's theory of
taste would be like pulling all the woof threads from a piece of cloth; there
would be nothing left to hold the warp threads together.

5

Beauties and Blemishes: David Hume

Hume's "Of the Standard of Taste" (1757)[1] brought the theory of taste closer to success than any other attempt before or after. Hume's essay was published at almost the exact midpoint of the period during which the theory of taste flourished—thirty-two years after the 1725 publication of Hutcheson's *An Inquiry into the Original of Our Ideas of Beauty and Virtue* got the theory of taste off to a philosophical start and thirty-three years before the 1790 publications of Alison's *Essays on the Nature and Principles of Taste* and Kant's third *Critique* derailed the theory of taste as a philosophical enterprise.

In his essay, Hume, on the one hand, finesses the difficulties of Hutcheson's less sophisticated theory and, on the other hand, avoids the obscurity and wrongheadedness of the third *Critique* and the bloated misdirectedness of associationism. It should be noted that Hume, well known for his use of the association of ideas, does not use or even mention this notion in "Of the Standard of Taste." I should also add that Hume's youthful mistake from the *Treatise* of claiming that utility (fertility of fields, etc.) is a kind of beauty does not make an appearance in the essay.

The superiority of Hume's theory in "Of the Standard of Taste" is exhibited as much by what he does not attempt to do as by what he does do. Hume makes no attempt to claim that there is a *faculty* of taste; he merely says that taste involves sentiment, that is, that taste depends on intrinsic valuing. He does say in his essay that "beauty and deformity . . . belong entirely to the sentiment, internal or external" (p. 235). I take it that his saying "sentiment, internal *or* external" indicates that he does not wish to try to tie taste to a particular, specific faculty or faculties. Hutcheson had argued that there is a specific faculty of taste and that it is an internal sense of beauty wholly different in nature from the cognitive external senses. Gerard,

1. David Hume, "Of the Standard of Taste" in *Essays Moral, Political, and Literary* (Indianapolis, Ind.: Liberty Classics, 1985), pp. 226–49. All subsequent internal page cites in this chapter to Hume are to this edition.

Hume's younger contemporary, argued that there are many different internal senses and that they are constituted by the ordinary functioning of the cognitive faculties. Later, Kant was to argue that there is a faculty of taste and that it consists of the extraordinary functioning of some cognitive faculties. Alison was to argue that there is a faculty of taste consisting of the imagination and sensibility. I believe that Hume saw the enormous difficulty involved in supporting the view that there is a faculty of taste, that is, a view that there is a *specific* mental structure or combination of mental structures that functions where matters of taste are concerned.

Hume also differs strikingly from the other taste theorists over the nature of the object of taste. Hutcheson, for example, specified a formula (uniformity amidst variety) that is supposed to be necessary and sufficient for something's being beautiful, that is, the overall beauty of an object. Kant was following Hutcheson's lead of specifying a formula in claiming that "form of purposiveness" is an object's beauty. Hume makes no attempt to specify a formula for the overall beauty of objects. At various points in his essay, Hume mentions a great number and variety of what he calls "beauties" and "blemishes," by which I take him to mean qualities or characteristics that can contribute to the beauty or ugliness of objects. I believe that Hume sensed the futility of trying to discover a formula that is necessary and sufficient for the overall beauty of objects: a futility that neither Hutcheson or Kant appreciated. In fact, in his essay, Hume does not address the question of how the overall or specific beauty of an object is to be determined.

Also, Hume makes no attempt to rule color out of the domain of the beautiful, as Hutcheson, Alison, and Kant do. Technical details of the philosophies of mind of Hutcheson and Kant caused or inclined them to conclude that color does not belong to the domain of beauty. Alison tried to rule out color in a different way. Nothing in Hume's philosophical system prejudices him against color—no internal sense of beauty connected only to form and no view that only a priori form can supply the universality required for beauty; he is free to place "lustre of color" on one of his several lists of "beauties." Hume must have realized, as anyone without a distorting theory who reflects for a moment would, that color is deeply entrenched in the domain of beauty and that it would be a mistake to try to rule it out.

Hume's essay, in comparison to other discussions of the theory of taste, is exceedingly brief and gives the impression of having been put together hastily. The brevity and apparent haste of the essay may be responsible for certain problems. His discussion of the principles of taste is incomplete and lacking in the formulation of any examples of the kind of principles he is talking about. His treatment of the principles of taste and his treatment of good and bad critics run together two distinct problems: the problem of the discovery of the principles of criticism and the problem of the discovery of good critics. Hume's essay, nevertheless, in comparison with the writings of the other taste theorists, is well organized and well argued.

Skepticism Disproved

Hume opens his essay with an extended account of the great variety and disagreement that exist concerning matters of taste. The disagreements he has in mind are disagreements about the taste qualities of objects such as poems, paintings, and plays. Hume concludes this lengthy account with the remark, "It is natural for us to seek a *Standard of Taste;* a rule, by which the various sentiments of men may be reconciled; at least, a decision, afforded, confirming one sentiment, and condemning another" (p. 229). This passage envisages two different versions of the standard of taste: (1) a standard of taste that is a *single rule* or *principle* that is sufficient for settling disputes or (2) a standard of taste that is a way of making a decision that is sufficient for settling disputes. The first possibility, "a rule, by which the various sentiments of men may be reconciled" says that it is natural to seek a *single* rule or principle to settle disagreements. Hutcheson and Kant were doing "what comes naturally," then, when they sought such a principle. Hutcheson's single principle, for example, is "Uniformity in variety always makes an object beautiful." Hume clearly rejects the master principle path and opts, I believe, for the other "natural" possibility envisaged in the passage: "a decision, afforded [that can achieve the] confirming [of] one sentiment and [the] condemning [of] another." Whether the standard of taste involves the application of single, master principle or the making of a decision (aided by a principle or principles from among a multiplicity of principles), Hume still has in mind the settling of disagreements about the taste qualities of objects such as poems, paintings, and plays.

The next step in Hume's essay is to formulate the position he regards as his principal opponent, philosophical skepticism regarding taste. This skepticism is the view that there can be no principle or set of principles of taste and that it is fruitless to dispute about taste. Although he speaks here only of taste skepticism, there is another philosophical position hovering in the background that Hume and theorists of taste generally oppose, namely, the view that beauty is an objective property of beautiful objects. Taste theorists generally want to carve out a compromise position between the objectivists and the skeptics. Hume rebuts the skeptical claim, saying,

> Whoever would assert an equality of genius and elegance between [the works of] Ogilby and Milton, or Bunyan and Addison, would be thought to defend no less an extravagance, than if he had maintained a mole hill to be as high as Teneriffe, or a pond as extensive as the ocean. (pp. 230–31)

Hume is using a "Disproportionate Pair" argument. He focuses on a pair of works of art that differ so greatly in value that it is impossible for anyone to think they are of equal value. The argument presupposes a principle or a set of principles of taste that underlies this impossibility. The pairs Hume mentions here may or may not be convincing, but pairs that do the trick are easily found. For example, consider the following pair, one a sonnet about loss and the other the closing lines of poem also about loss:

LXXIII

That time of year thou mayst in me behold
When yellow leaves, or none, or few, do hang
Upon those boughs which shake against the cold,
Bare ruin'd choirs, where late the sweet birds sang.
In me thou see'st the twilight of such a day
As after sunset fadeth in the west,
Which by and by black night doth take away,
Death's second self, that seals up all in rest.
In me thou see'st the glowing of such fire
That on the ashes of his youth doth lie,
As the death-bed whereon it must expire
Consumed with that which it was nourish'd by
   This thou perceivest, which makes thy love more strong,
   To love that well which thou must leave erelong.

FUNDY TIDE

On Scotia's shore his loved one waits
Throughout the foggy night.
Her hopes and prayers were dashed to bits
Beyond the harbor light.

His body washed ashore on Monday.
Oh fierce, infamous tide of Fundy.

When such a disproportionate pair is considered, it is easily seen that the one work is better than the other and that skepticism is disproved, and the question for Hume now becomes the discovery of the set of principles that underlies such comparative judgments and also judgments of taste generally. Note that Hume's kind of argument relies on an intuitive assessment of the overall beauty of each member of a pair of works of art so that one can conclude that one member of the pair is more beautiful than the other. Hume, however, never discusses in his essay the procedure for arriving at such overall assessments of the beauty of objects; he always focuses on the individual qualities or characteristics of objects—beauties and blemishes.

The Objects and Principles of Taste

After showing that differences in artistic value cannot be denied, Hume launches into the statement of his own theory, the first two aspects of which are (1) an inquiry into the logical nature of the principles of taste and (2) a discussion of the specific objects of taste and of the principles of taste. He addresses the question of the logical nature of the principles first: "It is evident that none of the rules of composition are fixed by reasonings *a priori,*

or can be esteemed abstract conclusions of the understanding, from comparing those habitudes and relation of ideas, which are eternal and immutable"
(p. 231). Notice that when Hume begins the exposition of his own theory,
he speaks of a plurality of rules. For Hume, the rules or principles he seeks
could have bases of only two sorts: (1) an a priori, relation-of-ideas basis or
(2) an a posteriori, matter-of-fact basis. Such principles will have the general
form of Hutcheson's master principle "Uniformity in variety always makes
an object beautiful," and a principle of this form, Hume must have thought,
obviously does not have merely an a priori, relation of ideas basis. He says
of the principles of taste, "Their foundation is the same with that of all the
practical sciences, experience; nor are they any thing but general observations, concerning what has been universally found to please in all countries
and in all ages" (p. 231). Notice again that Hume here implies that there is
a plurality of rules or principles. There is in this passage, however, some
confusion; Hume first says that the rules or principles of taste have experience *as their foundation,* but then he says that they *are* general observations
concerning what pleases. That is, he first says that principles of taste are
based on experience but then says they *are* descriptions of experience of what
universally pleases. If a principle of taste were merely an observation about
or a description of what pleases universally, then such a principle would
have the form "X always makes an object pleasing." A principle of taste,
however, must be about beauty or a beauty-making quality. A principle of
taste would have either the strong form of a necessary and sufficient principle —"X always makes an object beautiful"—or a weaker form—"X always
makes for beauty in an object."

In Hutcheson's theory, *the* principle of beauty is produced in the following way: He concludes first that there is a sense of *beauty,* which means for
him that whatever triggers the sense of beauty and produces its pleasure is
the property (or properties) that makes objects beautiful. He then concludes
that only uniformity in variety triggers the sense of beauty. Hutcheson's master principle—"Uniformity in variety always makes an object beautiful"—
then follows. For Hutcheson, the relevant general *observation* is that uniformity in variety universally and only produces the pleasure of *the sense of
beauty.* His principle of taste—"Uniformity in variety always makes an object
beautiful"—depends on the observation or description that uniformity in variety produces the pleasure of the sense of beauty but is not identical with
the description.

Hutcheson's theory has *the* sense of beauty to rely on to guide it to *the*
object of beauty and, hence, to *the* necessary and sufficient beauty-making
characteristic that is the subject of its master principle of beauty. Hume's
theory does not have such a taste faculty to guide it; his theory must rely on
the intuitions that function in the criticism of works of art to identify the
objects of taste. In effect, Hume claims that in criticism we can discover a
number of objects of taste, which he calls "beauties" and "blemishes," that
function as reasons to support evaluations concerning the beauty and ugliness of works of art.

In his essay, Hume illustrates the discovery of beauty-making and beauty-destroying characteristics by talking of the merits and defects of the poetry of Ariosto; his remarks imply that there are "beauties" and "blemishes" for the arts generally. Hume's many "beauties" play a role analogous to the role that uniformity in variety plays in Hutcheson's theory. The fact, however, that he specifies many such characteristics shows that Hume is not attempting to discover a single, master principle involving what is necessary and sufficient to make an object beautiful but that he is attempting to discover many principles, principles that involve characteristics that merely make for beauty or ugliness in objects. It may initially seem possible that Hume thinks that all the various "beauties" and "blemishes" he cites will in some way turn out to be instances of a single characteristic so that there is only one principle of taste. Although some of the characteristics Hume cites turn out to be different ways of referring to the same characteristic, nothing he says anywhere suggests that he thinks all of his "beauties" and "blemishes" can be reduced to a single characteristic.

Although Hume never gets around to formulating an actual example of one of the principles of taste, it is clear that for him such principles are universal, empirically based principles that have for their subjects either the "beauties" that please universally or the "blemishes" that displease universally. It is by now clear that Hume thinks there are a number of such principles of taste, for he always speaks in the plural when he speaks of such "rule*s*" or of "*their* foundation."

There is an important difference between Hutcheson's single principle and the collection of principles Hume's remarks imply. Hutcheson's principle is what I shall call a "strong" principle because it purports not only to be about what is necessary but about what is *sufficient* for making an object beautiful. Hume's principles are "weak" principles because they do *not* purport to be about what is *sufficient* for making an object beautiful but rather are about what contributes to making an object beautiful. Hutcheson's principle, together with the fact that an object has uniformity in variety, supposedly *entails* that the object is beautiful. The complete set of Hume's principles, together with the fact that an object has every characteristic specified in each of the principles, does not entail that the object is beautiful but only that the object has all the characteristics that contribute to making objects beautiful.

The "beauties" and "blemishes" that Hume cites in Ariosto's poetry at this early point in the essay are as follows. (Hume cites other beauties later in the essay.)

Beauties
Force of expression
Clearness of expression
Variety of inventions
Natural pictures of the gay passions
Natural pictures of the amorous passions

Blemishes
Monstrous and improbable fictions
Bizarre mixture of serious and comic styles
Want of coherence
Continual interruptions of narration

The four blemishes that Hume mentions reduce to disunity or low degree of uniformity and thus remind one of Hutcheson's theory. Hume's view, however, is very different from Hutcheson's. He views a low degree of uniformity as a blemish (i.e., a negative value), but negative value characteristics play no role in Hutcheson's theory as he actually formulates it. Hutcheson speaks of uniformity (in variety) always as a positive value.

The five beauties that Hume cites in the Ariosto passage do not reduce to one or even two or three or four. *Variety of inventions* is clearly Hutcheson's old variety. *Force of expression, clearness of expression, natural pictures of the gay passions,* and *natural pictures of the amorous passions* are four additional, different positive value characteristics. A little later in two different spots, Hume mentions five more beauties:

Luster of color
Exactness of imitation
Harmony
Design
Reasoning

Harmony, design, and reasoning are all perhaps ways of talking about uniformity, but luster of color and exactness of imitation are not kinds of uniformity or variety; they are two more different positive value characteristics. Exactness of imitation and the earlier mentioned natural pictures of the gay and amorous passions are similar, but they are not the same thing; both involve accuracy of representation, but the latter also focuses on the representation of valuable things—gay and amorous passions. Thus far, then, Hume has named one negative value characteristic and eight different positive value characteristics.

Low degree of uniformity (the negative characteristic)
High degree of uniformity (harmony, design, reasoning)
Variety
Force of expression
Clearness of expression
Luster of color
Natural pictures of gay passions
Natural pictures of amorous passions
Exactness of imitation

Hume's theory thus deviates sharply from Hutcheson's. He specifies a negative value characteristic and eight positive value characteristics, six of which are neither uniformity nor variety. With so many positive value characteristics in view (eight so far, and there will be more), Hume would not have thought that the presence of any one of the positive value characteristics, even in high degree, would be *generally* sufficient to make objects beautiful, although there might be particular cases in which one such characteristic in high degree would suffice to do so. Similarly, in the case of the one negative value characteristic mentioned (and there could be more), Hume would not have thought that the presence of this negative value characteristic, even in high degree, would be *generally* sufficient to make objects ugly, although in a individual case it might. (A low degree of uniformity would be a high degree of negative value.)

Hume realized, I think, that beauty as an overall evaluation of a work of art (or a natural object) is a threshold phenomenon; that is, such an object might have one or more beauty-making characteristics and still not be beautiful. On Hume's kind of theory, an object would be beautiful when it has one beauty-making characteristic in sufficiently high degree to make it beautiful, or when it has two or more beauty-making characteristics, each in high enough degree to suffice to make it beautiful, or when it has two or more beauty-making characteristics that somehow work together to make it beautiful. By contrast, although Hutcheson realized that the greater and lesser degrees of which uniformity (and variety) are capable can cause things to be of greater and lesser beauty, he did not realize that the beauty of an object is a threshold phenemonon, that the degree of uniformity (and variety) can fall below the beauty threshold, and that an object can have his complex beauty-making characteristic and still not be beautiful.

Hume never gets around to formulating any of the principles of taste of his theory. Given what he says about "beauties," "blemishes," and principles (and with the help of Frank Sibley's very useful remarks about principles in "General Criteria and Reasons in Aesthetics"[2]), it is possible to formulate examples of the principles of Hume's theory of taste for the domain of art.

> A low degree of uniformity, in isolation from the other properties of a work of art, always makes for ugliness in a work.
>
> A high degree of uniformity, in isolation from the other properties of a work of art, always makes for beauty in a work.
>
> Luster of color, in isolation from the other properties of a work of art, always makes for beauty in a work.

Principles can be formulated for each of the distinct beauty-making and beauty-destroying characteristics previously mentioned and for every other characteristic of the appropriate sort that universally pleases or displeases. The reason for the qualification "in isolation from the other properties of a work of art" is that a characteristic that in itself is a beauty-making characteristic or beauty-destroying characteristic might interact with another property

---

2. Frank Sibley, "General Criteria and Reasons in Aesthetics" in *Essays on Aesthetics* (Philadelphia: Temple University Press, 1983), pp. 3–20.

of a work of art in such a way as to reduce or cancel its own beauty-making or beauty-destroying capacity or interfere with the beauty-making or beauty-destroying capacity of the other property. For example, although luster of color is generally in and of itself beauty-making, in the case of a given work of art, luster of color or the luster of a particular color might not work well with one or more of the work's other characteristics.

The complete set of positive and negative principles would be the standard of taste for Hume, that is, would be the principles among which one can find the principle that would enable one to make "a decision [about a characteristic of an object], afforded [that can achieve the] confirming [of] one sentiment and [the] condemning [of] another." Hume implies this in a nativistic way when he writes, "Some particular forms or qualities, from the original structure of the internal fabric, are calculated to please, and others to displease" (p. 233). The question then becomes, "How is one to know which characteristics please and displease universally, that is, know which characteristics are the subjects of positive and negative principles of taste?"

Hume does not recommend an empirical survey of all persons to discover the universally pleasing and displeasing characteristics. Rather, he first advises great care in one's own reflecting as to which characteristics please and displease us. He recommends "a perfect serenity of mind . . . a due attention to the object" and the like to get around personal idiosyncrasies and allow the universal and original structure of one's own internal fabric to react in a free and unhampered way with pleasure or displeasure (pp. 232–33). Hume, however, seems to doubt that this procedure will do the complete job and advises us to attend to the great works of art that have survived the test of time; he mentions Homer. Time will have removed all the obstacles to correct judgment and "the beauties [and blemishes], which are naturally fitted to excite agreeable [and disagreeable] sentiments" (p. 233) will be revealed in great works such as Homer's.

Proving the Principles and Defective Cognition

But there is still a problem. Neither taking great care nor attending to the characteristics of the great works that have survived the test of time will work for those persons whose cognitive faculties and/or sentiments are defective. By taking the advice Hume has specified up to this point and following the procedures he specifies later, a person of sound cognitive faculties and sound sentiments can succeed in discovering the principles of taste, but a person who is cognitively defective appears to be in a different situation.

Hume tries to throw light on the problem of sound and defective taste sensibilities with the story of Sancho's two kinsmen. In the story, the two are asked to sample the wine from a newly opened hogshead. One kinsmen says it is good except for a slight taste of leather, and the other says it is good except for a slight taste of iron. No one else can detect either taste. When the hogshead is emptied, a key with a leather thong is discovered at the bottom of the barrel, and Sancho's kinsmen are vindicated. Hume claims that just as some wine tasters are sound and some are defective, some persons can discriminate what others cannot in the domain of the arts. In this domain, as in the case of Sancho's kinsmen, a merit—say, a high degree of uniformity—or a defect—say, a low degree of uniformity—may be present in such *mixed* and *small degree* (that is, present in a very subtle way) that some persons will not be able to detect it. As Hume sees it, the problem is to show such an insensitive person that he is wrong in the way that the key with the leather thong showed the insensitive wine tasters that the tastes of leather and iron were in the wine. Hume's answer follows.

> Here then the general rules of beauty are of use; being drawn from established models, and from the observation of what pleases or displeases, when presented *singly and in a high degree* [present in an obvious and unmixed way]. . . . To produce the general rules . . . is like finding the key with the leathern thong. (p. 235; italics mine)

Hume continues:

> But when we show him [the insensitive person] an avowed principle of art; when we illustrate this principle by examples, whose operation, from his own particular taste, he acknowledges to be conformable to the principle; when we prove, that the same principle may be applied to the present case, where he did not perceive or feel its influence: He must conclude, upon the whole, that the fault lies in himself. (p. 236)

Hume is wrong here. Producing a principle of taste that everyone, *including the insensitive person,* accedes to—say, "A high degree of uniformity, in isolation from the other properties of a work of art, always makes for beauty in a work"—will *not* show *cognitively* insensitive persons that they are wrong in the way that the key with the leather thong showed the insensitive wine tasters that they had missed something. The fact that the cognitively insensitive person acknowledges the relevant principle of taste and can be aware of, say, a *high degree* of *singly* presented uniformity in obvious, unsubtle cases does not show the cognitively insensitive person that he is missing the uniformity in a subtle case. Contrary to Hume's conclusion, if a person is cognively insensitive, "We [cannot] prove that the same principle may be applied in the present [subtle] case" because by hypothesis the person is cognitively insensitive.

Hume is at this point dealing with and confusing two different important questions: (1) How are the principles of taste to be discovered? (2) How can a cognitively insensitive person be brought to be aware of a particular, subtle merit or defect in a work of art so that all disputes about particular cases can be avoided?

The fact that merit and defect characteristics can occur subtly and obviously is involved in both questions. Consider first the question of the discovery of the principles of taste. Presumably, virtually everyone—and, hence, enough practically to count as universally—would be able to be aware of a candidate merit or defect when it occurs *singly* and in *high degree* (obviously).

The only question then is, "Does the awareness of the candidate characteristic evoke pleasure, displeasure, or neither?" If pleasure, the characteristic is the subject of a positive principle of taste. If displeasure, the characteristic is the subject of a negative principle of taste. If neither pleasure nor displeasure is evoked, the characteristic is not the subject of a principle of taste.

The fact that a cognitively insensitive person is incapable of being aware of a particular characteristic when it is in low degree and mixed with other characteristics (subtly) is irrelevant to whether that person agrees that that particular characteristic is a merit or defect. If that cognitively insensitive person can be aware of the characteristic when it occurs singly and in high degree, as virtually everyone will be, he has all the experience required to tell if its presence evokes pleasure, displeasure, or neither. Thus, all of the merits and the one defect Hume mentions (and all the merits and defects there are) can be known by virtually everyone when they occur singly and in high degree and, hence, can be judged as to their capacity for evoking pleasure or displeasure. The task of discriminating the cognitive content of the principles of taste is not such a difficult task. By the way, Hume's specification that a candidate merit or defect occur *singly* is his way of requiring *the isolation clause* in a principle of taste.

Then again, the task of discovering a general way of showing a person who is cognitively insensitive to the existence of a particular subtle characteristic that this subtle characteristic exists in a particular object may well be an impossibility. There does not seem to be an artistic equivalent of the key with the leather thong.

Hume has entangled two distinct tasks: the task of discovering the set of positive and negative principles of taste and the task of discovering a general way to convince cognitively insensitive persons that they have failed to detect the presence of a subtle value characteristic in an object.

Having failed to distinguish the two problems, Hume launches into a full-scale attempt to describe a good critic and the way in which cognitively insensitive persons can be convinced that a good critic is a good critic. He now appears to understand the search for the standard of taste to be a search for good critics.

Hume describes the characteristics of a good critic at considerable length. A good critic must be as sensitive to value characteristics in both their obvious and subtle forms as Sancho's kinsmen are to the characteristics of wine. There are a number of ways in which these sensitivities can be sharpened. A good critic is a person *practiced* in the experience of a particular kind of art and also practiced in the sense of having repeatedly experienced the particular work of art he is judging. The good critic must have made many *comparisons* of works of art so as to have acquired a knowledge of the full range of possibilities within a kind of art. In addition to having sharpened sensibilities, a good critic must not be *prejudiced* in any way that will cause the critic to misperceive the characteristics of a particular work of art. Hume then summarizes his description of the good critic and ties the notion of the standard of taste to his notion of good critic: "Strong sense, united to delicate sentiment, improved by practice, perfected by comparison, and cleared of all prejudice, can alone entitle critics to this valuable character; and the joint verdict of such, wherever they are to be found, is the true standard of taste and beauty" (p. 241). This passage raises a number of questions, but Hume pursues only one, namely, "where are such critics to be found? By what marks are they to be known? How distinguish them from pretenders?" (p. 241). The crucial case of the question Hume is asking is, "How are persons with defective cognitive faculties to identify good critics?"

The bulk of Hume's attempt to deal with this difficult question is largely futile and can be summed up with this passage: "Though men of delicate taste be rare, they are easily to be distinguished in society, by the soundness of their understanding and the superiority of their faculties above the rest of mankind" (p. 243). The problem with Hume's view here is that a person who lacks delicate taste cannot easily come to know that another person has it. For example, suppose I can see that another person has a sound understanding of, say, mathematics and music and is in these domains superior to the rest of humankind because I have a sufficient understanding of mathematics and music; my knowledge of the other person's mathematical and musical knowledge and abilities does not prove to me that this person can discriminate subtle characteristics I cannot in other domains, say, in poetry and painting.

Although generally Hume's attempt to show how good critics can be acknowledged by insensitive persons is a failure, he does make one remark that indicates how such acknowledgment can be achieved in a limited way. Near the end of his discussion of the present topic, Hume writes, "Many men, when left to themselves, have but a faint and dubious perception of beauty, who yet are capable of relishing any fine stroke, which is pointed out to them" (p. 243). Let us call this passage "Hume's key." When someone can point out to me some characteristic of a work of art that I had failed to discriminate and thereby enables me to experience the characteristic, then I have good evidence that this person is a better critic about that kind of characteristic than I am. This does not prove that the person is a good critic generally, just a better one than I am about that kind of characteristic. If, however, such experiences involving a wide variety of characteristics are repeated many times, then I have as good evidence as anyone could possibly have that my instructor is a better critic than I am, although not necessarily the good critic that Hume describes.

Hume's key fits only those cases in which the presence of a characteristic can be pointed out to someone. If a person cannot discriminate a characteristic that another claims to be present, then the person who does not experience the characteristic has no evidence that something is actually being pointed out to him and that the other person is a better critic than he is. Hume's key applies only in those cases in which an insensitive person has the potential for being sensitized; if a person lacks this potential, he cannot come to know the evidence that reveals that the other person is a better critic. Hume's key works only in those cases in which the artistic equivalent of the key with the leather thong is not needed. Although there is a way for some insensitive persons (those with a certain potential) to discover critics better than themselves, there is no general way for all insensitive persons to discover better or good critics. The story of Sancho's kinsmen has set Hume (and us) off on a quixotic quest for the nonexistent, artistic equivalent of the key with the leather thong.

Even if Hume has not succeeded in outlining a general method for recognizing good critics that will work for everyone, he has succeeded in giving a good account of the criteria of a good critic. More importantly, he has also given an excellent account of how the principles of taste are to be discovered. Candidate beauties and blemishes are to be experienced or envisioned singly and in high degree—experiences available to virtually everyone—to see if they produce pleasure, displeasure, or indifference. Hume apparently believes that there will be universal agreement about which characteristics are beauties and which are blemishes. He seems to take it for granted that everyone will find characteristics such as clearness of expression pleasant or want of coherence unpleasant when they are experienced or envisioned singly and in high degree, and I think he is, by and large, right. Hume's method of discovering a principle of taste and its results can be illustrated in the formulation of one of his principles: Clearness of expression (always capable of being experienced or envisioned in high degree), in isolation from the other properties of a work of art (i.e., singly) always makes for beauty in a work.

At the beginning of his essay, Hume characterizes the standard of taste as a way of making a decision that justifies or condemns the sentiments of persons. At the end of the passages just discussed, he has fleshed out this view by characterizing the standard of taste as the joint verdict of good critics, which is his specific account of the correct way of making a decision about human sentiments. It has been shown that there are difficulties with the discovery of good critics, so there are also difficulties with the discovery of the standard of taste conceived of as the joint verdicts of good critics. But before this problem can be addressed, the question of what such verdicts are about must be settled.

What exactly are such verdicts about? That is, what is the standard of taste about? I think that many readers of Hume's essay assume that he is talking about verdicts concerning whether particular works of art are good or bad. As noted earlier, however, Hume never addresses the question of determining whether works of art are good, bad, magnificent, or the like; in "Of the Standard of Taste," he discusses only the question of particular merits and defects in works of art. Whereas Hutcheson and Kant focus on the question of what makes works of art and natural objects beautiful, Hume focuses on the question of the various beauties and blemishes that are to be found in art. Hutcheson and Kant sought to discover the one characteristic that made an object beautiful, but Hume apparently regarded this as a difficult task that he did not want to engage in his essay. He does make the overall claims that Milton is better than Ogilby and Addison better that Bunyan, but he does not explain the details involved in the justification of the claims. Hume just does not here address the question of the overall evaluation of a work of art, that is, the question of how the beauties and/or blemishes of works of art work together to make them good, bad, or indifferent.

Now we return to the question of the nature of the standard of taste. Hume says that the standard of taste is the joint verdict of good critics. The joint verdict of good critics would be about the set of merits and defects to which works of art are heir, which is to say the joint verdict is about the complete set of the principles of taste. The difficulty of conceiving of the standard of taste as the joint verdict of good critics is that Hume does not succeed in giving us a general way of discovering good critics. It seems to me, however, that he does succeed in giving us a general way of discovering the principles of taste, the method of experiencing or envisioning a candidate merit or defect singly and high degree—a method available to everyone. Thus, if a standard of taste that is available to everyone is desired, then it could be said that the standard of taste for Hume's *theory* is the complete set of the principles of taste. Such a standard of taste would be the joint verdict of good critics, bad critics, and everyone else.

Principles of Taste and Differing Affections

At a relatively late point in his essay, Hume switches from talking about cognitive matters to talking about the affective responses of human beings to various taste characteristics. He shifts his attention to the pleasure, displeasure, or indifference that discriminated characteristics evoke. It is at this point that Hume first admits to a certain kind of relativity of taste.

He first asserts that there are two sources of blameless differing *in responses* to the characteristics of works of art, namely, "the different humours of particular men" and "the particular manners and opinions of [different] age[s] and countr[ies]" (p. 243).

In the discussion that follows, Hume really dismisses particular manners and opinions as a significant source of disagreement because he says that "a man of learning and reflection" will not be bothered by manners and opinions that differ from his; that is, there are correcting conditions that eliminate different manners and opinions as a source of real disagreement (p. 245). Hume, by the way, makes it very clear that morality is not a matter of opinion that differs from age to age, but more of that later.

It is the different humors of men—differences among human responses that do not admit of correction—that causes Hume to admit to a certain kind of relativity. He writes,

> A young man, whose passions are warm, will be more sensibly touched with amorous and tender images, than a man more advanced in years, who takes pleasure in wise, philosophical reflections concerning the conduct of life and

moderation of the passions. . . . Vainly would we, in such cases, endeavour to enter into the sentiments of others, and divest ourselves of those propensities, which are natural to us. . . .

One person is more pleased with the sublime; another with the tender; a third with raillery. . . . The ear of this man is entirely turned toward conciseness and energy; that man is delighted with a copious, rich, and harmonious expression. Simplicity is affected by one; ornament by another. (p. 244)

This passage makes it clear that Hume is now concerned with affective response rather than cognitive discrimination. He is not concerned here with the discrimination of the characteristics that are the subjects of the principles of taste, such as uniformity and luster of color, but with people's *reactions* to such perceived characteristics when they are perceived. The verbs he uses in the quoted passage—"more sensibly touched," "takes pleasure in," "more pleased with," "turned toward," "is delighted with," and "is affected by"— make clear that Hume is now concerned with the affective aspect of taste.

The relativity that Hume admits to here is, however, of a limited kind. Note that he does *not* say that a young man will be pleased by amorous and tender images and displeased by philosophical reflections and that an older man will be displeased by amorous and tender images and pleased with philosophical reflection. What he does say is that a young man will be "more sensibly touched" by amorous and tender images and that an older man "takes [more] pleasure in" philosophical reflection. Hume is saying that men of all ages take pleasure in amorous and tender images and in philosophical reflections, but that age and other conditions of life will shift their preference orderings. In the passage quoted and the text that surrounds it, all of the characteristics mentioned (conciseness, rich expression, etc.) give pleasure and are merits. I think Hume's view is that there is universal agreement about which characteristics are merits and which defects, but that people may differ in cases in which they have to make choices about which taste characteristics they will experience on given occasions. Thus, on Hume's view, there are no differings as to which characteristics are merits, just differings over which merits are preferred, given certain conditions. There are also no differings as to which characteristics are defects either, just differings over whether it is worth experiencing certain defects in order to experience certain merits, and the like.

Hume's relativism is then of a very limited sort. He does not raise the question of whether persons can blamelessly differ over whether a given quality is a merit or over whether a given quality is a defect. Hume apparently believed that once a person has a particular quality or characteristic clearly in view that his affective reaction could be of only one kind. Of course, he must have realized that as a matter of fact persons may react differently, but his view apparently would be that when persons so differ at least one of them is blameworthy. It is unfortunate that Hume does not address the question of the more radical kind of relativism in his essay.

I return to an earlier theme, the great multiplicity of merit characteristics that Hume mentions. In the passages in which he is primarily concerned with affective reaction, Hume mentions many more merits that persons may differ over in their preference orderings. He repeats some merit qualities already mentioned, but he adds the following new qualities: tender images, wise philosophical reflections, the sublime, raillery, conciseness, energy, rich expression, simplicity, and ornament. So, there are eleven more merits, none of which is easily or obvious reducible to those already mentioned, to be added to the eight positive value characteristics that Hume mentions earlier in the essay. Hume has thus mentioned nineteen distinct merit characteristics and one defect characteristic thus far, which means that so far his theory appears to underwrite at least twenty principles of taste explicitly. His procedure of casually mentioning merits without any hint of the possibility of reducing any of them to one or a small number of merits suggests that Hume thought that there are a large number of irreducible merits. He may also have thought that there are a large number of irreducible defects, but here the evidence is not so clear, as all the defects he mentions appear to reduce to one defect.

Morality and Art

Until the very end of his essay, the characteristics Hume cites as merits and defects are largely of the sort that in the present day would be called *aesthetic* qualities—uniformity, luster of color, force of expression, and the like. In a lengthy passage at the end of his essay, he shifts his attention and focuses on the moral contents of art as defects (or merits).

Although Hume argues that the depiction in works of art of ordinary manners and connected phenomena differing from one's own is blameless and not a defect, he goes to considerable length to try to show that the representation of immorality without the appropriate moral point of view is blamable and a defect in a work of art. He writes that, "where vicious manners are described, without being marked with the proper characters of blame and disapprobation; this must be allowed to disfigure the poem, and to be a real deformity" (p. 246). Hume's statement leaves open two distinct possibilities: (1) the case in which an author presents vicious manners without any moral point of view and (2) the case in which an author presents vicious manners in an approving way. Certainly the second case is less debatable as a defect than the first. In any event, the example Hume gives later is an instance of the second case. He notes that the kind of defect he is talking about is to be found in the works of many of the ancient poets and tragedians. By implication, there are other cases of a similar kind. For example, Hume's view must also be that (1) where virtuous manners are described and marked with the proper characters of praise and approbation, that this must be allowed to ornament a work of art and to be a real merit; (2) where vicious manners are described and marked with the proper characters of blame and disapprobation, that this must be allowed to ornament a work of art and to be a real merit; and (3) where virtuous manners are described and marked with the improper characters of blame and disapprobation, that it must be allowed to disfigure a work of art and to be a real defect.

Continuing his discussion of morality and art, Hume contrasts speculative opinion with moral opinion; the latter he clearly implies may be right or wrong, but speculative opinions "are in continual flux and revolution" and are scarcely subject to correction (p. 246). Consequently, there is no basis for regarding a speculative opinion in a work of art that differs from one's own opinion as an artistic defect. Hume includes religious belief within the domain of speculative opinion, and remarks, "Of all speculative errors, those, which regard religion, are the most excusable in compositions of genius. . . . The same good sense, that directs men in the ordinary occurrences of life, is not hearkened to in religious matters, which are supposed to be placed altogether above the cognizance of human reason" (p. 247). Hume notes, however, that speculative opinion can become entangled with moral matters and thereby become subject to blame (or, by implication, praise). Under the guise of citing the blameworthiness of one of the moral attitudes of Roman Catholicism, Hume cites the blameworthiness of one of the moral attitudes of Christianity (and many other religions). He writes, "It is essential to the Roman catholic religion to inspire a violent hatred of every other worship, and to represent all pagans, mahometans, and heretics as the objects of divine wrath and vengence" (p. 247). Hume then describes an artistic example of "this bigotry," taking care to select his example from the French theater. The cited example, presumably by a Roman Catholic playwright, comes from one of two French plays named by Hume. In the passage of the play referred to, a Hebrew priest's violent condemnation of a Hebrew woman for having spoken to a priest of Baal is approvingly presented by the playwright. Hume's example exhibits a double layer of religious bigotry directed at an extinct religion—the bigotry of the approving presentation by a Christian playwright of the bigotry of the Hebrew priest.

Thus, Hume identifies at least two apparently different kinds of artistic merits and defects: aesthetic ones and moral ones. He does not indicate in his essay if the moral merits and defects are tested in the same way that aesthetic merits and defects are, that is, by being experienced or envisioned singly and in high degree to see if they evoke pleasure or displeasure. The question being raised is whether Hume regards moral merits and defects to be matters of taste and therefore on the same footing with such characteristics as uniformity and force of expression. I doubt that he does regard them as being on the same footing, but he does not discuss the matter in his essay. In any event, Hume does identify both aesthetic and moral factors as merits and defects.

So, in addition to the principles of artistic evaluation involving aesthetic qualities, there are for Hume principles of artistic evaluation involving moral characteristics. An example of such a principle would be: The approving representation of immorality, in isolation from the other properties of a work of art, always makes for disvalue in a work. I use the term "disvalue" here rather than "ugliness" because moral defects (and merits) have the appearance of not contributing to ugliness or beauty.

The Evaluation of Works of Art

In his essay, Hume, unlike Hutcheson and Kant, is not concerned with trying to determine the way in which works of art are to be evaluated in either the sense that a work of art is good, bad, mediocre, or magnificent or in the sense that one work is better than another. Rather, as already noted several times, he is concerned with trying to determine the procedure for discovering which characteristics of works of art are merits and which are blemishes. The questions of (1) how the artistic beauties and blemishes of a work of art "add up" to determine the overall value of the work—that is, whether it is a good work, a bad work, or an indifferent work—or (2) how merits and defects of works determine that one work is better than another are left unexamined by Hume. So, two central questions of the theory of taste are left unaddressed by Hume.

If Hume had addressed either of these two questions, he could not have done so in the way that Hutcheson, for example, could have or did. Consider first the question of comparing the beauty of two different works of art. Hutcheson claimed that the possession of a single complex property (uniformity in variety) is generally sufficient to make an object beautiful. No matter how difficult in practice, in principle at least, on Hutcheson's theory, comparing the beauty of two different works would be a matter of determining which of the works has more of the single property that is supposedly sufficient for making objects beautiful. The situation with Hume's theory is, however, very different. He claims that there are many different beauties and blemishes that works of art may have, and although he does not tell us how they do it, it would have to be the beauties and blemishes of works of art that determine if a work is beautiful or ugly. So, the comparing of the beauty of two different works of art on Hume's theory cannot be simply a matter of determining the degrees of a single property. As noted, Hume fails to address this problem, but his contemporary Gerard did give it some attention, and what he says fits Hume's theory. I quote Gerard's remarks on comparisons in full:

> an analysis of the several combinations of qualities which are agreeable or disagreeable to taste, would enable us to compare and to fix the rank of all those objects which please by means of the same combination: the degree of these qualities, which belongs to each of them, can generally be ascertained with abundant accuracy; and every sentiment which is disproportioned to the acknowledged degree of pleasing qualities in its object, may confidently be condemned as wrong and perverted. The only difficulty would be, to decide between objects which, possessing different qualities, yield distinct species of pleasure. In this, attention to these qualities, it must be acknowledged, can give us no assistance. But this is a case in which it is seldom necessary to decide; there is often an impropriety in attempting it. To render objects capable of being

compared, they must have something in common: it is only objects which have some quality in common, that can be compared in respect to the degree of it.[3]

Gerard here anticipates some of the things Bruce Vermazen says in his important article "Comparing Evaluations of Works of Art."[4] Gerard, like Vermazen, says that the same property in different works can be compared. Gerard, like Vermazen, also says that when two works of art have different valued characteristics, they cannot be compared. Gerard, unlike Vermazen, says that works with the same valued properties can be compared. One of Vermazen's most important points is that even when two works have exactly the same valued properties, it may not be possible to compare them if the rankings of the valued properties fall into certain patterns, but Gerard does not show an awareness of these kind of cases.

Given what Gerard says, it can be seen that there is no general way on Hume's kind of theory to compare the overall values of *all* works of art. Given what Vermazen says, it can be seen that such comparisons are even more limited than Gerard thought.

The other question that Hume's essay does not address is that of the way that the merits and defects "add up" to a specific overall value for a work of art. On Hutcheson's and Kant's theories, there is a straightforward, if simplistic, answer to this kind of question: A work is beautiful if it has the single property that is sufficient for making objects beautiful. For Hume's theory, it cannot be this simple. Again, although Hume does not address the question, Gerard has a little to say on the matter that fits Hume's kind of theory. Gerard writes,

> Our gratification must in every case be balanced against disgust; beauties against blemishes: before we have compared and measured them, we can form no judgment of the work. . . . in every performance, beauties and blemishes are to be found in different parts. A contracted mind fixes on one or the other. . . .
>
> But a person of true taste forms his judgment only from the surplus of merit, after an accurate comparison of the perfections and the faults [of a work].[5]

Gerard's remarks are, of course, only a beginning that hints at the solution of the problem of how specific, overall evaluations of works of art can be made. For a more complete discussion of how a theory like Hume's can deal with the problem of the specific evaluation of individual works, see Chapter 9 of my book *Evaluating Art*.[6]

3. Alexander Gerard, *An Essay on Taste*. 3d ed. of 1780, Walter J. Hipple, Jr., ed. (Delmar, N.Y.: Scholars' Facsimiles & Reprints, 1978), p. 259.

4. Bruce Vermazen, "Comparing Evaluations of Works of Art," reprinted in *Art and Philosophy*. W. E. Kennick, ed. (New York: St. Martin's Press, 1979), pp. 707–18.

5. Gerard, *An Essay on Taste,* pp. 138–39.

6. George Dickie, *Evaluating Art* (Philadelphia, Pa.: Temple University Press, 1988), pp. 129–55.

6

General Evaluation

Hutcheson and Hume

In this chapter I shall attempt to illustrate how Hume's theory of taste is far superior to the other four theories discussed.

The main defect of Hutcheson's theory of taste, viewed from the point of view of our intuitions about beauty, is that it focuses on only one, albeit complex, property as beauty-making. According to his theory, all properties except uniformity in variety are excluded from the domain of beauty. The most obvious, unfortunate exclusion is that of color, which on Hutcheson's view is to be excluded because a color is a "simple" idea.

The reason that simple ideas such as color are excluded from the domain of beauty on Hutcheson's theory is because he held that the internal sense of beauty is triggered only by complex ideas. He assumed that it is the external senses such as vision and hearing that, in addition to functioning cognitively, can also function affectively and *respond* to simple ideas to produce pleasure. On his view, color and other simple ideas can produce pleasure, but these ideas are not beauty-making because they do not interact with the sense of beauty to produce their pleasure.

Hutcheson's exclusion of color and other simple ideas from the domain of beauty results from his conclusion that there is an internal sense of beauty that is triggered only by complex ideas. His argument for the existence of an internal sense of beauty, as was shown in the final section of the Hutcheson chapter, is inconclusive. His argument depends on his two assumptions: (1) that the objects to which the external senses respond are always simple ideas and never complex ones and (2) that every pleasure derives from a sense. However, since the assumption that every pleasure derives from a sense is implausible, Hutcheson's argument does not go through and his exclusion of color and other simple ideas is unjustified. Of course, even if Hutcheson's argument contained no obvious flaw, it would be a mistake to conclude that color does not belong within the domain of beauty.

Hume makes no attempt at all to claim that there is a specific internal sense of beauty or that beauty is always a matter of complex ideas. The overwhelming majority of beauties and blemishes he cites are complex ideas, but he does cite luster of color (a simple idea) as one of the beauties. Moreover, in the one place in his essay where the question of internal or external sources of pleasure arises, Hume casually says that taste qualities relate to sentiment (pleasure) from either internal or external sources. He writes,

> Though it be certain, that beauty and deformity, more than sweet and bitter, are not qualities in objects, but belong entirely to the sentiment, *internal or external;* it must be allowed, that there are certain qualities in objects, which are fitted by nature to produce those particular feelings.[1]

Although Hume's remark leaves open the possibility that there are internal senses and that he may agree with Hutcheson that pleasure (sentiment) derives from a sense, he does not tie simple ideas to the external senses and complex ideas to internal senses. In fact, his remark makes clear that he thinks that beauty and deformity are connected to sentiment or pleasure independently of an internal or external source. The main point here is that Hume's theory does not exclude color or other simple ideas from the domain of beauty; his theory thereby fits our intuitions about beauty-making characteristics.

Independently of the question of whether simple ideas are beauty-making, Hutcheson does not justify his conclusion that uniformity in variety is the only complex idea that is beauty-making. As noted in the final section of the Hutcheson chapter, he simply ignores all complex ideas except uniformity in variety. And, while his contention that uniformity in variety is beauty-making is right and his argument for it persuasive, his failure to discuss any other complex idea leaves open the possibility that other complex ideas are beauty-making. In fact, our intuitions about beauty are that there are many complex ideas that are beauty-making, such as elegant shapes, delicately curving lines, and the like, a conclusion that dovetails with those of Hume's essay.

Hutcheson's view that the sense of beauty is not triggered by any simple ideas and is triggered only by uniformity in variety is as unintuitive as it is inconclusive. Moreover, as shown in the final section of the Hutcheson chapter, his argument that a sense of beauty exists at all is also inconclusive.

Hutcheson's view that there is an innate sense of beauty that responds to a feature or features of objects has the great advantage from the traditional point of view that it avoids relativism by tying the beauty-making feature(s) to a specific, innate faculty that all humans are alleged to have. The great disadvantage of Hutcheson's view is that the argument he uses to try to establish the existence of the sense of beauty is an inconclusive one.

Hume must have seen that Hutcheson's argument does not support his

---

1. David Hume, "Of the Standard of Taste," in *Essays, Moral, Political, and Literary* (Indianapolis, Ind.: Liberty Classics, 1985), p. 235. Italics are mine in quotation.

metaphysical conclusion that there is an internal sense that is the foundation of the theory of beauty. And, he no doubt thought that such a claim cannot be supported. In any event, while Hume leaves open the possibility of internal as well as external sources of pleasure, his theoretical commitments are only to the phenomena—pleasure and the objects of experience that evoke pleasure. An important consequence of his relying only on the phenomena is that it allows for the rise of the threat of relativism, a threat that Hume combats with his conception of principles of taste and his way of discovering them. In the end, however, he acknowledges a certain kind and degree of relativism. In effect, Hume trades unfounded metaphysics for a degree of relativism.

In his *An Inquiry into the Original of Our Ideas of Beauty and Virtue,* Hutcheson attributes the value that representation in art has to representation's being an element in a particular kind of uniformity. According to his view, the resemblance between a representation and its subject matter constitutes an instance of uniformity (of the complex object: representation/resemblance/subject matter); representation is seen as an element in this complex object of beauty. Since uniformity is valuable (beautiful), the elements of the uniformity have dependent value. In his later work, Hutcheson changes his view and claims that representation in art is valuable because it triggers a sense of imitation.[2] On this view, representation is valuable independently of considerations of uniformity.

Hutcheson's later account of the value of representation involves the difficulty of relying on the existence of a sense of imitation, a metaphysical view that is as unfounded as that of the existence of a sense of beauty. His earlier account of representation's value, independent of the difficulty of its ultimate reliance on the existence of a sense of beauty attuned to uniformity, also involves the following difficulty. When we value a representation, we focus on and value its resembling its original and not on the unity of the object constituted by the representation and its subject matter as its two terms.

By contrast, relying only on the phenomena, Hume's view is that not only do we independently value representation but also we value representation in two different ways. He explicitly notes that we value accurate representations ("exactness of imitation"), and he implies that we value the representation of some things because we value the things that are represented ("gay and amorous passions").

There is an interesting parallel between one of Hutcheson's arguments and one of Hume's, arguments in which both philosophers focus on the simplest cases of perceivable characteristics. There may be a historical connection between the two arguments, but I shall not try to show that there is. Hume may have taken Hutcheson's argument, refined it, and used it in his essay. The Hutchesonian argument is his attempt to show that the sense of beauty is universal in all human beings. After he thinks he has proven

2. Peter Kivy, *The Seventh Sense* (New York: Burt Franklin & Co., 1976), pp. 33–34.

that there is a sense of beauty and that its sole object is uniformity in variety, Hutcheson gives an argument to show that the sense of beauty is universal. The argument assumes that there is a sense of beauty in some persons with uniformity in variety as its sole object and that the sense of beauty is the only possible source from which the pleasure taken in uniformity can be derived.

Hutcheson proposes the following argument or test for the universality of the sense of beauty: focus only on cases of great simplicity of perceivable uniformity, avoiding all complex cases, so that *everyone* will be able to distinguish the uniformity in the cases focused on. In one of the many cases of easily perceivable uniformity he uses, he asks, "Who was ever pleased . . . [w]ith unequal legs or arms, eyes or cheeks in a mistress?"[3] "No one," he thinks is clearly the answer. Using this case and many like it, he correctly concludes that when uniformity is perceived, everyone prefers greater uniformity to lesser uniformity. And, because, as noted earlier, Hutcheson thinks he has already shown that the sense of beauty is the only possible source of the pleasure taken in uniformity, he incorrectly concludes that he has proven that the sense of beauty is universal in human beings.

Hume uses the consideration of simple cases of perceivable characteristics—that is, perceivable characteristics occurring singly and in high degree—as a test of whether a characteristic is the subject of a principle of taste.

In their arguments, both Hutcheson and Hume focus on *simple* cases of a perceivable characteristic or characteristics. Hutcheson uses the consideration of simple cases of uniformity to try to show that the sense of beauty is universal. His argument fails, showing only that greater uniformity is universally preferred to lesser uniformity. Hume restricts his parallel argument solely to drawing conclusions about characteristics of experience rather than trying to infer an underlying faculty, thus steering the argument away from the metaphysics of faculties. Hutcheson's argument proves that uniformity is the subject of a principle of taste. Hume's version of the argument proves that uniformity and many other characteristics are subjects of principles of taste.

The Associationists and Hume

Gerard's theory is more similar to Hume's than is Alison's. Consequently, I shall begin my discussion of the associationists by comparing and contrasting Gerard's theory with Hume's, focusing at the very beginning on features that Gerard's theory does not share with Alison's.

Gerard, like Hutcheson, commits himself to a metaphysics of specific, internal senses of taste. But, unlike Hutcheson, he claims to know that there are internal senses of taste on the basis of introspective examination and thereby to be able to know and describe the workings of these metaphysical

---

3. Francis Hutcheson, *An Inquiry Concerning Beauty, Order, Harmony, Design.* Peter Kivy, ed. (The Hague: Martinus Nijhoff, 1973), p. 77.

structures. Gerard, however, is no more entitled to claim that there are specific, internal senses of taste than Hutcheson is, and his claim to a knowledge of the workings of such internal senses is also unjustified. Hume, while appearing to leave open the possibility that there are internal senses, does not place any weight on the notion of internal senses and denies that taste properties are tied to them exclusively. Moreover, Hume does not attempt to give any account of how the pleasures of taste are produced; here, as elsewhere, he restricts himself to the phenomena.

Gerard and Hume both multiply the number of taste properties, the former specifying about a dozen and the latter mentioning about twenty distinct taste characteristics. Gerard gives the impression, like Burke, that he is giving or trying to give a *complete* list of the taste properties. Hume's casual mentioning of "beauties" and "blemishes" throughout his essay gives the impression that he is not trying to give a complete list but rather that he is just mentioning some of many. Both men advance the theory of taste by expanding the number of taste properties.

The main defect of the associationist point of view—shared by both Gerard's and Alison's theories—is the polar opposite of that of Hutcheson's. The chief problem with Hutcheson's theory of beauty is the claim that only one property is beauty-making for objects, a conception that fails to account for innumerable objects of beauty. The main defect of the associationists' theory of taste is the claim that by association any object can be made beautiful, sublime, and so on, a conception that hopelessly dilutes the notions of beauty, sublimity, and other taste characteristics.

Gerard loosened the links between taste and the material world by introducing the association and coalescence of ideas into the theory of taste, but he does retain some connection between taste and the world, speaking of the splendor of unassociated color and of other examples. Alison severs all connection between taste and the material world, claiming that the objects of the material world in and of themselves can never be beautiful or sublime.

Gerard does not seem to comprehend one of the implications of his use of the association (and coalescence) of ideas. After giving an exposition of his views on the internal senses and his account of how the association of ideas supposedly works in the taste domain, he tries to develop a notion of the standard of taste, a notion that is completely at odds with the associationist approach. If, for example, any object can become beautiful for anyone on the basis of association, then the notion of a standard of taste for beauty makes no sense. Gerard's theory is then an unintegrated mixture of a view like Hume's, in which certain properties are put forth as the taste characteristics that make objects beautiful, sublime, and the like, and an associationist theory that claims that any object can acquire taste characteristics independently of what it is like. By contrast, although Hume in the *Treatise* uses the notion of the association of ideas in connection with taste, in his mature theory expressed in "Of the Standard of Taste," he does not. He does not even mention the association of ideas in the later work.

Alison's theory, in contrast to Gerard's, is an integrated one in that there is no talk of senses tied to particular taste properties of the material world that make objects beautiful or sublime; his whole discussion is given over to trying to show how association (together with coalescence) functions to make objects beautiful or sublime. Alison does not even mention the notion of a standard of taste.

Although his view is an integrated one, Alison's whole theory actually consists of one implausible claim piled on top of and derived from other implausible claims. He claims to discover that all experiences of beauty and sublimity begin with the evocation of a simple emotion followed by a train of unified associations with attendant emotions and pleasures. He then claims that it is obvious that characteristics of the material world in and of themselves cannot evoke emotion and that because this is so, it must be that the objects of beauty or sublimity derive their beauty or sublimity from being signs of or expressive of qualities of mind, the only possible kinds of thing that can evoke emotion. From this he concludes that characteristics of the material world in and of themselves cannot be beautiful or sublime. He also concludes that the association and coalescence of ideas are at work between the characteristics of the material world and qualities of mind to produce the beauty and sublimity that objects have. It is even alleged that beauty and sublimity can be produced when the quality of mind involved is not beautiful or sublime, so that beauty and sublimity are produced, so to speak, out of nothing, that is, out of associated ideas, neither of which is beautiful or sublime.

I do not need to argue here against the various elements of this theory because I have already done so in the last section of the Alison chapter. For present purposes, the falsity and implausibility of Alison's theory are sufficiently revealed by remembering that according to his theory there is no difference between the beauty aspect of beauty-of-color experiences of blind persons such as Dr. Blacklock and those of sighted persons.

I want to reflect here on what lies behind and motivates Alison's theory, on what drives him to such extremes of implausibility. He is trying to connect the theory of taste to theology, to connect the beauty and sublimity of the material world to God. He wants the theory of taste to intimate what at the very end of his book he calls, "the alliance . . . between earth and heaven."[4]

I think Alison wants the theory of taste to be a sort of extension of the design argument for the existence of God. This augmented version of the design argument begins with the clear evidence of a special kind of order— the experience of beauty and sublimity—and supposedly ends with God's mind as an integral aspect of the beauty and sublimity of natural objects. When at the beginning of his book, Alison (implausibly) claims, unlike the other theorists of taste, that emotion is an essential part of the experiences of beauty and sublimity, he is already preparing the way for the notion of

---

4. Archibald Alison, *Essays on the Nature and Principles of Taste,* 5th ed. (London: Ward, Lock, and Co., 1817), p. 323.

qualities of mind and ultimately for his theological conclusion involving qualities of God's mind, because he will later argue that emotion can be evoked only by qualities of mind. The first stage of the argument goes as follows:

1. There are experiences of beautiful and sublime (material) objects, such experiences essentially involving emotion, and the (material) objects of these experiences are man-made and natural.
2. Material objects cannot in and of themselves be beautiful or sublime because matter by itself cannot evoke emotion.
3. Qualities of mind alone can evoke emotion, so the only material objects that can evoke emotion are those that are signs of or expressive of qualities of mind.
4. Therefore, beautiful and sublime material objects are so because they are signs of or expressive of qualities of mind.

If Alison's dubious premises are granted, the qualities-of-mind conclusion of the first stage of his argument follows. Alison, however, wants to draw an additional, theological conclusion, for he writes in summing up at the very end of his book that "all the works of human art or design, are directly significant to us of the wisdom, the invention, the taste, or the benevolence of the artist; and the works of nature, of the power, the wisdom, and the beneficence of the divine artist."[5] Thus, he concludes that the beauty and sublimity of the natural world are signs of or expressive of ("significant . . . of") qualities of God's mind. Hutcheson and Gerard connect beauty, sublimity, and the other taste characteristics to God in believing that God created the beauties and other objects of taste for human enjoyment. Alison goes further; he connects beauty and sublimity not just to God's creative agency, he connects God to the beauty and sublimity of natural objects logically. On his view, it is part of the meaning of beauty and sublimity of the works of nature that they are signs of or expressive of qualities of God's mind.

But even if Alison's premises and the conclusion of the first stage of his argument that beautiful and sublime material objects are so because they are signs of or expressive of qualities of mind, his further, theological conclusion does not follow from them. Alison's general thesis that material objects are beautiful or sublime because they are signs of or expressive of qualities of mind just does not have any particular connection to theology. The qualities of mind signified or expressed by beautiful and sublime natural objects could just be those of human or animal minds—as they supposedly are in the examples that Alison gives. When, for example, Alison speaks of the delicacy of the myrtle, the delicacy allegedly derives from the resemblance of aspects of the myrtle to aspects of an individual with a mind, but the mind in question need not be a divine one. Furthermore, Alison nowhere attempts to supply the premise or premises that would be needed to allow for his theological conclusion. His theological capstone is a non sequitur.

5. Allison, *Essays on the Nature and Principles of Taste,* p. 315.

Alison was, no doubt, counting on the common, eighteenth-century view that the natural order of the world implies design; he must have thought that he could assume the existence of God on this basis and that it was but a small step from the conclusion that beauty and sublimity are signs of or expressive of qualities of mind to the conclusion that the beauties and sublimities of the natural world are signs of or expressions of God's qualities of mind. It is, however, a giant, unsupported step, and Alison's theory of taste as an augmented design argument fails.

Of the comparisons made so far in this chapter, Alison's and Hume's theories offer the strongest possible contrast.

As just noted, in the mature statement of his view, Hume does not make use of the association (and coalescence) of ideas in the way common to Gerard and Alison, a move that hopelessly dilutes the taste notions. Nor does he, as Alison does, claim that trains of unified associations are an essential part—or even a part—of the content of taste experiences. In "Of the Standard of Taste," Hume seems to have abandoned any attempt to use the association of ideas in a positive way.

While Hume does not have much or anything to say about emotion in "Of the Standard of Taste," he clearly does not claim, as Alison does, that emotion is an essential aspect of such experiences. Alison, in fact, is isolated and atypical in his claim about emotion; neither Hutcheson nor Gerard makes a similar claim about emotion. Incidentally, of the theories discussed in this book, Gerard's is the most complete, fine-grained, and adequate in the treatment of emotion in taste experiences. I suspect that Hume agrees with Gerard on this matter and that he just did not take up the issue in his brief essay.

Hume's view is certainly at odds with Alison's that the beauty and sublimity of material objects are *always* signs of or expressive of qualities of mind. Hume, of course, does not deny the beauty-making or sublimity-making significance of those characteristics that are expressive of qualities of mind; he specifically mentions, for example, "amorous and tender images" and "conciseness and energy" as beauties and these characteristics are expressive of qualities of mind. Then again, Hume cites many nonexpressive characteristics as beauties, for example, uniformity, variety, luster of color, and exactness of imitation.

Finally, the author of *Dialogues Concerning Natural Religion* obviously has no desire to connect the notion of God to the theory of taste and, therefore, has no motive to try to tie beauty-making or sublimity-making characteristics solely to qualities of mind as part of an overall strategy to insinuate that God is essentially connected to beauty and sublimity.

Kant and Hume

Kant is following the Hutchesonian tradition in claiming that there is a faculty of taste and that it responds to a specific feature of experience, although in his case the specific feature is the form of purposiveness. Hutcheson argues for the existence of a faculty of taste universal to all human beings in order to underwrite the objectivity of judgments of beauty and to guarantee against relativism. The existence of a faculty of taste as conceived of by Kant would, of course, provide the same kind of guarantee, but he does not feel the need of such assurance. Kant *begins* both of his arguments for the existence of a faculty of taste with the premise that judgments of beauty, although subjective in a sense, are objective in the sense that they demand assent. Using this premise plus others, Kant concludes that there is a faculty of taste and that it is the understanding and the imagination in harmonious free play.

I showed in the last section of the Kant chapter that both of Kant's arguments for his conception of the faculty of taste are inconclusive. It seems to me impossible to establish that there is a faculty of taste as conceived of by Hutcheson, Gerard, or Kant; in any event, none of these eighteenth-century philosophers gives a persuasive argument for his claim.

Hume manages to establish taste objectivity without the notion of a faculty of taste by scaling down the notion of what a judgment of taste is about. For Hutcheson and Kant, a judgment of taste has the form "This object is beautiful." As noted at the end of Chapter 5, Hume does not say how judgments about the overall judgments of beauty are to be accounted for. He does, however, say how judgments of taste of the form "This characteristic is beauty-making" are to be accounted for and how principles of taste are to be discovered and justified.

Kant is also following the Hutchesonian tradition in claiming that there is only one specific beauty characteristic that interacts with the faculty of taste and that it is sufficient for making an object beautiful. According to Kant's theory, an object's having the form of purposiveness ensures that it is beautiful. There are at least two grave problems with this view.

The first problem is one shared with Hutcheson's theory, namely, that an object's simply having a beauty-making property cannot ensure the object's beauty; it has to be established that the beauty-making property is present in sufficient degree to surpass the beauty threshold. It is not possible for Kant's theory to take account of the threshold requirement because having a form of purposiveness is not something that can vary by degrees and thereby accommodate the notion of a threshold. Hume does not get to the point in his treatment where the question of the beauty threshold comes up. His theory, however, is admirably equipped to deal with the notion of a threshold because he claims that there are many beauty-making and beauty-destroying properties and that they are of a kind that varies by degrees. The question of how an object's overall beauty is determined comes up explicitly, although briefly, in Gerard's theory, and the notion of the beauty threshold is implicit in his discussion. Hume's theory sufficiently resembles Gerard's to make it clear that the notion of a beauty threshold is implicit in his theory also.

The second grave problem with Kant's view is that the form of purposiveness (systems) is just not a beauty-making characteristic. The forms of some systems ("natural purposes") are not beautiful at all, and although some systems ("natural purposes") have beautiful forms, these forms are not beautiful because they are systematic ("purposive"). The heart of Kant's theory is an irrelevancy. He has been carried into irrelevancy by the overweening influence of his teleology on his theory of taste. Kant's theory somewhat resembles Alison's in this respect.

There is not the least chance that a trace of teleology will show up in Hume's theory of taste. Several passages in "Of the Standard of Taste" have a slightly teleological ring. Hume writes, for example, that "there are certain qualities in objects, which are *fitted by nature* to produce . . . particular feelings" (italics mine).[6] Such a remark by Hutcheson, Gerard, Alison, or Kant would be a teleological claim, for they conceive of nature as God's creation. When Hume uses the expression "fitted by nature," "fitted by" has no connotation of an intentional action of any agency.

Kant, together with Hutcheson, was afflicted with the worst possible case of the great, eighteenth-century, philosophical, color-blindness plague. Kant's view is that there are no beauty-of-color experiences! Alison, also afflicted, at least allows for beauty-of-color experiences, but astonishingly concludes that because this beauty is derived from associations that it is completely available to blind persons! Gerard does very briefly note that some colors are inoffensive to the eye and that there is what he calls "splendor" of color, but he seems to think that the great bulk of the beauty of color is derived, as Alison thinks all is, from associations. Only Hume, of the five philosophers under consideration, does not explicitly deny beauty of color, treat it as merely a matter of association, or treat unassociated beauty of color as a minor sort of beauty of color. Admittedly, Hume merely mentions "lustre of color" as one of the beauties he cites without any real discussion of beauty of color, but he does not qualify his remark in any way that suggests that he thinks beauty of color unimportant. Hume's essay is, of course, very brief, and he makes no attempt to develop a detailed theory. Unfortunately, virtually all the examples he focuses on in his essay are of a literary nature, and such examples steer the discussion away from considerations of visual matters.

6. Hume, "Of the Standard of Taste," p. 235.

Index

Addison, Joseph, 21, 125, 136
Aesthetic: Kant judgments of taste are, 107, 110, 111
Aesthetic ideas: Kant on, 112–14; unite artistic and natural beauty for Kant, 112
Alison, Archibald, vii, 30, 33, 47, 123, 151; introspection is his method, 58–59; obscurity of theory of taste, 3, 4
A priori: concepts (the categories) of the mind, 89; Kant's new sense, 89
Ariosto, 128, 129
Aristotle, 115
Art: Hume on morality and, 138–40
Art, fine: Kant on, 111–13
Association of ideas, the, 5, 146; accidental association, 64, 67; Alison and inferential association, 56, 62, 67; Alison and trains of associated images, 55–56, 58–59, 60, 62, 73–74; coalescence of ideas and, 30–43; coalescence of ideas makes associationism possible, 71, 76–81; creates beauty and sublimity for Alison, 61; and disagreement over taste for Hutcheson, 12, 29; and expression in Alison, 65; general account of, 22–23; and Gerard, 33; Gerard ignores, 46–47; Hume does not use in "Of the Standard of Taste," 123, 149; Hume on, 36; Hutcheson's use of, 30; meaning and Gerard's use

of, 36; natural and accidental, 22–23; a necesary condition of taste experience for Alison, 56; sublimity and Gerard's use of, 35, 37

Baumgarten, Alexander, 85
Beauty: Alison on beauty and emotion, 57, 70; Alison on beauty as the expression of qualities of mind, 68; Alison on beauty of color and blind persons, 68; Alison's account of beauty in music, 65–67; Alison's account of beauty of color, 67–68; Gerard and Alison's notion of acquired beauty is a fantastic one, 81; Gerard on acquiring beauty by the association of ideas, 40–41, 70, 72; Gerard on beauty of color, 39–41; Gerard on beauty of figure, 37–38; Gerard on beauty of utility, 38–39, 71; Gerard on comparisons of, 140–41; Gerard on overall, 141; Gerard's acount of beauty, 37–41; Hume and beauty as a threshold concept, 130; Hume does not address question of overall, 124, 126, 130, 135, 140, 141, 150; Hume does not mention utility as, 123; Hume does not rule out beauty of color, 124, 143, 151; Hume on beauty of utility, 38; Hutcheson and beauty as a threshold concept, 26; Hutcheson and degrees of, 130; Hutcheson on absolute